FELDPOST

FELDPOST

THE WAR LETTERS OF FRIEDRICH REINER NIEMANN
A GERMAN SOLDIER ON THE EASTERN FRONT

TRANSLATED AND EDITED BY
DENIS HAVEL

AFTERWORD BY
WHITNEY STEWART

FONTHILL

denn dieser dein Bruder war tot und ist wieder lebendig worden; er war verloren und ist wieder funden.

Lucä 15:32

To those never found—DMH

Fonthill Media Language Policy

Fonthill Media publishes in the international English language market. One language edition is published worldwide. As there are minor differences in spelling and presentation, especially with regard to American English and British English, a policy is necessary to define which form of English to use. The Fonthill Policy is to use the form of English native to the author. Denis Havel and Whitney Stewart were born and educated in the United States of America; therefore American English has been adopted in this publication.

Fonthill Media Limited
Fonthill Media LLC
www.fonthillmedia.com
office@fonthillmedia.com

First published in the United Kingdom and the United States of America 2016

British Library Cataloguing in Publication Data:
A catalogue record for this book is available from the British Library

Copyright © Denis Havel and Whitney Stewart 2016

ISBN 978-1-62545-015-9

Typeset in 10pt on 13pt Sabon
Printed and bound by CPI Group (UK) Ltd, Croydon, CR0 4YY

Acknowledgments

No work is ever the product of a single hand. In this respect, *Feldpost* is no different. I must first acknowledge the family of Reiner's nephew, Dr Hans C. Andersson, who first entrusted me with the translation of Reiner's letters and then further entrusted me with the telling of Reiner's story. Special acknowledgment must be given to Hans's wife, Whitney Stewart, without whose dedication and literary and technical skills the story of Reiner would never have proceeded beyond the pen-and-paper stage. My thanks go also to Paweł Wyszomirski and Łukasz Gudkiewicz for their invaluable work with Whitney in the former Glowaczow battlefields, and to Sarah Shachat, who helped prepare this manuscript. Also, gratitude to Juanita Havill (my sister) and Dr Christiane Andersson, who dropped all their own projects to review my manuscript. And lastly, I must acknowledge the contributions of my longtime friend, Naomi Cox, whose insights and deep understanding made it abundantly clear that Reiner's story must be told and that it was my *Pflicht*—my duty—to do so.

Denis M. Havel
August 2015, Mt Carmel, IL

CONTENTS

A Note on Style, Translation, and Presentation

Obviously intelligent and well-educated, Reiner came from a highly cultured family and wrote a high style of German that one might label academic—a style he had not quite mastered by the young age of twenty. He composed his letters almost exclusively in *Hochdeutsch*, with dialect or even local colloquialisms making but rare appearances. With his father being a professor, Reiner writes no simple letters home. They are lengthy, oblique, and complex—at times almost incomprehensible, although that may owe more to the conditions under which they were written than to any lack of mental discipline on Reiner's part. He employed the *Sütterlinschrift* style of cursive, a style removed from German school curricula more than half a century ago and which is mostly indecipherable to the younger generation of Germans and translators. Fortunately, his handwriting was broad and distinct, allowing easy recognition of the nearly extinct form.

His *Feldpost* comes to us in three forms:

1. The original handwritten letters on the standard Wehrmacht stationery.
2. The occasional handwritten postcards—some military, some civilian.
3. The typewritten copies made by the father for the family *Rundbriefe*.

Oddly enough, the typed versions presented the greatest difficulties for the translator. Reiner's father typed the letters at night, after a long day of work and often under conditions hardly better than Reiner's when he wrote his letters (i.e., constant interruptions by air-raid alarms and mad dashes to the cellar). Mistakes were unavoidable and often crept into the copies. Words were miscopied, left out, or transposed; sometimes, entire lines were transposed or were obviously missing, which resulted in a confusing text that could cause even a German to seriously consider Mark Twain's suggestion that German might best be read while standing on one's head. However, by following the logic of the sentence or paragraph, the translator could satisfactorily work out most of the obvious errors.

With hundreds of pages of personal letters of a young German soldier, the question of how best to present them to the reader had to be addressed. As a story of human interest, the letters could easily stand on their own. Provided with sufficient annotation, the reader could easily read the story of Reiner as written in his own words. However, Reiner's story played out upon a stage set for him by historical events and took place within the context of the greatest conflict in human history. With that in mind, it was decided to provide the reader with a broader framework in which to read Reiner's words.

A brief historical and biographical sketch of the Niemann-Elmering family will introduce the reader to the world and family into which Reiner was born, and in which he grew to young adulthood. The background sketch will draw upon the unpublished memoirs of Lütte Andersson, Reiner's eldest sister (who passed away in New Orleans on 6 January 2014) and upon a selection of pre-war Niemann family letters. Each section will begin with a summary of the overall German military situation followed by a more detailed description of the immediate military context in which Reiner found himself, i.e. the 58th Regiment and the 6th Infantry Division. These descriptions are drawn from the regimental and divisional histories and from other relevant Wehrmacht records. Then Reiner will tell his story. By such an arrangement, the reader will not only have a sufficient context for Reiner's letters, but also the opportunity to compare 'history-as-written' with 'history-as-experienced' at the individual level. What will not be provided is any analysis, speculation, or judgment concerning what kind of young man Reiner was. That will be left to the reader.

Introduction

The *Feldpost* of Friedrich Reiner Niemann offers the historian and lay reader alike an uncommon documentation of the Second World War as experienced by a young German soldier serving on the Eastern Front. True, all soldiers of any nation write letters home—that is hardly uncommon. What is uncommon about Reiner's correspondence is its extent and completeness. In his thirty-eight months of service in the Wehrmacht, this dutiful son of a close-knit family wrote over 100 letters to them. Except for one noticeable time gap, they represent a weekly and at times daily account of his wartime experiences. That they even exist today is partly due to their having been part of the Niemann Family *Rundbriefe*. In a world before Facebook and continuous texting and tweeting, some families in Germany made copies of letters and circulated them among friends and relatives scattered throughout the country. The Niemann family adopted this practice in late 1942, when their eldest son, Wolfgang, was transferred with his anti-aircraft unit from Germany to Italy.

With his older son in Italy, his younger on the Eastern Front, and his two daughters no longer at home, Reiner's father painstakingly typed copies of the family letters and circulated them among the siblings (*Rundbriefe*). This method provided his children with relatively timely news of one another and increased the likelihood that at least one copy of each of Reiner's letters would survive. Survive they did—they made it through the front, the terror bombings of Cologne, the chaos of defeat, the Soviet occupation zone, a journey across the Atlantic, and lastly the ravages of Hurricane Katrina as it struck New Orleans in 2005. The letters seemed to have as many lives as their author himself.

Reiner was but one of the millions of young men who were born after the First World War but condemned by their youth to suffer in a second great war. Like the others, he would have chosen a very different future for himself, but it was not for him to choose. They could only suffer, endure, and hope to survive. Millions did not.

Neither a statesman nor a general, a diplomat nor a historian, Reiner served as a common soldier—a *Landser*. Although he was an officer candidate for a period, the highest rank he achieved was that of *Obergefreiter* (Corporal). As such, his view of the war was strictly personal and limited. He was a *Schütze* (rifleman) in the 58th Infantry Regiment of the 6th *Rheinisch-Westfälischen Infanterie* Division, and, as any rifleman will attest, his world was his squad and the half-dozen or so members of it. He knew his comrades by name and background; his company commander by name and sight; and his regimental commander perhaps by name, mostly by rumor, but hardly by sight. Everything else was outside his world, a world that rarely extended more than a few hundred meters beyond his foxhole or trench. A distant tree line, a hill, a riverbank—those were the boundaries of his world, and what lay beyond them was none of his concern.

Further restricting Reiner's scope of observation was the situation on his sector of the front (Army Group Center). When he first arrived in the spring of 1942, the German *Blitzkrieg*, with its rapid advances across wide tracts of Russian land, had already come to a halt before Moscow in the previous winter's frost and cold. Reiner spent his entire time at the front solely engaged in defensive warfare—*Stellungskrieg*. For him, *Blitzkrieg* had truly become *Sitzkrieg*. Although he was sent to the front four times, he saw remarkably little of Russia or Poland. He rarely saw a civilian, a city, or even a village. He saw only what was visible from a foxhole, over the parapet of a shallow trench, or through the firing slit of a cramped bunker. This is certainly restrictive, but also instructive, as his letters reflect just how little the front-line soldier knows of where he is and of what is going on.

Though his view was necessarily limited, it was all the more focused for that. International politics, ideologies, and military strategy were all beyond Reiner's world. While the great leaders in Washington, London, Moscow, and Berlin were making their decisions to reshape the world, Reiner and his comrades were making more immediate and—to them—far more important decisions. Their concerns were food, shelter, the safety of their families at home, and survival for one more day—hoping that if enough of these days were strung together, they just might survive the war.

Reiner's *Feldpost* does not constitute a memoir—those reflective, polished accounts written long after events, with observations and insights broadened and deepened by age and maturity, but in which originality has been necessarily distorted by those same factors. His letters were often written as events occurred—indeed, at times when the shells were actually falling—and they reflect how he felt at the time, not ten, twenty, or even thirty years later. In this, they are as fresh and as close to a real-time account as can be achieved. They may lack in reflection, organization, perspective, and at times even comprehension, but they do not lack in honesty. How could they? If he was confused, then he was honestly confused. If he was mistaken, then honestly so. If he was seemingly oblivious to the reality of his situation, then, again, he was honestly so.

Invariably, when dealing with any German who lived during those times, the inevitable question arises: was Reiner a Nazi? He was born in 1922. He was eleven years old when Hitler came to power, and consequently he passed through the important formative years of his adolescence under the Nazi regime. Although he had been a member of the *Jungvolk* and the *Hitlerjugend*, his letters show no evidence that he was a Nazi and not even the slightest hint that his attitude or world view was in any way influenced by Nazi ideology. The efforts of political indoctrination appear to have been wasted on him.

If Reiner harbored any National Socialist sentiments, he certainly would have felt free to express them in his letters without fear of reprisal if the political censors read them. He would not have been concerned that any such pro-Nazi utterances would have been detrimental to his military career. Although he belonged to an old, tradition-bound line regiment of the old army, he was simply too far down the pay scale for any pro-Nazi remarks to have raised an aristocratic eyebrow. Some German soldiers and even some of the younger officers were ardent Nazis, strongly imbued with the ideas of National Socialism. One can read their support of Hitler and the regime in their letters. Minister of Propaganda Goebbels would often make the most of such *Feldpost* from the front. Reiner simply appears to have not been one of them. In the hundreds of pages of Reiner's writing, the name Hitler appears but once, in the form of the obligatory '*Heil Hitler*' above his signature on Reiner's formal request to be transferred out of the *Landesschützen* (home guard), where he was convalescing from a wound, back to his original Wehrmacht unit. The words '*der Führer*' never appear. Likewise, words like 'Greater Germany', 'Third Reich', and other expressions associated with Nazi-speak make no appearance in his letters. By contrast, as the war continues, his letters express an increasing pessimism concerning the outcome of the war and Germany's future. It is even difficult to discern any form of nationalism or youthful patriotism in his letters, something one might expect during wartime. There is no talk of the German mission to unify Europe and preserve western Christian culture or of one's individual duty to defend *Volk* and *Vaterland*. There is no discussion of the justness of Germany's cause (nor any discussion of its unjustness either). Reiner remained mostly silent on the war, its reasons, and its importance. Reiner was the product of the Niemann family, not of National Socialist Germany, and a young man whose sensibilities appear to have been shaped more by the eighteenth century than by the twentieth.

No claim can be made here that Reiner's letters somehow represent the 'typical' German soldier, or what the 'average German solder' felt or thought. Reiner's letters represent only Reiner, and he was anything but typical or average. Indeed, he was unique, but then all the young men of that war were unique. Whether American, Russian, German, or British, each had his own individual set of experiences and reactions to them. Each had his own worries and fears, hopes and ambitions. Not one was 'typical' or 'average'. Each was an individual.

What emerges from Reiner's *Feldpost* is a portrait—a self-portrait—of a young man who could have been any parent's son, anyone's brother. That he wore the *Feldgrau* was an accident of birth. That he suffered through the Second World War was an accident of history.

1

Beginnings

Friedrich Reiner Niemann—Reiner, to his family—composed his war letters not only within the historical context of the Third Reich and the war on the Eastern Front, but also within the context of a family. This family framework exercised a greater influence on Reiner than the twelve years of National Socialism and the six years of war. Reiner did not write his letters into a void; he wrote them to a father, a mother, a brother, and a sister. Therefore, a certain knowledge of the Niemann family—its origins and structure—is necessary for any appreciation of the letters and the young man who wrote them.

Reiner's family was both extended and close-knit despite being spread across Germany, from West Prussia and Silesia in the east, to Cologne and the Rhineland in the west. Reiner's world included his parents and three siblings, in addition to myriad paternal and maternal aunts and uncles. The family also had a few close friends, and Reiner's father had a circle of professional and intellectual acquaintances. However, aside from this, Reiner and his siblings grew to adulthood and developed their individual character and outlook on life within the family boundary. That a family unit should exert such a powerful and lasting influence upon the children may seem commonplace in normal times; however, considering the time in which the Niemanns lived, with the constant assault upon the family structure by a totalitarian regime and the physical and moral destruction from the war, the Niemann family's ability to preserve its character and moral balance is remarkable.

Reiner was not born to be a soldier. He did not spring from one of those classic Prussian-German families with a centuries-old tradition of military duty to the Fatherland, or from a family with any particular devotion to the concept of Germany; quite the contrary. Reiner's father was a professor of art, his mother the daughter of a successful landowner. There was nothing in Reiner's background to prepare him for the brutality of war, but there was much to shield him from its brutalizing effects.

Reiner grew up in a comfortable and educated middle-class home, surrounded by music, literature, philosophy, religion, and, of course, art. It was with these, and his family, that he continued to surround himself during the war, in order to maintain his humanity—if not his sanity.[1]

Had there been no Hitler, no Third Reich, and no war, Reiner's life would have been quite different. He might have become an architect, a musician, or perhaps even a writer, but history, and those who sought to shape it, sent him down a harsher path.

Born in Kassel on 19 May 1922, Reiner was the youngest of Alfons and Lotte Niemann's four children. His parents, his two sisters (Lütte and Heidi), and his elder brother (Wolfgang) were his closest companions throughout his life. Wolfgang was also his dearest friend.

By the time Reiner was born, his parents had already gone through enough drama to be a story in itself. Alfons was born in 1886 in Oppeln, Silesia, and Lotte in Neumühle, West Prussia, in 1888. They could have both been considered 'Easterners', but they came from very different worlds.

Lotte's family was 'landed gentry' of West Prussia. She was the eldest child (of seven) of Adolf Elmering, a successful and respected owner of a *Rittersgut*—not just any estate, but one with a name. In this case, it was 'Neumühle'. Her world was one of relative comfort, advantage, and stability.

Alfons, however, lived more modestly. He was the son of a railroad employee and the youngest of seven children. His father's unpleasant and quarrelsome nature eventually cost him his job and the family its security. As a boy, Alfons often went hungry, but he was fortunate that his sister Grete, seventeen years older, recognized his artistic talent and saw to it that he received the necessary schooling and training. After high school, Alfons earned a scholarship to attend the Breslau Academy of Art.

In class-conscious Imperial Germany, two people from such different social strata would rarely have the chance to meet, let alone marry. But meet they did in 1909, while Alfons was a student at Breslau. As one would say now, the chemistry was immediate. Within a year, Lotte and Alfons were engaged.

The announcement of their engagement was not well-received in either household. That Adolf Elmering's treasured daughter should marry a penniless artist, a young man without prospects, whose head was not only full of ideas but *new* ideas, was not to be countenanced. The reaction in the Niemann household was no more encouraging. They believed: 'We are poor people. It does no good to get involved with a rich man's daughter.'[1]

Both families insisted on a five-year engagement, hoping it would bring the young couple to their senses. Instead, however, the world around them lost its senses and plunged into the First World War. Alfons had been excused from military service during his normal call-up in 1906 due to the slightness of his stature, but after the heavy casualties of the first year of the war, he was suddenly found to be hale and healthy in 1915. He was assigned to the 6th *Bataillon* of Jaegers.

With such uncertainty about them, Alfons and Lotte saw no point in extending their engagement and promptly married. Alfons was sent off to the trenches on the Western Front in early 1916, just in time to be shoved into the meat grinder of Verdun. In March, during the horrific fighting around the so aptly named '*Le Mort-Homme*', his left arm was shattered.[2]

Lotte's reaction to the news was a simple '*Gott sei dank!*' Thank God indeed, because now her husband was out of the slaughter. He would never go back to the trenches; he would survive.

Unfit for front-line duty, Alfons spent the remainder of the war painting murals on the walls of military barracks and aerodromes and beginning his family. His first child, Liselotte (Lütte), was born in 1916.

With the end of the war in 1918 and his release from the military in January 1919, Alfons was free to complete his studies and return to his family. A second daughter, Adelheid (Heidi), was born in 1919, and his first son, Wolfgang, in 1920. In 1921, he accepted a position at the *Kunstgewerbeschule* and moved his family to Kassel. He was now Professor of Graphic Arts, and in 1922, the father of a second son—Friedrich Reiner.

Reiner was born into a suffering Germany still reeling from its defeat in the First World War—2 million dead, countless war invalids, hunger, starvation, a collapsed economy, and a collapsed society. There had been revolutions from the left; there had been revolutions from the right. However, the force that would shape Reiner's fate had not yet raised its monstrous head above the horizon. True, within a year of Reiner's birth, a near farcical attempt at revolution erupted in a Munich Beer Hall by a rag-tag group calling themselves 'National Socialists'—whatever that term meant—but it ended with a volley of lead, its perpetrators either dead or fled. The event merited hardly a single morning's headline. The event had nothing to do with the Niemann world in Kassel.

The Niemanns had concerns of their own. The newest member of the Niemann family, Reiner, was a sickly child beset by a host of childhood maladies, including asthma. His eldest sister, Lütte, recalls her little brother in her memoirs as 'a sensitive, pale, and thin little thing with large blue eyes in his pretty, pale face and having the thinnest legs and the skinniest little body'.[3]

Reiner was a *Sorgenkind* (or 'worry-child') for the family, and in typical Niemann fashion, they all pitched in to take care of him. His mother spent hours at his bedside, telling him stories as he struggled to breathe. His siblings did all that they could to look after their baby brother. In time, he outgrew his maladies to become a strong, healthy boy who excelled in swimming, boxing, and gymnastics. He became the tallest and the physically strongest of the family. In the later years of the war, with disaster looming from all directions, the family turned to this once 'thin little thing' because of his strength.

The Niemanns weathered the turbulent times of the Weimar Republic somewhat better than many German families because Alfons held a job with a secure salary.

They did not escape entirely unscathed, however. Lotte's share of the inheritance of her father's 500,000-mark estate had been reduced by hyperinflation to a mere 750 marks of the new currency. Though Professor Niemann certainly never brought his wages home in a wheelbarrow, when he did come home with his salary, every member of the household old enough to walk scattered throughout the city to various shops to quickly purchase the household necessities before the prices rose.

Despite this, Reiner's childhood was a happy one—once he had outgrown his afflictions—with parents very much devoted to the upbringing and development of their children. In Kassel—the 'Heart of Germany'—the family enjoyed a comfortable apartment, newly built on the *Friedrich-Ebert-Strasse*, two 'house daughters'—not servants, but educated young girls of good families—hired to help with the chores and the children, and the first washing machine and vacuum cleaner in the area.

It was a family life and childhood of happy memories, with two daughters and two sons who were as close to one another as can be imagined. Having grown up on her father's country estate, Lotte insisted that the children spend much time in the fresh outdoors to escape the 'unhealthy' city air. Those were the days when families did things together, and so on weekends there were always the family outings and picnics as they hiked among the hills and woods surrounding Kassel—fond memories for a child, indeed.

Then there was the culture. Reiner was surrounded by it. It was as much a natural environment for him as were the surrounding hills and woods, through which he would likewise take long hikes. Literature, religion, music, and art— next to his parents and siblings, they would be his closest companions throughout his life. It was a good life and a good childhood there in Kassel, but all that would soon change.

They had been through much, Alfons and Lotte. They had managed to marry against their families' wishes; they had survived the First World War and had made it through the ups and downs of the Weimar period. They had created a family, a home, and a future that seemed to hold promise, but then came the Nazis and the beginning of a family tragedy.

It is easy to understand that to a man like Alfons—educated, cultured, and artistic—a political movement whose face was that of brawling, torch-bearing, semi-literate thugs would hold little appeal and elicit feelings of both contempt and dread. However, there was also another reason; his beloved Lotte, Reiner's mother, was part Jewish. Lotte's mother, Elisabeth *neé* Berendt had been half-Jewish, which made Lotte, as quarter-Jewish, a second-degree *Mischling*, under the Nazi Nuremberg laws. If that fact had been discovered, it would have placed her under certain restrictions; had she not already been married, she would have needed special permission to marry Alfons. The issue was a constant worry, but nothing ever came of it. The secret was kept.[4]

Ironically enough, Alfons ran afoul of the Nazis. In 1932, he had been offered and had accepted a professorship at the prestigious Academy of Fine Arts in Breslau. After the Nazi seizure of power in 1933, he was informed that his continued employment there was contingent upon his joining the Nazi party. He refused, and so at the age of forty-eight, with a wife and four children, he found himself without a job—and seemingly without a future. In addition to his dismissal, he had been slapped with a *Berufsverbot*, an official ban forbidding him to practice his profession. However, the ban was soon lifted—in a fashion. He was allowed to accept a teaching position at a high school, the *Apostelgymnasium* in Cologne.

For Professor Alfons Niemann, this was a considerable demotion, especially since he was only paid the salary of a new teacher. Nevertheless, perhaps in Catholic Cologne, which had never been friendly territory for Hitler and the Nazis, and with colleagues who for the most part were priests and monks, he would be safe from official harassment.[5] Safe from harassment perhaps, but not from bitter professional disappointment. All his ambitions and artistic ideas would have to be put away in a drawer to gather dust. Although he did his best to hide his disappointment from his family, he became unsmiling, introverted, and depressed. Alfons was no longer the same man and never would be, because the failed artist in Berlin had yet more misery to visit upon the Niemann family.

In 1934, the family packed up, left the happiness of Kassel, and headed into an unknown world in Cologne and a life under National Socialism. True, the father was unhappy and the mother was a bit more careworn, and life might be slightly more restricted due to their diminished income, but they would be together.

Reiner was eleven when Hitler and the Nazis schemed their way into power and began their quest to reshape German society. Throughout the country, the German family found itself in competition with a state that believed that it should shape and determine the lives of Germany's youth. For the first time, Reiner and his siblings would be exposed to influences not determined by the family but through the compulsory membership in the various Nazi youth organizations. For Lütte and Heidi, there was the *Bund Deutscher Mädel* (BDM), and for Wolfgang and Reiner there was the *Jungvolk* and *Hitlerjugend*. There was a lot of hiking, camping, and singing in these organizations—supposedly healthy, innocent, youthful activities—but it would be hiking without the family, camping without the family, and God only knew what songs they would be singing. Then, of course, there would be the political indoctrination. In the case of the Niemann children, the state was too late; their political and social attitudes were already formed. Alfons and Lotte had created a '*Festung Niemann*', a wall of western culture and values surrounding their children, which National Socialism would find difficult to penetrate.

What of Reiner during this period of 'German National Renewal'? He leaves us little written evidence concerning his childhood and early adolescence. Except for obligatory thank-you letters to ancient aunts and uncles, what child leaves behind a lengthy collection of correspondence for future historians to ponder? Reiner is no exception. Most of what is known about Reiner in the decade before the war is gathered from his school records, references to him in his mother's letters to her sisters and cousins, and a few notes he penned about himself.

In a 1939 résumé, Reiner offers the reader a brief biography:

Mein Lebenslauf (Niemann)

I was born on 19 May 1922, in Kassel, the son of the university professor Alfons Niemann and his wife Lotte Niemann, neé Elmering. I was baptized in the Lutheran confession. Easter of 1928, I entered the local Public School #13, and after four years I entered the Reformrealgymnasium I in Kassel. When the Art Academy in Kassel closed in 1933, my father took a position as a drawing instructor at the Apostelgymnasium in Cologne. We moved here in April 1934, and I entered the Quarta of the Oberrealschule in the Hansering on May 1. In March 1936, I entered the Jungvolk[6] and temporarily held the position of *Jugendschaftsführer*.[7] In 1937, I was transferred to the Hitlerjugend.[8] In the summer of 1938, I received the Youth Sports Badge. My interests lie in various areas; especially music but also in art, literature, as well as the technical fields and natural science.

Having entered the *Jungvolk* at the upper age limit (fourteen), he was, as he stated, temporarily a *Jugendschaftführer*. As for his time in the *Hitlerjugend*, except for receiving the Reich's sport badge, he mentioned no other accomplishments. Much has been written about the various Nazi youth organizations; apologists assert these were no different from any other youth group, while others claim they were nothing less than paramilitary organizations training the German youth to be the killer-wolf-children of the Führer. Whatever the truth, Reiner's involvement seemed to have had little effect on him. 'My interests lie in various areas; especially music but also art, literature...'

In a 1938 letter to her cousin Hänse Wagner, Lotte Niemann discussed the relative merits and character of her four children and said, 'Reiner has the greater natural openness, accepts himself, and is probably the most gifted of the four.'

His giftedness, however, is not particularly borne out by his school record. He was an average student. Like most young men, he excelled in those subjects that interested him, and he muddled through the rest. His final report from the *Oberrealschule* in Cologne shows that he received a comprehensive and typical education of the day—math, science, languages (English and French), literature, music, art, and religion. His marks in religion, music, and art are particularly good, as are his marks in sports, swimming, and boxing—two sets of talents not commonly associated with one another and revealing a certain dichotomy in his nature that later served him well at the front. One was set to preserve his sanity, and the other would preserve his life.

A few years after the Nazis took power in 1933, a certain peace and stability seemed to appear in German life, though in many respects it was the peace of the grave as the regime eliminated its opponents. The economy had revived, the 1936 Berlin Olympics was a great success, and life was good—except if you were Jewish, a member of another targeted minority group, or openly critical of the government. Perhaps a National Renewal was actually happening. However, as the 1930s came to a close, events revealed the riskier aspects of the Nazi regime and its Führer. German troops entered the Rhineland and annexed Austria with no great fuss. Then, in the fall of 1938, Hitler demanded that Czechoslovakia turn over its German-speaking region, the Sudetenland, to Germany. A European crisis arose as Hitler threatened military action; the frightening possibility of another European war sent a chill through the German nation.

However, Reiner was preoccupied with happier events. He had recently turned sixteen and was focused on his immediate musical world. He described this in a 23 September 1938 letter to his aunts (Alfons' two sisters) in Bad Flinsberg, Silesia:

Meanwhile, here in Cologne my share of everyday life has already begun, that is to say: Music. It began last Saturday with an evening of music arranged by the Collegium Musicum in honor of Father's birthday. They performed motets by Schütz and chorales by Bach with one to two people singing each part. The motets had six parts and the chorales had four. At dinner that evening, people ate at a huge table (twice the size of our dinner table) with six people on each side and four at each end. It was all very nice and a most natural and pleasant atmosphere reigned over it all—especially in view of the present times. The following Monday I went to my piano lessons. On Wednesday, I picked up the last roll of film with the three-person group pictures we had taken on Sunday. The close of Sunday's event had provided an opportunity for a group picture (the first time since forever) but then later it occurred to me that such a group shot had been taken at Löhn. On Thursday, I began practicing the F-flute intensively—mostly Johann Fischer. As for the rest, I only played the *Matthäuspassion*, which I copied from a borrowed book. My plans for next summer will be to go to Hamburg and North Germany. Only if Bohemia's mountain region becomes German will I perhaps travel to your region. Perhaps Uncle Fritz will want to go with me on a paddleboat trip on the Elbe. Who knows? Once again, I thank you, send my greetings, and hope to see you again soon.

Urgent telegrams were shooting back and forth between European capitals, and British Prime Minister Neville Chamberlain met Hitler three times in Germany in a desperate attempt to prevent the crisis from plunging Europe into war. Despite this, Reiner seldom mentioned political tensions or Nazi disruptions of the social fabric; he was concerned with a possible change in vacation plans.

Over the next year, other changes came to the Niemann family; the children left the family circle, some through the natural process of growing up and beginning their own lives, others because of world events. Lütte and Heidi left to continue their education. Wolfgang went into the *Reichsarbeitsdienst* (Labor Service). Then, after a brief stint at the technical school in Charlottenburg, he went into the *Luftwaffe*, where later he commanded an anti-aircraft battery in Italy. Only Reiner was at home when the war broke out in 1939. In the spring of 1940, he too was called into the *Reichsarbeitsdienst*.

Reichsarbeitsdienst

In the spring of 1940, Reiner left the Niemann family nest to make his first journey outside the family circle. Thereafter, he only returned for brief visits. He had completed his high school exams in February, and in April, he began his compulsory service with the *Reichsarbeitsdienst* (RAD), or National Labor Service. The RAD was one of those new ideas of the Nazi party to help further their concept of a *Volksgemeinschaft*. Upon completion of high school, German youth were required to perform six months of National Service. For the young men, that meant living outdoors in camps, performing manual labor on state work projects, or helping to bring in the harvest.

Times had changed since Reiner's brother, Wolfgang, had performed his labor service. Gone were the days of bringing in the harvest and flirting with farmers' daughters. The world was at war, and the German Panzers were smashing across the French border. Reiner performed his labor service on foreign soil close to the front. Instead of donning the sharp RAD uniform, he wore the *Feldgrau*, instead of a stylish forester's cap, he wore the *Stahlhelm*, and instead of carrying a shovel and scythe, he wielded a rifle.

On the coarse, brown Wehrmacht stationery, he wrote his first *Feldpost*:

2 June 1940

Dear Parents,

Today we had our first assembly in order to receive our pay. In addition to our 'Defense Pay' of one mark, we also receive 'Front Pay' of the same amount, so that makes a total of two marks per day, which is eight times what we got in Hasenfeld and is certainly not unwelcome.

At the moment, we are enjoying a fine Sunday afternoon, listening to the record player: Strauss, the Marseillaise, chansons, and quotations from Molière and others. Recently I was sitting in the village church playing French church music on a harmonium, which was there in place of the organ that had been removed. It sounded much different, but it worked out better than I could have imagined. As I played, I was alone in the church that had no windowpanes, and the walls were unplastered. I had my rifle and gasmask and must have presented a rather paradoxical picture. The church appeared to be old, but it was full of modern, kitchy figurines of Joan of Arc and other French saints.

31 July 1940

From: *Arbeitsmann* Reiner Niemann
Feldpostnummer 10789
To: Herr Student of Architecture Wolfgang Niemann at Beun.
Dear Wolfgang,

Yesterday those men who had a high school diploma and who had registered at a university were assured that they would be discharged on August 20th. This order came down from the higher authority, and the conditions will be strictly adhered to, so it won't apply to me. Consequently, I have written to Hänse [Reiner's mother's cousin, Hänse Wagner] so that the parents can register me for this trimester in Berlin, since I don't think this card will reach you in time. If you are in Berlin, you can register me, but only if you are certain that the parents know that you are in Berlin. I've told them not to register me if you are in Berlin. Perhaps you could contact each other. If you already have, then you don't need to wait for this letter. I want to be an architect but the main thing is that I obtain my certificate of registration from the T.H. [*Technische Hochschule*, Berlin] Otherwise, I won't get released. Since July 20th, we've been moved three times. I hope you can take care of this.

Apprenticeship

After high school and labor service, Reiner confronted the life situation common to most young men at the age of eighteen. They are free to make their own decisions and carve their own future. What will they make of it?

Reiner wanted to follow his brother's footsteps and study architecture, but there was still a war of sorts going on and of course the matter of his eventual conscription into the Army. True, the major enemy, France, had been defeated, but there still remained the pesky problem of the British Empire. However, one cannot plan one's life based on matters beyond one's control. Would it not be best to complete as much university training as possible before conscription actually occurred? Who knew, Germany and Britain might come to some agreement and peace would break out. Perhaps then the authorities might cut him some slack and allow him to complete his education before having to perform his military service—or even excuse him from it altogether. In any event, he couldn't simply sit on his hands and wait.

Reiner did not attend university—presumably, he registered too late—but he apprenticed with the famous architect Dominikus Böhm, a friend of his father's (Reiner's family was obviously well-connected in certain areas). Not only did Reiner work under Böhm, he lived with the Böhm family in southern Germany and learned directly from the master himself.

It was a good time for Reiner, this last year before conscription. He began learning his profession from one of the greatest, and on weekends he went sightseeing, visiting the art museums of Augsburg and Munich and, more importantly, the many historic village churches—architectural jewels tucked away in the Bavarian hills and valleys. He even struck up a brief acquaintance with a young woman, a certain *Fraülein* Thiem.

The war, such as it was, continued. There was the occasional British bombing raid, but tucked away in southern Germany, beyond the range of the RAF, such raids were little more than radio reports and morning headlines to Reiner. The raids were more of a nuisance than anything else, so there was yet a chance for peace.

What Reiner did not know (indeed, what the German population did not know) is that their Führer was secretly preparing for the real war, the war that he believed he and the German nation were destined to wage—the conquest of Russia and the destruction of Bolshevism. While Reiner was enjoying his days in southern Germany, the Führer's headquarters in Berlin was drawing up plans. Broad red lines on huge maps marked out objectives and defined the fate of millions. Millions of German soldiers were transferred to the east and hidden amid the forests along the Russian border.

Peace never really stood a chance.

Munich
3 May 1941

Dear Parents,

I'm sitting in a Munich tavern having my fourth beer (because the beer is so good here). I'm just back from visiting a Munich art exhibit with my friends. The impressions were somewhat mixed. Most of the art was barely better than kitschy or plastic paintings, and most of them (some twenty-five to thirty) have already been sold to some *Gauleiter*[9] Adolf Wagner. They were typical beer faces[10] that you would find in the worst art shops. The rest of the art left me cold.

[Undated]

Dear *Fraülein* Thiem,

After working with an uncle of mine, an architect from Breslau, on the plans for the University of Pressburg, I am recovering from my exertions, which have hindered my letter writing. When I am in Breslau again, I will write you more about it.

Greetings,
Your Reiner

Jettingen
Mid-June 1941

Dear Wolfgang,

I've been here a quarter of a year, and you wrote me one and a half months ago. Today is Sunday, and the weather is lousy so I can finally write you back. Believe it or not, this is the fourth time I've started a letter to you. My time is so fragmented and because of my incurable laziness about writing that by the time I finish a letter, it is disjointed and no longer relevant. It's funny that the less one writes, the more he thinks about the people he hasn't written, and often, thinking about them is better than writing because often letter writing is little more than filling up pages. I often think of you when I'm biking, not because of a twinge of conscience for not having written, but because now I have to ride without you. Many a profiteer may be seen in church but that doesn't make them any more Christian. That's me in many ways, especially in regard to your thoughtfulness in sending me a birthday letter, which I really enjoyed. In the meantime, the workers have been here twice, the corn has grown, Crete has been conquered, and we have been at war with Russia for a week.[11]

2

Operation Barbarossa

The war with Russia that Reiner just happens to mention in the letter to his brother ('...we have been at war with Russia for a week.'), almost as an afterthought, was the greatest military operation in history—Operation Barbarossa, the German invasion of Russia.

At 3.15 a.m. on the morning of 22 June 1941, three German Army groups—*Nord*, *Mitte*, and *Süd*, or North, Center, and South—with 3 million men, 3,580 armored vehicles, and 7,184 artillery pieces, supported by 1,830 aircraft, crossed the Russian frontier, initiating what would become the greatest conflict in human history. When it ended four years later, both nations were devastated. Germany lost 3 million of its sons; Russia lost some 13 million.

Some wars begin by mistake—a misjudgment, a diplomatic misunderstanding. Other wars are viewed (always in hindsight) as having been preventable at one point or another. The Russo-German War of 1941–1945 was neither. It was inevitable. There were two opposing ideologies, two dictators—one seeking expansion to the east, the other seeking expansion to the west. There would be war, sooner or later; Stalin, who was rebuilding his army, preferred later, but Hitler, always the impatient gambler, chose sooner.

Named for the legendary medieval German king and Holy Roman Emperor Friedrich Barbarossa, the German war plan was as ambitious as it was audacious. A nation of 80 million was to defeat a nation of 190 million in a single, swift campaign, concluding its operations before the dreaded Russian winter set in—not so much out of consideration for the adverse weather, but rather that Germany's limited resources meant it would not prevail in a protracted struggle.

On the northern flank, *Heeresgruppe Nord*, under *Generalfeldmarschall* von Leeb, with twenty-one infantry, six motorized, and two Panzer divisions, was to push through the Baltic countries, drive north, and take the city of Leningrad.

In the center, *Heeresgruppe Mitte*, under *Generalfeldmarschall* von Bock, with thirty-five infantry, six motorized, and nine Panzer divisions, was to smash through the Soviet frontier defenses, destroy the Russian forces north of the Pripet Marshes, and advance on Moscow.

On the southern flank, *Heeresgruppe Süd*, commanded by the venerable *Generalfeldmarschall* von Rundstedt, with thirty-three infantry, three motorized, and five Panzer divisions, was to drive into the Ukraine to the Black Sea, seizing the Donets Basin that was so essential to Germany for the raw materials of war.

All these objectives, however, were but points on a map. The primary objective of Operation Barbarossa was to destroy the Red Army whether close to the border or deep within the interior.

Having tested its *Blitzkrieg* concept of war in Poland and after having perfected it in France and the Low Countries, the Wehrmacht now applied it to the Russians with devastating results. The hard-hitting, swift-moving Panzer and motorized divisions would smash through the enemy lines, plunge deep, and then turn inwards to link up with other Panzer and motorized units that had broken through at other points of the front, creating huge pockets of encircled Russian troops. The footslogging German infantry would follow in the wake of the Panzer forces, sealing off the pockets and destroying the enemy troops trapped within.

The 4.5 million Russian troops along the border were caught completely by surprise that June morning. Their responses to the German attack were confused, disjointed, and ineffective.

Heeresgruppe Nord advanced out of its East Prussian bases, swept through the Baltic countries where they were hailed as liberators (the Soviet Union had forcibly annexed the Baltic nations the previous year), broke through the 'Stalin Line' located along the old Soviet frontier, and raced north. They broke through each line of defense that the Russians hastily established. Pskov fell on 9 July. The Luga Line was smashed after hard fighting by the third week of August. 'Novgorod the Golden' fell to the Germans on 16 August. By 11 September, forward elements of *Heeresgruppe Nord* had reached the high ground just south of Leningrad and could actually look down into the city and see the waters of the Gulf of Finland beyond. So began the siege of Leningrad, which would last for 900 days.

On the central and southern fronts, the German advances had been even more spectacular. With the wide-open space of the steppes, the Panzers exploited *Blitzkrieg* to the fullest. Time and again, they broke through the Russian lines and encircled entire groups of Soviet armies. The resulting battles of annihilation took even the German generals by surprise—first at Minsk, where four Soviet armies had been trapped on 8 July, resulting in nearly 300,000 Russian prisoners. The Dnieper was crossed on 10 July, and Smolensk fell on the 16th. At Kiev, 665,000 Russians fell into German hands on 19 September. The encircled pockets of Vyazma and Bryansk yielded another 663,000 prisoners. By 17 October, the way to Moscow lay wide open.

In the first four months of Operation Barbarossa, the successes of the Wehrmacht were astounding. Western Russia was overrun, Kiev and the Ukraine had been taken, and Leningrad had been cut off and besieged. The Russian Army lost upwards of 2.8 million men. The Germans took 1.5 million prisoners. In many areas of the conquered territory, especially the Ukraine, the German soldiers were welcomed as liberators from the hated Communist regime. The German generals, normally a rather sober-minded set, found it difficult to restrain their elation. Perhaps the Führer had been right when he had remarked that 'one only needed to kick open the door and the whole rotten structure would collapse'. Just one final thrust, and Moscow would be theirs.

Despite the chaos into which the world had been plunged and the havoc the German Panzers were wreaking all along the front in European Russia, Reiner expressed no great concern in his correspondence as he continued his apprenticeship under Professor Böhm in the relative safety of southern Germany:

Jettingen
9 July 1941

Dear Parents,

I've just killed two flies with a swatter and who knows how many more I'll have to kill. Since I am out of stationery, I just use regular paper and a typewriter. Just think—next Sunday I'll be going to Memmingen and visiting Hilde Gessner [Heidi's friend]—I've already written her. Here they've already made big plans for August. The whole household will be going to Vöcklamarkt, which is only some 40 km from Salzburg and lies in the foothills of the Alps. A famous altarpiece is supposed to be located nearby. In August, there is of course the famous Mozart festival in Salzburg. This vacation is supposed to last two weeks—with my luck, I'll probably be called up in August!

Outside, the June bugs are constantly buzzing about now. I leave the windows open wide, first to let in the evening breeze; and second, so I can catch a June bug and put it on Gitta's bed. (I always called her Fräulein Frasquita.) She hasn't yet taken revenge for my last prank. One really can't help oneself from wanting to aggravate her—she talks so much. The other day she hung up a flycatcher in the room. It didn't catch many flies, only paper wads. But she talks so much, and always without thinking and always so flatteringly of the Böhms. I recently made it clear to her that the reason we have wars is that people talk too much. If something is not true, then talking is the same as lying. But if it is true, I suppose one should talk. Otherwise, things would be worse.

Jettingen
24 July 1941

Dear Mother,

On Monday, *Frau* Professor [Böhm] left to go to Cologne in order to pack up most of her things. The Böhms are so worried about air raids. Frau Böhm will probably meet Father there. Yesterday three of us went fishing in the Mindel in a rather primitive fashion. We were using a ten-meter long net, and for me it was fun despite our slim catch. We caught four whitefish, two trout, and one grayling. We had no trouble eating them all today, but I am already hungry again. I recently swam in the Mindel, but you could barely swim because you had to swat off the swarms of gadflies that buzzed around your head. It was even worse when you got out of the water.

The 6th Infantry and Operation Barbarossa

While Reiner was busy swatting flies and irritating Fraülein Gitta or netting fish in the quiet waters of the Mindel, his future comrades-in-arms of the 6th Infantry Division were crossing the East Prussian border into the Soviet Union as part of Operation Barbarossa. Assigned to the 9th Army, they formed the northern flank of von Bock's *Heeresgruppe Mitte*. On Day One of the invasion, they fought through the surprised Russian border outposts and advanced 42 km. The next day, they advanced another 45 km and crossed their first major obstacle, the Nieman River—that same river that Napoleon had crossed in 1812 to begin his ill-fated invasion of Russia. On 24 June, the 6th Infantry pushed forward another 30 km— over 100 km in just four days, and all on foot. These first few days characterized what Operation Barbarossa would be for the German infantryman—marches of 30–50 km a day, day after day, under the blazing sun of high summer. First along the leg-killing, sandy treks of the Baltic countries, and then the choking dust of the primitive Russian roads. The only break from the mind-dulling marches came when they had to assault Russian positions. The fast-moving Panzer divisions might grab the headlines and be featured to the German public in the *Wochenschau* newsreels, but in reality, 75 percent of the invading German forces were infantry divisions. Napoleon had once remarked that an army marches on its stomach. The Germans knew better; an army marches on its feet.[1]

In three weeks of combat and 500 km of marching, the 6th Infantry Division had reached the Russian fortifications of the 'Stalin Line', at Polozk. They broke through this barrier with its concrete bunkers (many cleverly disguised as harmless barns and farm houses) on 15 July, crossed the Duna, and advanced another 350 km to the city of Rzhev on the Volga. The city fell to the Germans on 16 October, and the men of the 6th Infantry continued their eastwards march, little realizing that in a few months they would be back in Rzhev, a city whose name would be forever bound to theirs in the history of the Russo-German war.

Despite the incredible successes achieved during the first months of Operation Barbarossa, the Germans were beginning to have problems of their own. Having advanced 1,200 km, their supply lines were just that much longer; the deeper they plunged into Russia, the wider the front became for their already over-extended lines. They too had suffered heavy losses. By 1 November, the invading German forces had lost 686,000 men (20 percent of their original force), one half of their vehicles and 65 percent of their tanks. Their equipment was wearing out; the men were exhausted.

The Führer's headquarters might have been euphoric, the generals confident, but the common German soldier—the *Landser*—knew that it had been no walkover. It was he who had had to 'kick open the door', and he who had found the Russian soldier to be a tough, stubborn, and at times fanatical opponent. And then there was the country itself—there seemed to be no end to it. Accustomed as he was to the confines of cities and towns or the limited vistas of Alpine valleys and forests of Germany, the German soldier now found himself lost in the vast expanse of the Russian land, with only the sky above and the endless steppe below.

In addition to the wear and tear on the equipment and the exhaustion of the troops, another factor now came into play—the Russian climate. First to arrive were the autumn rains. They were initially welcome relief from the heat and the throat-clogging dust of the Russian roads, but then the world dissolved into the bottomless Russian mud—the *Rasputiza*—and the German advance came to a halt. Then, on the night of 6 November, came the first frost. It, too, was a welcomed relief at first, as the ground froze and the advance could resume. However, the thermometer continued to fall, and by 13 November it had reached –20 degrees centigrade. The Russian winter had arrived.

As with all other divisions along the front, the 6th Infantry continued their march through the dust, the rains, the bottomless mud, and then, finally, the frost. They advanced another 100 km beyond the Volga, and after heavy fighting, they reached Tutani, on the Tma River, on 2 November. That is as far as they would ever get. They were now 1,000 km from where they had started on the morning of 22 June, but more important to the men of the 6th *Rheinisch-Westfälischen Infanterie* Division was that they were 2,000 km from their *Rheinisch-Westfälischen* homes.

Although the war was 2,000 km away, deep in Russia, it was now actually coming closer to the Niemann family. The night raids by the RAF were becoming more than a nuisance. Reiner's brother, Wolfgang, was serving in an anti-aircraft battery near Essen. In October, Reiner's apprenticeship with Professor Böhm ended. He had received his notice to report for military duty.

Einberufung: Conscription

The date of Reiner's conscription into the Wehrmacht is recorded in his service record as 20 October 1941. He was eight months short of his twentieth birthday, the normal age of conscription. As he put it in a 2 November letter to his brother, Wolfgang, 'although it was fully expected, I did think it came rather quickly.' And for good reason.

The Russian campaign had been raging for four months, and although the Wehrmacht had achieved great successes, Leningrad had been reached but not taken. The Ukraine had been entered but not subdued, and Moscow was still several hundred kilometers away. The German plan called for Russia to be defeated before winter, and winter was but weeks away. More important to Reiner's conscription was that the Wehrmacht had already lost 686,000 men. Little wonder that his conscription 'came rather quickly'.

Being within the VI *Wehrkreis* (military district), Reiner was assigned to the 58th Infantry Regiment of the 6th *Rheinisch-Westfälischen Infanterie* Division. It was an old division, the 6th. Its three regiments (58, 18, and 37) were the proud tradition-bearers of famous German regiments of wars past. It was certainly 'Old Army', its officer corps made up of *Grafen* (counts), *Freiherren* (barons), and any number of *vons* (men from Germany's military aristocracy). Drawing its recruits from the Rhineland and Westphalia, it combined the steadfastness of the Westphalian peasant with the technical skills of the recruits from the urban centers of the lower Rhine. It was also half-Catholic and half-Protestant, and so required the services of two divisional chaplains of the respective confessions.

In the war so far, the 6th Division had achieved an illustrious record. Although it had taken no part in the Polish campaign—posted instead to guard the western border of the Reich against a French attack—when it was let loose in the Western Campaign in May 1940, it was unstoppable. It went through the Ardennes, across the Maas, and then across the Somme at Amiens. Then there was a plunge southwest, across the Seine, all the way to the Loire valley, and then a turn back north to the Cotentin Peninsula and the channel—a victorious march of over 1,000 km.

In Operation Barbarossa, they had so far achieved no less, albeit this time against much stiffer opposition. On the day that Reiner, still dressed in his civilian clothes, walked through the barracks gates in Osnabrück[2] and crossed the boundary between civilian and soldier, his future comrades of the 58th were crossing the Volga some 1,500 km away. The war diary of the 58th Regiment records for that day:

> Using Russian boats found in the area, the Regiment began transporting the foot soldiers over the river in the late afternoon of 20 October to establish a bridgehead on the northwest bank of the Volga.

Reiner was assigned to the 3rd *Kompanie* of the 58th Regiment's training and replacement battalion. Despite the heavy casualties, the Wehrmacht was still demanding that its troops be thoroughly trained before being sent to the front (where they would receive even more training before entering combat). The Wehrmacht had no use for half-trained cannon fodder. Reiner was trained for some seven months before he arrived at the front. He was also accepted as a *Kriegsoffizier-Bewerber* (KOB), or officer candidate. His training was intensive, extensive, thorough, and methodical. It takes more than practical training to turn a civilian into a soldier, something the Wehrmacht well understood and at which it excelled—no matter the recruit's background.

So began Reiner's *Feldpost* and his life as a German *Feldgrau*.

Osnabrück
2 November 1941

Dear Wolfgang,

My first impressions here in the barracks. On 20 October, we recruits arrived here after a train ride that we enjoyed to the fullest. We all engaged in lively conversation the entire way. In the afternoon, I went with the recruit transport from the Rhine and Ruhr area to our new home, the Winkelhausen-Kaserne. It had all been a good trip in beautiful sunny weather. We talked among ourselves and got to know each other.

At the train station in Osnabrück, we were divided up. Some were sent to the 37th Regiment and others to the 58th and the M.G. [machine gun] company. Then as we marched through the city to the barracks, we were reunited with each other and joined by other recruits we didn't know. But then there was a hold up, and we couldn't proceed any further. We were left alone with our own thoughts, which can hardly be expressed even with strong language.

As they were arranging the Guard, and we assembled on the parade ground for the first time, waiting to be assigned to our units, I felt somewhat out of place and embarrassed in my civilian clothes in the presence of all those in uniform who watched us from the windows or as the war-wounded or decorated veterans strode by. They greeted us, strong and proud with a certain elegance, which encouraged us, even though we sensed in them a hint of smug superiority. Our superiors received us upon our arrival with consideration and concerned themselves with us like older, experienced comrades. As I later became acquainted with the military tone, I had the feeling that I would be well looked after and resolved to give it my best.

I hadn't been home for the past half year before my calling up. Instead, I was in South Germany and Silesia working with various architects, getting practical experience in preparation for my architectural career. However, I was ever mindful of my imminent conscription. And although it wasn't fully unexpected, I did think it came rather quickly. So, as I marched through the city with my comrades, I kept my eyes open for buildings of architectural interest.

Osnabrück
8 November 1941

Dear *Fraülein* Thiem,

Thank you for your letter. It's a rather strange correspondence that you and I carry on with one another. It began with a mix-up: then it became like a conversation in polite society—that is, casual, conventional, lacking in urgency. And now we've reached a crisis that came about from an error. Isn't that sufficient for you? It wasn't an actual error but rather a difference of opinions concerning the facts that you misunderstood during my last day in Cologne. Due to our mutual reserve, it is clear that I must explain the event, and I don't feel that it will exhaust me. If you so desire, I will continue with our correspondence and hope that it will soon be more than this forced and informal tone that it has at the moment.

In order for you to better know with whom you're dealing, and since I showed my cards first—as you know, I would like to become an architect. As long as I was a civilian my main activity was playing the piano, not waltzes, tangos, foxtrots, and the like, but the music of Bach and his predecessors.

Osnabrück
30 November 1941

Dear Parents,

Yesterday evening I organized my mail and determined that Father was correct in his number of his letters. I had #11 down twice and skipped #12, so now it's been corrected.

Today the local theater is presenting *The Magic Flute*, and I want to try to get into town to see it, even if it's sold out. Tomorrow we have combat practice and will go to the range on the train. Since we must be up by 3.45 a.m., we only have passes until 9 p.m. this evening, and that is how long the opera lasts. That is the second problem, if I should go. The third problem is that tomorrow we also have to have our gear in perfect shape. Consequently, today's letter will not be a long one, especially since I still need to write Wolfgang a birthday letter.

Osnabrück
30 November 1941

Dear Wolfgang,

I don't know if this letter will reach you as quickly as your postcard reached me yesterday since you are no longer in your old anti-aircraft position but rather in an officer training course, and I am now in the barracks. I don't know if this is an improvement or not, but at least it is a change, and when I was in the RAD, a change was always something positive. So that this letter should reach you on the right day, I am writing it today—especially because I also have time to write today. I will leave it up to you as to when you open it. So, with the clumsy hands of a soldier, I write you to congratulate you on your birthday [3 December] and on your official promotion.

Osnabrück
7 December 1941

Dear Professor,

I send you my congratulations for your approaching birthday and my wishes for your continued good health. Unfortunately, it must be with a letter, and a letter for which I do not have the necessary spare time. That's because we have vigorous training the entire day. Even in our free time, one's ability to concentrate is greatly curtailed by the constant radio noise, accordion racket, and the usual unrest and disturbance in our quarters. So, you will have to put up with the type of letter that might arise out of such conditions.

You have probably learned from *Frau* Dunkel that I have finally been called up, but that's not that bad for I am in the 'Queen of all Weapons', the '*Kindergarde*'[3] [Children's Guard], that is the infantry. At the moment, I find myself in the less than pleasant realm of the recruit. Here in the fields we are taught 'Lie down!' 'Up!' 'Forward!' We wade through streams in water up to our belts and all this in rain or shine. And so it goes, day after day.

At noon, we have exercise, target practice, instruction, and assembly with all our new equipment. Since we are not allowed to leave the base, on Saturdays half the men usually get drunk, which leads to us getting even stricter training the next week. Once a week we have to make a long night march, and we average two air raid alarms a week that disturbs our sleep. Thank God, we can at least sleep in the cellar. That is, if we can, because we are crammed together there on sacks of straw. But when you think about what will and must be demanded of us at the front, you have to endure and actively take part, and give up, for now, all civilian interests including music, art, etc.

The Attack On Moscow

While Reiner was making the transition from civilian apprentice-architect to soldier, Operation Barbarossa reached a critical point. With the arrival of the Russian winter, the German High Command had to make a crucial decision: halt the advance, have the troops dig in for the winter and go over to the defense, or make one final push to take Moscow. Hitler naturally chose the latter and ordered the offensive to resume on 19 November. With weakened divisions (the average strength per division had been reduced from regulation 15,000 men to 5,000) and exhausted, hungry, and frozen men, the attack on Moscow went forward.

The Germans fought through the cold and the snow; they somehow fought through the last two defensive lines before Moscow. Nevertheless, the thermometer kept falling: 30 degrees below, then 40 below, then 50 degrees below zero. Vehicles froze, tanks froze, and weapons froze; hands and feet froze. Finally, on 5 December, the attack on Moscow froze to a halt. Forward elements of the attacking German divisions had reached to within 8 kilometers of the city and claimed they could see the spires of the Kremlin—it was probably a mirage floating in the icy ground mist. It would remain a mirage, for except as a prisoner of war, no German soldier would ever enter Moscow. Operation Barbarossa had failed. Russia had not been defeated in a single swift campaign, which left those at the Führer's headquarters asking themselves, 'What now?'

Stalin soon answered their question. Assured by his intelligence network that Japan had no intention of joining its German ally in the war against Russia, and that Japan was instead planning to attack the American and British forces in the Far East, Stalin felt confident about withdrawing some thirty divisions of his far-eastern army to throw them into battle against the exhausted and overextended German forces. These well-trained divisions were superbly equipped for winter warfare and would spearhead the great counter-attack Stalin was planning. Nor were these the only troops he possessed. Despite having lost the equivalent of 229 divisions since the beginning of the war, the Russians had been able to amass 350 divisions for the offensive that would throw the German invaders back if not destroy them altogether. However, some of these divisions were nothing more than cannon fodder, with little or no training and many of the men not even having weapons. However, this was of little consequence to the Soviet high command. When the offensive got rolling and the casualties rose, there would be more than enough rifles to go around.

The great Soviet counter-offensive began on 6 December on the Central or Moscow Front. Over the next several months, it spread along some 900 kilometers of the Eastern Front, from Leningrad in the north to Belgorod in the south. That first winter of the war saw some of the most bitter and brutal fighting of the entire war, and all of it under the harshest of winter conditions as German and Russian troops battered one another among the snow drifts in –30 to –40-degree weather.

The German Front was broken through at many points. German soldiers repeatedly found themselves cut off and surrounded. They would fight their way out only to find themselves surrounded again. Hitler demanded that the front be held. 'Not a step back!' The troops would defend and die where they stood. Field marshals and generals were fired, and new ones were brought in to save the situation. However, under the avalanche of relentless Russian attacks, the Germans were driven back— some 120–190 kilometers at various points along the front.

By the end of March, however, the Russians, like the Germans before them, had exhausted themselves, and the great Soviet counter-offensive came to a halt in its own blood. By now, the war had cost the Germans 1 million casualties, with 210,000 dead. Russian casualties ran to some 5 million, perhaps extending as high as 6 million. With both sides having fought themselves to exhaustion, it was now the turn of the Soviet high command to ask 'What now?'

Shielded by the official propaganda, the German public knew little of the depth of the crisis that gripped the Eastern Front. As far as they knew, their sons were still advancing victoriously or at least bravely holding the front. In a 19 December letter to her cousin, Reiner's mother lamented, 'Unfortunately our two soldier sons cannot be with us at Christmas.' The two girls, Lütte and Heidi, were there, and Wolfgang, in nearby Essen, managed to obtain a thirty-six-hour pass to be home on the 26th. Reiner did not make it home for *Weihnachten*.

Reiner's training intensified and he qualified as a KOB (*Kriegsoffizier-Bewerber*), or an officer candidate, and was scheduled to begin his initial officer's training. Although Reiner read the same newspapers and viewed the same weekly newsreels as the German public, he probably heard numerous accounts about what awaited him in Russia from the returning wounded convalescing at the barracks.

21 December 1941

Dear Parents,

Earlier I was in town, but unfortunately all the shops were closed. I came home immediately so that I could take care of the Christmas mail, and I found your letter from Sunday as well as the new reading material and the three pretty postcards, for which I thank you. I'll almost wager that the Barlach card came from the Book and Art Shop at the Minoritenkirche. Right?

While in the city, I went past the Deppen & Sons glassworks, with whom Böhm used to carry out his plans for his stained-glass windows. From the street, one could see the panels of one of the windows Böhm designed. It stood in a room near the window. This is just another sign of how small the world really is.

Osnabrück
31 December 1941

Dear Parents,

Just a short letter today to let you know what is going on in my life. On 3 January, we will be going to Senne, a large training ground near Paderborn. We will be there for two weeks and will have rigorous training every day. We should have free time on Sunday and passes, but with all the repairs to our equipment that we'll have to make, as well as getting caught up on sleep, we won't have much time to write, nor will we feel like writing. However, if it's not that bad, then you will surely hear from me.

I enjoyed your postcard with the artistic corn on it. I'm interested in how Heidi does it. I miss her personal notes, her conscientiousness, and her exactness. In any event, I've been able to recognize Cologne again through a telescope, and it seems to me that when seeing the total of it, one has the best picture of the city.

Since Christmas, we haven't had any heavy duty because our commander really hasn't had the desire for it. For example, early this morning we were to have night maneuvers, but it was cancelled because of ice.

From: Osnabrück-Haste
Winkelhausen *Kaserne*
3/58 (3rd *Kompanie*/58th Regiment)

To: Grete & Ella Niemann
Bad Flinsberg
Isargebirge
5 January 1942

Dear Aunts,

Sorry, just this card with my hearty thanks for your Christmas package with the delicious cake and the other good things to eat and smoke.

For three days now we have been here on the exercise field at Senne near Paderborn. Today our NCO course began and after four weeks will be continued in Osnabrück.[4] The duty here is hard and without breaks. We go out to the training field at 9 a.m. and usually don't return until 5 p.m. Even on Sundays, we don't have free time nor a chance to go out like before, because there are always plenty of things to clean or repair. Otherwise, things are great with us here. We sleep in stone barracks that are well heated. Paderborn is 8 km away and is easily reached by bus, but for the time-being, we don't get any passes to go there. I send you my quick greetings and my many good wishes for the coming year.
Your Reiner

Osnabrück
22 February 1942

Dear Professor Baum,[5]

I just came back from a beautiful ski trip that I took with three comrades. It was wonderful. Although on Sundays we are allowed to sleep until eight o'clock in the morning, we got up early and at first light, we were crossing the fields and going through an almost Hessian-like beech forest. It made me think of the beautiful ski trails along the *Hohes Gras* and the *Habichtswald*, and it occurred to me that I have wanted to write you for a long time. Recently Father sent me your Christmas calendar, which now hangs on my locker door and reminds me every day of the old days. I thank you for it, and for the Schelmann stories, which I read many years ago.

At the beginning of January, we were at the training grounds at Senne near Paderborn and not that far from Kassel. I had applied for a Sunday pass but nothing came of it because we were sent back that Sunday to Osnabrück for psychological evaluation. Then we returned to Paderborn. On 26 January our officer course began which is why we underwent psychological evaluation in order to approve us for further instruction. The course lasts until the end of March and is why I write so seldom and above all so disconnectedly. Our platoon leader is a fine *Leutnant*, who sees to it that we do not go stale intellectually. He takes us to the theater, to concerts, poetry readings, and dances at the Palucca dance school. Every week we arrange a social evening at a neighboring girls camp[6] where we sing and play music, which would be better if we practiced more. We read Rilke poems, and novels by Wiechert.

Osnabrück
14 March 1942

Dear Wolfs,

Have you received the civilian articles yet? I left them in Cologne with the trunk as agreed. My parents would either want them sent back or have you bring them with you if you are going to meet them in Cologne. I don't know if that's possible on short notice. However, if you need them, then send me or my parents a short note. And now I thank you once more for your friendship. You know yourself what good friends you've always been to me and to my parents.

Anyway, everything worked out fine. I arrived in Cologne right at midnight, went home, and woke the family but they are used to that because of all the air raid alarms. Then we had a nice time together, emptying a bottle of wine and then we went to bed. Unfortunately, at least for me, all day Sunday was under the shadow of me having to depart and that rather ruined the short time I had at home. I get distracted at home and don't do any of the things that I had intended to do. I like to bury myself in beautiful books, pictures, and music, but I tell myself that the more you attach yourself to your former life, the more difficult it will be later to accept the crassness of your military duty. So, I remained aloof and distant on that beautiful Sunday and was not able to allow anyone to bring me out of myself or to improve my mood. There was nothing else I could do. In the evening at 8.45 p.m., my train brought me back here without having to make any stops, and by 4 a.m., I was in bed only to be awakened at 5.30 a.m. The next evening, we had night maneuvers and frequent air raid alarms that lasted for the rest of the week. Consequently, I haven't gotten any sleep, but that's part of the bargain.

First Time Out:
Letters from Rzhev (I)

The Summer Battle of Rzhev

The Russians were determined to retake Rzhev. The Germans were no less
determined that they would hold the city. There was one battle for Stalingrad,
which lasted six months; there were six battles for Rzhev, which lasted for a year
and a half. But who today has heard of Rzhev?

A city of 54,000 inhabitants (1939) that lay on both banks of the Volga, Rzhev
had been contested throughout its 1,000-year history. Located on the upper
Volga and rich in timber, over the centuries it had been held by the principalities
of Novgorod, Lithuania, Poland, and finally by Muscovy. In 1942, however, the
struggle for the city had nothing to do with timber. While the Russian winter
offensive had driven the Germans back all along the front, Rzhev had held like a
bulwark among the flood of Soviet attacks and now remained the sole German
position on the Volga. It formed a projecting salient some 530 km long, and 150
km northwest of Moscow, and as long as this salient remained in German hands,
Moscow would always be threatened. Similarly for the Germans, as long as they
held Rzhev, it could always serve as a springboard for any future offensive against
the Soviet capital.

When Reiner first arrived at the front in the spring of 1942, there had already
been three battles for Rzhev. A fresh recruit from the training grounds, he was
about to enter the fourth or 'The Summer Battle of Rzhev'. His military records
show that he arrived at the city on 13 May 1942 and was assigned to the 1st
Kompanie (*Oberleutnant* Leder) I *Bataillon* (*Oberstleutnant* Hollinde)[1] 58th
Regiment (*Oberst* Furbach) of the 6th *Infanterie* Division.[2]

Although an officer candidate with some officer training, his rank was that of
Schütze, or private. The unfortunate gap in Reiner's correspondence, which began
in February and extended over the next two and a half months, leaves the reader
uninformed about Reiner's first experiences and impressions of the Eastern Front.

However, excerpts for the *Kriegstagebuch* (war diary) and Heinz Löhdorf's '*Geschichte des 58ten Regiment*' do provide information as to what his days would have been like this first time out:

> From 13 April—21 May only the usual skirmishing and sudden shelling by artillery and mortars is to be noted. During this period we had thirteen dead from the artillery...
>
> The weather during this time was so capricious as to prevent any undertaking by friend or foe. Only the artillery had any work to do....
>
> 22 May: renewal of artillery attacks on our position, also far to the rear. *Leutnant* Hotan of 2 *Kompanie* was killed....
>
> 23 May—During the night of May 23, the 1st *Kompanie* under *Oberleutnant* Leder relieved *Kompanie* Kurrath....
>
> 24 May—16 June: Mostly quiet. Only sporadic artillery and mortar fire by both sides and enemy patrols. The regiment suffered no losses. At night enemy air activity by U2's [nicknamed sewing[3] machines or night owls]....
>
> 17 June: Heavy fighting. By noon, four attacks with nine tanks (T-34) supported by fighter-bombers are beaten back with no dead on our side....
>
> 19 June: Regiment visited by *Generalfeldmarschall* von Kluge.[4] Otherwise just the usual artillery and mortar fire....
>
> 8 July: I *Bataillon* relieved by part of Infantry Regiment 37....
>
> 11 July: Regiment back on the front. Relieves Infantry Regiment 693....
>
> 11–16 July: Usual artillery and mortar fire. Regiment has four killed....
>
> 17 July: Enemy patrol hit by counter-patrol. Enemy loses eight dead and one prisoner.
>
> 19–21 July: Front remains quiet. Night of 20th aerial attack costs one life....
>
> 22 July: Planned relief of the regiment by Infantry Regiment 11 begins at 02:00. March to rest area northwest of Ssytschweka begins....
>
> ...after months of hard fighting we are looking forward to a time to rest and restore our equipment in order to be ready for future assignments.
>
> 30 July: All these hopes and wishes only last until noon because Ivan[5] has broken through the lines at the juncture of 256th and 87th divisions. In this emergency, 9th Army immediately thinks of Regiment 58. We fall in for what will become a costly mission.

The 6th Infantry's period of rest and replenishment had been cut short by the opening attacks of the 4th Battle of Rzhev. The remnants of the Russian divisions trapped far behind the front from the Third Battle of Rzhev had barely been rounded up when the Russian commander of the Kaliner Front, General Konew, launched another offensive to retake Rzhev. He had forty-one infantry divisions, fifteen infantry brigades, and thirty-eight armored brigades at his disposal, in addition to over 3,000 tanks. On 30 July, after a ninety-minute bombardment of the German positions, the Russians launched a two-pronged attack—one from the north, aimed at taking Rzhev, and a second from the east, aimed at the right flank of the Rzhev salient.

The northern attack broke through the German lines at the juncture of the 256th and 87th Infantry divisions just west of Rzhev. The 6th Infantry division was ordered to fall in and head north at all speed to close the gap in the German lines. Such was the crisis and the haste that the division was sent off piecemeal and without much of its heavy equipment.

First to go was Reiner's I *Bataillon* of the 58th. They were loaded on a train at Ssytschewa and rushed north to Rzhev, where they were dumped off and sent into battle with only the ammunition they could carry in their belts and one hand grenade per man. They were to seal off the hole in the German lines near Polunino. Just after midnight on 1 August, they went into the attack in the rain and the dark. Somehow, they managed it. They fought their way through three lines of Russian entrenchments and closed the gap. The Russians left behind 200 dead and fifty-one prisoners. It had cost the Germans eleven dead.

The next day, 2 August, as other units of the 58th Regiment arrived, the troops dug entrenchments in the swampy ground the best they could. At 1.50 p.m., Russian infantry, supported by two heavy and three light tanks, attacked in the sector of the 2nd *Kompanie*. The attack was repelled with the loss of twelve dead. Reiner's company commander, *Leutnant* Voss, was wounded. During the course of 3 August, two more Russian attacks were repelled, costing another four dead. *Leutnant* Voss's replacement, *Leutnant* Berghaus, was killed.

As the sun rose on 4 August, it promised another day of bloody combat for Reiner and the men of the 58th Regiment. Heavy movement along the Russian lines throughout the morning indicated a renewal of their attacks against the positions of the 58th. At 1.45 p.m., Russian bombers attacked the village of Polunino. Ten minutes later, a heavy and accurate artillery bombardment rained down along the entire sector of the III *Bataillon* and Reiner's 1st *Kompanie*. The Russians launched their first attack at 2 p.m., with two battalions of infantry supported by thirty T-34 and KV-1 tanks.[6]

At around 2.30 p.m., three of these tanks broke into the German positions while the remainder stayed back and blasted away at the German infantry. The Russian infantry was thrown back in hand-to-hand combat. The Germans destroyed nine Russian tanks. Three Russian tanks were damaged but drove off under their own power.

At 3.00 p.m., Russian tanks with accompanying infantry renewed the attack. Only one platoon of infantry moved to within hand-grenade range before they were repulsed. Undeterred, the Russians launched yet another attack at 4.00 p.m. with three battalions of infantry supported by ten tanks. German artillery and infantry fire stopped the Russian infantry, but Russian tanks broke into the German positions and spent the remainder of the afternoon driving back and forth through the German lines, firing at anything that moved, until they were finally driven off.

The Russians launched their last assault at 7.50 p.m., and three of their heavy-duty K-1 tanks tore a hole in the German lines, inflicting heavy casualties. Later, in the dark of the night, German engineers hunted down these monsters, destroying one and disabling another. The third tank escaped. The fighting on 4 August finally died down after midnight. The war diary of the 58th Regiment includes the laconic entry '*Das Regiment verlor heute 30 Tote*'—'Today the Regiment lost thirty dead'. But not Reiner.

A brief note from Alfons to the family:

Dear Loved Ones,

Reiner has been wounded! The news hit us like a bolt of lightning. But it's not too serious.

You should be receiving news of this soon. Because in Reiner's letter he so vividly described the defensive situation on the northern Russian Front—for the first time and because many letters will make his stay in the hospital a bit more pleasant, we must all write to him soon.

Alfons

From Reiner:

Warsaw, 13 August 1942

Dear Parents,

I hope you all have received my postcards and aren't too worried about me in regard to the fighting around Rzhev—which must have started near the end of July. What happened with me is as follows: On 21 July, we were relieved by another unit and pulled out of the front. Then in two days, we marched 90 km to the south and moved into rest quarters in a deserted village that was more lice- and vermin-ridden than ever before. Because of the rain and the swampy terrain, we couldn't even pitch our tents. The higher command would not leave us in peace. They hounded us and drilled us in water that was almost over the tops of our boots—all under the name of 'Tactical Maneuvers'. This finally reached a high point and end point on 20 July when we were sent out in the pouring rain to engage in live-fire maneuvers from 5 a.m. until 11 a.m. We didn't have a stitch of dry clothing, either on our backs or in our huts. And so we sat until 2 p.m., soaking wet in our filthy huts and watched the stream slowly rise and cut us off from the rest of the company. Then came the order for us to be ready in forty-five minutes. How we all cursed about that.

While we were packing our kits, the Russians had to go out in the rain and build a causeway over the stream. But it wasn't done quickly. We couldn't march off until evening, and only for two kilometers because we could see that neither the baggage train nor the foot soldiers would be able to cross the river. So, we marched off, without our baggage, in another direction. Still in the pouring rain, we marched two kilometers through swamps with water up to our belt buckles. Then, fifteen kilometers on a road to the next supply depot. This turned out to be only eleven kilometers from our original starting point in the village.

At eight the next morning, we rolled out and reached our initial position at three in the afternoon. That evening we went into action, without having been fed or resupplied. For us, everything went well. Our company remained in reserve that night while in the morning the other two companies went into attack and began suffering casualties. That was, I have to think about it, the 30th of July. The evening of the 31st, we advanced and on the first of August had our first combat. The evening of that same day, we relieved the other two companies in their forward positions, and after more than two days received our first cold rations. It would be another two days before we got any hot food and that was just Army stew.

For two days it was quiet on both sides, but on the 4th of August, the fighting broke out, and it doesn't seemed to have stopped yet. The morning around 10.00 a.m., I left our position to go back to the village,[7] which lay some eight hundred meters off, in order to fetch some water. There was no great hurry, so I spent some four hours rummaging through houses looking for anything useful. Then shortly before 2.00 p.m., as I was getting ready to head back, accurate artillery fire suddenly began hitting the village. I took cover in an anti-tank bunker. After ten minutes and as many explosions in the immediate area, the houses to the left and the right were burning and the bunker was in shambles. Even the stairway had collapsed. Despite the artillery fire, we scrambled out because the house next to us was threatening to collapse on us. There was more to come. I crawled about in wide circles through the burning village and then when it finally quieted down, I sprinted the eight hundred meters over the open ground and back to our position. Then Ivan showed up with his 52-ton tanks[8] with their 173 mm guns and began driving back and forth across our trenches. I took over the mortar whose crew had all become casualties and began firing on the five tanks that were in my company's sector. Because I had no cover, after two hours I got hit with shell fragments. I was then ordered to take a message to the rear and was told to remain there.

At midnight, I arrived at the collection post for the wounded in Rzhev. We were loaded onto a train August 6th and left around 2 p.m. On the way, we were attacked by fighter aircraft, which killed eight of the wounded, and destroyed one of the locomotives. And then began the seven fat years. On the morning of the 10th of August, we arrived here and were deloused, bathed, and put into beds, and did that ever feel good.

Now I'm waiting for a train to take me to Germany. Every day they call out, 'Who's going to Frankfurt am Oder, Dresden, Halle, and so on.' Since no trains are going to the west (Cologne or Rhineland), I will probably choose to go to Breslau, Berlin, or even Kassel. Should I have no luck with this, I will choose South Germany. If you have any suggestions, please write as soon as possible. But then maybe I'll already be gone. I can't complain about things here except that when I first arrived I ate far too much. I'll have to be careful now. Unfortunately, I've lost all my equipment and personal items, above all my diary and letters. They were all left behind in our forward position, so I've probably seen the last of them because the company pulled out on the 4th of August. Actually, I've been quite lucky to have this insignificant wound because the fighting around Rzhev was just getting started, and I fear that few of the company will survive. Perhaps I will even get leave and see you all soon.

Auf Wiedersehen,
Reiner

The Summer Battle of Rzhev Aftermath

For now, Reiner was well out of the bloodbath of Rzhev. After eighty-three days at the front, he went back to Germany. He spent the next two and a half months in the hospital until he was assigned to the convalescent company of his regiment in Münster. There he remained until classified KVF[9] and sent back to Rzhev. When Reiner wrote 'not many of the company will survive', he was not far wrong. When the I *Bataillon* was briefly pulled off the front line on 18 August, Reiner's company was down to only one officer, four *Unteroffiziere* and eighteen men—and the summer Battle of Rzhev still had two more months to run.[10]

By the time the 4th Battle of Rzhev ended in mid-October, the Russians had gained little ground. True, they had reached the Volga on either side of the city, but the Germans still held Rzhev. It had cost the Russians 380,000 dead and wounded, with another 13,770 taken prisoner. This 4th Battle of Rzhev was quickly followed by a 5th, the 'Winter Battle of Rzhev', which began on 25 November and ended on 15 December. Over this period, the Russians lost another 200,000 men. Again, the Russians had gained little, and the Germans still held Rzhev.

In these last two battles of Rzhev, German divisions like Reiner's had been reduced to nothing by casualties, then rebuilt only to be reduced to nothing once more. The Russians had lost over 500,000 men—but who today has ever heard of Rzhev?

Reiner's military records state that he was wounded on 8 August 1942 near Rzhev and that he suffered an *Artilleriegeschossplitterverletzung* (shell fragment wound) in his upper right arm. He was treated at the main dressing station at Rzhev before being transported by hospital train to the military hospital in Warsaw on 10 August. On 24 August, he departed by hospital train to the Reserve Military Hospital at Gars am Inn, Germany, 40 kilometers east of Munich, where he arrived on the 27th. Six days after being wounded, he was promoted to *Oberschütze* (Private First Class) and awarded the *Verwundetenabzeichen* (wound badge in black) for his first wound.

In early October, shortly before Reiner was classified *Kriegsverwendungsfähig zur Ersatzeinheit* (fit for reserve duty) and released from the hospital on 19 October, his mother made the long journey from Cologne to Gars to visit her son in the hospital. Reiner arrived in Münster on 22 October and was assigned to the *Genesendenkompanie Infanterie-Ersatz-Bataillon 58*, the Convalescent Company of the Replacement Battalion of the 58th Regiment.

Osnabrück
9 September 1942

Personnel Company, Replacement Battalion, 58th Regiment
To: *Oberschütze* Reiner Niemann
Reserve Hospital Gars am Inn

Due to your arrival in hospital, you have been transferred to the Infantry Replacement Battalion 58, Osnabrück, effective on 27 August 1942. After recovering, you will report here.

A sufficient convalescence leave will be granted you either by the hospital or the replacement battalion. Upon completion of your leave or after release from the hospital, you must proceed without any delay to the Infantry Replacement Battalion 58 Osnabrück. If you do not comply with this order to return without delay, then you will be considered Absent without Authorization and subject to punishment.

Captain and Company Commander [signed]

[Undated]

Dear Parents,

I had just mailed a letter, four pages, and then came your letter with Mother's travel plans. Because I am not yet able to get out, I haven't been able to look into living accommodations and food. I will see to it tomorrow and find out what there is as far as accommodations in private homes are concerned, and send you a telegram. The food supply in town will certainly be better than in Cologne, and I can get additional bread here at the hospital. Because it's not rationed, there is plenty of it. The same with meat. I can always save some from lunch and dinner, without it being deducted from my daily ration, although we don't always get so much every day that I can do it. But with unpeeled potatoes, it can be done because there are always extra potatoes. Don't worry about this illegal method of getting food, and don't think I can't do it. I don't even have to be secretive about it because around here it's normal for the men to take extra meat, put it on bread, and save it for evening supper. There is always bread here, even between meals, and fruit can be bought. So, come on.

Telegram

Gars

Address: Professor Niemann, Cologne, Klettenberggürtel 15.

Private accommodations possible, but plentiful. Food: bread, potatoes, and often various spreads. If necessary, more can be had with ration stamps. Better than in Cologne.

Gars

10 October 1942

Dear Parents,

It seems strange to me to be writing to you and Mother since once again she is in a different world, a world that I can only reach with my thoughts. Unfortunately, now my home is much further away than Cologne, and the difference between Russia and Germany is so great that the differences between the various regions of Germany seem almost non-existent. I don't know if you can understand or not but I no longer feel that I can take the train back home. I would need a moon rocket or some other fantasy vehicle. Often I have dreams about home. I see myself showing Father my Russian coins, or I see myself quarreling with Wolfgang or as I sit with Lütte and Knud [Lütte's husband][11] at a musical performance and grow angry and then embarrassed because I so tactlessly expressed my unrequested opinions of these wartime productions. And then they try to help me out of my embarrassment, painful though it may be.

Gars
14 October 1942

Dear Aunts,[12]

Mother left here five days ago and she travelled back to Cologne without stopping off in Kassel or in Magdeburg at Aunt Annemie's to rest. After she left, autumn arrived here and not just for my hospital stay but for the entire region around Gars. When Mother left here, it was rainy and dreary, and now it's become quite cool and frosty, and I am no longer angry about being discharged. I've held this position here with my light wound a long time—two and a half months—and now beautiful autumn is here. When you stand in the steep mountains that they have around here, you can see the pine forests completely spotted with pinecones such that you would think you had never seen so many before. Often, the tops of the trees are so heavily weighted by these bundles of cones that they bend over like shafts of wheat and must lean on their neighbor. The sun shines through the leaves of the beech trees and causes them to shine bright green and orange. It's almost like walking barefoot, soundlessly, over the thick moss of the gently lit forest floor. The glittering spider webs slide across your brow and often cling to your eyes.

Soon, however, I won't be able to take such walks in this beautiful region. My time here is almost over, but I shouldn't think of the future because it only disturbs the present moment. I would like to do something about it, but soon it will be marching time again.

Cologne
23 November 1942

Dear Wolfs,

As you already know, I'm at home now on convalescent leave. Yesterday was the high point of my leave. Eight days ago, Wolfgang managed to get a long leave. And Lütte and her soldier boy and his mother were here, and that was really wonderful. However, today they left. I just saw them off, and now I am sitting at home thinking about my own departure on Thursday and what will follow. You will be my only consolation because my unit has been transferred to the Schlieffen Barracks in Münster. So, I can surprise you from time to time with a visit. That gives me some human support between my bleak military duties. I'll be able once again to hear the sounds of the piano instead of military commands and the shrill sounds of the whistle that are always ringing in my ears. Above all, I would like to see the many Gothic and Baroque structures, under your guidance of course. But I have many other plans: to nose about the work of an architect, and do research on the construction firm[13], to have music for the piano and flute forwarded to me, to go to concerts and hear beautiful music. I hope that gradually I will be able to do all this before I am packed off to the front again. For the time being, I am giving you ample warning.

Greetings,

Your Reiner

[Undated]

Dear Aunts,

I hope to get my next leave at Christmas time and maybe even get to Flinsberg. At least it's being considered and if the conditions allow, we might be able to celebrate Christmas with you. But perhaps I shouldn't get my hopes up. It all depends on us three soldiers and our leaves. The rest of the family has gone to bed, and only poor me is still up, completing the letters that were delayed because of family celebrations. I am already tired, but I promise you that I will write you more often from Münster. Until then, I will send my greetings.

Münster
8 December 1942

Dear Aunts,

Fortunately, I am once again with the troops and hopefully I won't be leaving them anytime soon.[14] Our unit has been moved here from Osnabrück, which isn't all that bad because there are people here I can warm up to and Münster is a charming city, much more so than Osnabrück. The Wolfs, the *Bauernhaus* architect for whom Uncle Fritz [Niemann] has worked, I visit every day and play the piano and feel completely comfortable with them. Perhaps this is good for them as well, a relief from their monotony that allows them to forget the heavy shadow that hangs over them. I've also visited Sophia Vocke [a family friend], and they are completely the opposite of the Wolfs. She has no trouble seeing the good side of life. She draws portraits and with the money she gets from it, she buys herself playthings: a lapdog for 300 marks and a harmonica. It's funny to see how she uses things to make life pleasant. She has two children, many visitors, her dog, a grand piano, and a beautiful apartment. I wish everyone could be like her in these difficult times. I haven't yet seen all that much of Münster. It's usually dark by the time I get to go out. Thank God, the old city hasn't suffered much damage from the bombing.

Second Time Out:
Letters From Rzhev (II)

The year 1942 revealed that Germany had reached the limits of its military power. The tipping point in the balance of the opposing powers occurred early the next year. The advance of the Italo-German forces in North Africa towards the all-important Suez Canal had finally reached its limit and halted along the Egyptian border. In October 1942, at the Battle of El Alamein, the British 8th Army forced the Axis forces into a full-scale retreat back across the North African desert to Tunisia. Not only had the United States entered the war against Germany in December 1941, but it had also landed an army on the west coast of North Africa in November 1942, which drove east to link up with the British. Rommel's *Afrikakorps* now found itself bottled up in Tunisia with the Allies in front and the Mediterranean behind them. Hitler's orders to the trapped German forces were predictable—'victory or death'. There would be no evacuation. By May 1943, both an army and a campaign had been lost.

Limits had likewise been reached on the home front. In January 1943, the Wehrmacht required 800,000 new recruits, but despite the most rigorous call-up and combing-out of factories of non-essential workers, only 400,000 could be found. Foreign workers were brought in, willingly and unwillingly, and boys now manned the anti-aircraft batteries defending German cities and industries as the former crews were sent off to the front. Eventually, the German armed forces reached a peak of 11.2 million men in the spring of 1943, but that was the limit; from there, the number would only decline. The war was also being brought home to Germany, and not just by the ever-lengthening casualty lists and lines outside of shops. The British Royal Air Force was ramping up its terror-bombing campaign on the German population. On 28 March 1942, a concentrated force of over 200 British bombers hit the city of Lübeck. In May, Rostock was attacked over a period of four nights, and on the 30th, the British launched a 1,000-plane raid over the ancient city of Cologne.

The campaign in the east, however, was the most illustrative of the limits and overextension of German military power, and it also saw the most serious consequences. A year earlier, in Operation Barbarossa, the Wehrmacht had been able to launch its attack along the entire front, whereas in the summer of 1942 it could only concentrate sufficient forces to attack on the southern sector. Unlike Barbarossa, which had been intended to defeat the Soviet Union, 'Operation Blue', as it was called, had the more limited goal of seizing the Russian oilfields of the Caucasus in order to be able to continue the war—not necessarily to win it. However, even that limited objective proved to be too much.

It was a two-pronged offensive with one army, von Paulus's 6th, advancing east to the Volga and the other armies of Army Group South driving south into the Caucasus. Stalingrad on the Volga was reached in August but the city was not taken, and as the German forces drove deeper into the Caucasus, their flank became ever longer. Von Paulus's 6th Army at Stalingrad was to protect their flank but who would protect his? So overextended was the German Army that it had to depend on Italian, Hungarian, and Rumanian armies to protect the German 6th Army's flank north and south of Stalingrad. The consequences of this overextension were soon in coming.

On 18 November, the Russians launched their massive counter-attack. The Italian, Hungarian, and Rumanian armies north and south of Stalingrad collapsed, and four days later the two pincer arms of the Soviet attack met at Kalatch and the German 6th Army was cut off and encircled. Von Paulus was ordered to hold out—not because of stubbornness on the part of Hitler, but rather to buy time for the German armies in the Caucasus to retreat back north to avoid being cut off as well. And so the men of the 6th Army in Stalingrad dug in and held. Attempts were made to supply them by air; attempts were made by German forces to break through to them, but all failed. The men froze or starved to death until 31 January, when Von Paulus finally surrendered. An entire army was lost, with 107,000 German soldiers marched into captivity. It was the greatest disaster of arms that the Wehrmacht had yet suffered in the war. With some truth, the claim can be made that the German reverses in North Africa and at Stalingrad represented the turning point in the war. From then on, Germany was in retreat—but no one knew that at the time. All that was known was that the war and the dying would continue.

Stalingrad had fallen. Rzhev would still hold out—at least for a little while longer. When Reiner returned to the front on 25 January 1943, the fifth or 'Winter Battle of Rzhev' had ground to a halt only a month before. Not much had changed. His regiment and division were still at Rzhev, although they were no longer in the Kolberg *Stellung* in front of the city. They had turned over their sector to the 129th Infantry Division and had been moved some 5 km west to the Lepeticha Bogen, where they took up position on the south bank of the Volga. Reiner now wore the *Verwundeten Abzeichen in Schwarz* (wound badge in black) and had been promoted to *Oberschütze* (Private 1st Class). More correctly, he was an *Obergrenadier*, because on 29 October 1942, his division and regiment

had likewise received a promotion of sorts. To boost morale, Hitler had decreed
that henceforth all infantry divisions and regiments would be renamed grenadier
divisions and grenadier regiments, and the enlisted men's ranks of *Schütze* and
Oberschütze would become *Grenadier* and *Obergrenadier* respectively. Not
that the divisions and regiments would receive any additional *Grenadiers* or
Obergrenadiers. Reiner's regiment consisted of only two half-strength battalions (II
Bataillon had been dissolved earlier) and had a combat strength of about 800 men.

However, they had received the new light machine gun (MG-42), with a rate of
fire of 1,500 rounds per minute, and specialized winter clothing and camouflage.
No longer would they be reduced to wearing blankets, tablecloths, and bed linens
stripped from Russian huts. Now they could resemble genuine German soldiers
rather than beggars and vagabonds when the snows arrived. Reiner was assigned
(25 January) to the 3rd *Kompanie* (*Leutnant* Martin Kruse) of the *I Bataillon*,
58th Grenadier Regiment and was to begin his eight-week required tour as a
squad leader before attending more officer courses in Germany. Fate, however,
changed all that.

The next chapter begins with excerpts from the *History of the 58th Regiment*
and its war diary that illustrate the immediate situation that Reiner encountered.

Löhdorf: History of the 58th Regiment

The Christmas celebrations were not disturbed. A Christmas tree stood in
each bunker, and holiday packages arrived on time. Comrades who had no
family received the 'Führer packages'. All were deeply moved and beautiful old
Christmas songs rang out. This was our 4th Christmas of the war.

The last few days of the year 1942 were decidedly quiet and without any
events. The casualties for December were 47 dead and 28 missing.

The first of January was celebrated by the firing of all our weapons and
except for the usual disruption fire, Ivan remained quiet. Even so, we had 9
dead and 2 missing.

On Jan. 5th an assault party led by *Leutnant* Kleinemeier broke into the
Russian position north of Kolonie. In man-to-man combat, the enemy position
was rolled up but *Leutnant* Kleinemeier was wounded and died at the main
dressing station on Jan. 9th.

On Jan. 14th the regiment was relieved in part at night from the bridgehead
position in order to move a few kilometers further west and to take up the Volga
position. It was minus 32 degrees.

On Jan 15th the rest of the regiment was relieved. So on Jan. 18th, our
regiment occupied the Volga sector. We were on the south bank and Ivan was
on the north bank. He wasn't as close to us as he had been in the '*Stadtgut*',
'*Handtuch*', or the '*Panzerstrasse*' positions. The new sector was considerably

more quiet than our former sector. Only the harassing fire bothered us. On 30 Jan the regiment received 9 Iron Crosses 1st class, 112 Iron Crosses 2nd class, and 50 war services crosses, 2nd class.

Reiner's correspondence:

Berlin
15 January 1943

Yesterday, instead of reaching Berlin at 8.30 p.m., the train didn't arrive until 10.00 p.m. It wasn't in a hurry, just like us three KOBs [officers in training]. We went to the Vockes and slept there unconcerned. Today we got up around 8.00 a.m., drank coffee and went sightseeing in Berlin, that is to say, we sat in the Nussbaum,[1] Berlin's oldest bar, drank a beer and wrote postcards. Later we met up with an old tour-guide who told us about the city and the things worth seeing. Then around 12.30 p.m., we went back to the train and it headed to Posen, which we hope to tour when we get there. The day after tomorrow, we should be in Warsaw. So far everything has gone as planned.

Brest-Litovsk
17 January 1943

And now we are in Brest and with luck will be able to see the city. So far, we haven't had to sleep in the train at night. We left Berlin around 12.30 p.m. and arrived in Posen around 5.10 p.m. where we received our first rations and got a hot meal in the evening. Then we went to the weigh station where we were hospitably received. I slept in a bed with a hot water bottle, and the other two KOBs slept on sofas. The next morning we got up around nine, had hot rolls for breakfast, and then went to see the city. All but one of the churches had been closed by the Gestapo, so we could only see them from the outside. I passed by most of the shops. There was hardly anything worth buying, even in the bookshops. I did, however, find a little practical illustrated dictionary. As for the modern architecture, only the brick water tower was of any interest to me. I had seen it in a picture before. On the other page, I have tried to draw it for you. It may look different. I have only tried to capture the general impression. Overall, it seemed well built and proportioned. We left Posen around 2.30 p.m. and arrived in Warsaw around 10 p.m. and spent the night. We left around 6 a.m. and arrived here [Brest] around 11.00 a.m. I'll write you more later. For now, I send you my greetings.

Minsk
20 January 1943

Now I have enough time to give you a complete description of my travels from Münster. I got back from my leave around 3 a.m. and immediately began packing. I had packed most things and lay down around 5.30 a.m. to catch two hours of sleep. But at 7 a.m., things were hectic because we were told of all the things we had to do before we shipped off. At the cobbler's, I had to pick up my boots. At Barrack 13, I had to exchange my socks, and at Boelcke Barracks, I had yet to retrieve my laundry, then at Fourri, a loaf of bread. I also had to turn in my pass and get my new papers. Then back to Boelcke Barracks to sort out my personal items and get them packed. By the time I was finished, there was no time left to get over to the Wolfs to get my things there packed and ready to go. There would have been time, however, for the train that was supposed to leave at 10.00 a.m. didn't leave until 11.42 a.m. The Battalion office didn't get our papers ready in time, so they sent us off without them. With all this, I guess I was lucky to be able to get my things at the Rossius's sent off. When I get back to the Vockes, I will write the Wolfs and explain the circumstances. The three of us then went to the train station where a cyclist finally came with our papers from the Battalion. Then we departed for Hamm and around 2.10 p.m. headed for Berlin where we arrived around 10 p.m., an hour and a half late. My progress from there you will already know from my other letters. Right now, I want to eat for it is lunchtime and the food has already been brought in. I'm sitting here in the soldiers' home and things are rather pleasant here. Hardly has one sat down and there is coffee and buttered bread. Then at exactly 1.00 a.m., lunch. Here it's rather similar to how it was in Brest. I couldn't find a train because they were overloaded. Because of that, we stayed two days in Brest. We arrived there on the morning of the 17th and that afternoon went to a movie, *Der Meineidbauer*, an over-dramatic, almost laughable film ruined by the heavy use of technology at every chance. We spent two days in Brest, eating and sleeping, and we left on the 19th in a rather empty, poorly heated train and arrived here this morning around 3.00 a.m. The cold here is bearable since we don't have to stay outside that long. It's about –25C and about 25 cm of snow on the ground, which crunches loudly. In the train, the windows were always covered with thick ice and if you opened them, then the walls would be covered with frost. At the time, things are going fine with me. I take every opportunity to amuse myself, get my share of food, and delay my departure.

26 January 1943

Dear Parents,

And now I am here.[2] Today I'll remain here in the rear with the supply troops and tomorrow afternoon I go up to the front. It gets dark here two hours earlier than with you and during the day one can't go up to the front line positions. We are still in the same old area, but I don't get to go back to my old company [the 1st]. That's because of the squad-leader confirmation process,[3] and I'm not too happy about it. How this process will go, I don't know, but it won't be an easy time. Otherwise, the front is quiet and well provided with bunkers and other defenses. The provisions for the trip here were so good that I still have plenty of bread left. And we are all well supplied here. Each day 600 gr. of bread, and every fourth day, 750 gr. per day. The mid-day soup is rather thin because there are no potatoes. For the cold, we are supposed to have felt boots and camouflage snow suits, at least those who have to stand watch duty or go on patrol. All in all, we are well provided for and the weather is beautiful, especially for skiing. The landscape around here is also rather beautiful, so we were all in good spirits when we arrived here yesterday. But I'll write more about this later. First, my field post number is 09175D. If you can, please send me nice things to read.

Your Reiner

[Undated]

As I was writing the letter this morning, the other KOB was still here. He is already fed up with the situation here. I guess it's my own natural stubbornness that allows me to come back and re-adjust to the front. Since my earlier writing, I've been able to wash up and further get used to my surroundings. At the moment, I'm writing this letter with a big cigar in one corner of my mouth and a well-pleased smile in the other corner. My comrade has already left for the front lines, and I am to go up tomorrow. Unfortunately, we won't be in the same company. I've just had a Russian lesson from the twelve-year-old son of the household here. With the help of your tourist dictionary and the illustrated dictionary I picked up in Posen, something may come of this. I would like to stay longer in the village here and learn more Russian. For the most part, I've overcome my aversion to anything connected with Russia. Yesterday, it was a joy to go skiing through the winter landscape. As always the sky was as blue as it is with us during the summer. The slanting rays of the setting sun cause every ridge or drift of snow to cast a distinct shadow. The entire landscape is sharply delineated into golden red and blue. In Wjasma, I first saw the incredible play of the reflecting light of the winter sun. Like in a mist, one could see from the left and right side of the sun a stream of light that grew wider and brighter as it descended to the earth. It's all very amazing and joyful to see. Sometimes in the distance, you see a train on the horizon sending tiny rings of smoke up into the sky.

Of my trip here, there is nothing special to report. To Wjasma, I traveled in a well-heated passenger train and from there in a heated cattle train.

Right now, I want to get some sleep, for the last time in a house and on a real bed without being wakened by sentry duty. So goodnight, my loved ones. Just think it was one year ago that I began my KOB course.

Your Reiner

28 January 1943

Dear Parents,

Now I am really back at the front. I have already slept one night on the front lines. Yesterday when I arrived, the *Leutnant*, who is a theologian, told me I would be taking over a squad whose *Unteroffizier* was on leave. This will be no easy task. For one thing, it's a large squad: twelve men and two machine-guns, and for another, it has several 'lifers' and several Iron Cross holders. So, I tell myself, '*Friss, Jude, oder stirb*' ['eat, Jew, or die']. So far, I've been accepted well enough and the area is quiet, and I also trust my superiors. If in the next fourteen days nothing happens, everything will be fine.

28 January 1943 [evening]

As a new squad leader, I have just finished my first trench duty. I have to admit that when the platoon leader was making clear all my duties as a squad leader, I was getting fed up. Here on the front line, every leader receives his instructions from his superiors, he salutes and says, '*Ja und Amen*', knowing full well he can't carry out the orders without getting a bad reputation among his men. For me, as a KOB and probably the youngest member of the squad, this would be fatal. Most of the officers understand this, but the Colonel is too far removed from the NCOs. That's why during an inspection everyone is leading each other by the nose, and it's all a sham. It's like in civilian life where you have all your tests and final exams. After the platoon leader had explained the most important of my duties, I was at a loss to figure out how I could ever perform them. But now after having done my trench duty and being treated with respect by the men, my self-confidence has grown, and I am feeling a bit superior and pleased with myself. But maybe it's not all that great. One can always exploit human weakness like pride and self-importance to get from them performance of which one never thought himself capable. But enough of that. Being a squad leader does have its advantages. I don't have to stand in the cold on sentry duty, so I'm safe from freezing and because less is demanded of me physically, I can survive on the rations. The main advantage is that after spending a certain time here, I'll be able to get away. I am quietly hoping to get a leave in April, so I can spend

Easter with you at home. We'll just have to see. Otherwise, things here are like they always are in Russia. True, I don't have any lice yet, but there are plenty of other bugs to ruin a night's sleep. Sleep here is not a pleasure as it is at home, or even in the barracks. Here it is an outright necessity that you cannot do without. Soon enough I'm sure I'll have lice and everything else, but then maybe by then your first letters will be here.

Your Reiner

2 February 1943

Dear Parents,

As of today, I have been here a week and am in the middle of everyday matters. At the moment, the ground is not frozen, but it is snowing and the trenches are full. Consequently we have to work night and day, three hours of sleep is all we get. When working outside, one is completely drenched with sweat on the inside and when you come inside to thaw out, you get completely drenched on the outside. I don't worry about lice or other bugs; the wet clothing runs them off. Otherwise, everything is all right. I have worked myself in as squad leader without anything going wrong to this point. Recently Ivan attempted a raid on a neighboring position. Imagine this: of sixty men, Ivan left forty-five lying dead in front of the position and five were taken prisoner.[4] We only lost one badly wounded and two lightly wounded. Our position still remains quiet, hardly anything else seems possible. I send you my greetings and you don't need to send me any candles. We have plenty here.

Your Reiner

4 February 1943

Dear Mother,

Right now, I have some time, so I will begin your birthday letter. It's early morning and all the night sentries have been relieved, only one man stands watch during the day. Since we have twelve men in the bunker and only eight beds, some of us have to stay up and write. I've just sent a card to Böhm and have had time to look at the pictures from my last leave. I've thought about the fact that just three weeks ago I had returned to the barracks from my leave in Cologne and was packing my gear. Two weeks ago, I was in Smolensk, and one week ago, yesterday, I had arrived here at the front. In five weeks, I should be an *Unteroffizier* and most importantly, maybe in seven weeks back home on leave. I believe it will all work out. I was thinking that if Wolfgang still has to go to Africa, he wouldn't be able to leave before then and with his susceptibility to jaundice he couldn't tolerate the tinned army rations there. I also think that you must not worry so much about your sons. You should have a very happy and pleasant birthday, without all the usual running around and daily torments. In the evening, I hope you can have a glass of good wine with your dutiful daughters in a warmly lit living room, and not in some cold air-raid shelter. I don't think that anyone could wish you anything better for your birthday.

8 February 1943

It's high time that I write you a letter and get it off in the mail so that you receive it in fourteen days. Our lives continue here with all the daily travails and troubles. It's difficult to keep the trenches cleared of snow and muck. For the moment, the cold is not all that bad. I wish it were colder. Then we wouldn't have to work so hard day and night. Work as a squad leader is not all that hard, just never-ending. At night, I have to check the sentry posts of the platoon every two hours and during the day there are so many things to do that one meets himself coming and going. The men have so little sleep that they are grouchy and reluctant. You have to stand right there behind them to make sure the work is done and then afterwards look after the tools yourself. Plenty of cigars come in that are never smoked. But that's just the way things are, and I'll just have to get used to things like lice, bugs, and all the other discomforts of Russia. There is one good thing here: I can roast my bread ration and it almost tastes like a fine delicacy, which I'll certainly miss when I'm no longer here. Actually, I may get away from here sooner than expected. An officer course is supposed to begin April 1st, and even if my eight-week term here isn't finished, I may be able to attend it. Supposedly, the course is no longer held in Berlin, or even in Germany, but rather in Belgium. But that is another matter. A couple of days ago, the squad that I lead was divided into two squads, although we are all still in the same bunker. That lightens my responsibilities. For now, I only have four men and one machine-gun. I have been issued a brand new sub-machine-gun. I am otherwise distinguished from the men in that I don't wear the thick, clumsy winter clothing but rather the less restrictive white-camouflage cloak and trousers. In addition, I also have padded long underwear. I don't wear all my winter clothing, but still I don't freeze. Those who do sentry duty have recently been issued hot water bottles with a chemical package, which when one adds snow or water to it, will maintain a temperature of 50–60C. These are carried about in our pockets, but lucky is the man who does not need them, especially as concerns the human body.

Your Reiner

13 February 1943

Dear Parents,

It's two o'clock in the morning and outside is a raging snowstorm. I've just come inside from trench duty and am cheering myself up with some schnapps in the warm bunker. One of the men was already lightheaded enough to offer me six cigarettes for a canteen of water. Our evening 'Volga Stew' is heavily salted and so we had long since drunk up all our coffee. So naturally, I went out and made my way some 50m through the deep snow and driving storm to the stream and fetched the water. Now I have six cigarettes and am in an even better mood. (Please send cigarette paper as we have plenty of tobacco. My pipe is broken.) You should see how things are here, though mostly we are in good humor. Well now, it's time for me to climb into my vermin-sack. The bed bugs won't bother me that much. My clothes are still wet and I sleep too deeply. In an hour and a half, I have to go back outside, the last of four times every night. I send you all my greetings and good night!

Your Reiner
Punktiert: Pause in letters possible. Replacement in sight.[5]

17 February 1943

Dear Parents,

It is early morning and I have just finished my last two-hour trench duty. I am still fairly fresh, if not completely rested. But when one unexpectedly receives such a long nice letter as I did yesterday, then one must sit down and write. Thanks so much for it. Right now, I have the use of a bunker light made of paper, a tin holder, and wax, which soon enough will be completely liquid. But now, to the letter.

The air-raid during our last farewell is such a thing. I hadn't yet reached the bus stop on Sülzberger Street when the all clear sounded. I still had an entire hour before the train left, and I considered going back, but I realized the extra half-hour at home would not be worth the awkwardness of a second farewell. So, I just remained in the train station. One should not mindlessly rummage about in emotions of a farewell, and public farewells are always stiff, awkward, and more often than not lead to later regrets and self-incrimination on the part of the participants, as Father and I have both done. As hard as departures and farewells may be, we all understand how we feel. But enough of this, there is no point in trying to think logically about emotions for there is no logic in the world of emotions. Conversation and writing require logic.

I've been here for three weeks and it doesn't seem that long. Certainly at first, it was difficult for me to play squad leader, but I've settled in and become accustomed to the situation so that my life isn't that difficult now. At first when I was more or less dropped in among eleven men, I really had no idea how I was going to manage. The situation is better now that they divided the squad so that I only have five men to lead and one machine-gun. My life is much more bearable now. Also, twice a week I have KOB instruction back at the battalion, but I have it under control and will let you hear from me every 4–5 days.

Among the candidates here, is one from the old course we had with Lt Iffland, and he told me about my former classmates. Of the twenty-nine men, four have been killed and several others crippled; one is at weapons school and another was sent for the first time to the front in January. I've also had a chance to see my two comrades who came here with me. One had bad luck and was wounded again on February 3rd. He had only been a squad leader for three days and had just started his term. He was the one I attended courses with in Selenitschino when we were in the rear area for three weeks. He had been so angry to learn that he wouldn't be returning to his old company. The other KOB comrade is with the machine gun company and as such is out of danger. My situation has been fairly easy because we haven't been attacked by any assault groups or patrols. We seldom have casualties and then only from an occasional sniper or mortar round. The reason is that during the night the Russians stay some three hundred meters away and some four hundred meters during the day. Even the cold hasn't been that bad. Tonight it's barely below freezing and yesterday during the day it got up to around 5C and here the snow melts quickly. We will probably have more cold weather again but –30C is more preferred by us than raging snowstorms at 5C.

As concerns winter clothing and candles, we actually have more than we need. We often move our positions about and there is constant changing of personnel. How does it stand with my letters from my trip here? Has the letter from 17 January from Brest or the one from 20 January from Minsk arrived— or perhaps both? For Mother's letters, I am especially thankful. Does she have a new pen or something? Her penmanship is much different than before. It's much rounder and less cramped than before. It is similar to Heidi's smooth, even, perfectly formed letters or also like *Frau* List's. But I'll quit harping on this for it is nonsense. Even so, something has changed, maybe Mother is in a better frame of mind for her writing is definitely younger, more confident, and free as well as more concentrated and focused, especially when you consider the time she was writing: 11.30 p.m. I enjoyed the letters and yes, I remember Uncle Karl's expressive eyes, which seemed strange in his otherwise serious, reserved and stern face. Is this all nonsense that I'm writing? Well, I'll just leave it as it is and close this letter. Soon more, and I send you all my greetings.

Reiner
Punktiert: I am northwest of Rzhev Volga in no-man's-land. Front calm.

22 February 1943

Dear Parents,

By now Mother's birthday is over and I have spent a lot of time thinking about home, and in celebration of her birthday I read a good portion of *The Story of Sali and Vrenele*. It's probably my favorite story that Father used to read to us when we were children, busy with our scrapbooks. I can remember the smallest details—that's how well I listened.

Here everything is pretty much the same except the food has improved over the past few days. Instead of the wretched 'Volga Stew', we're getting a good, thick stew you can almost stand your spoon up in. On occasion, we even get some chocolate. The small book and your letters #2 and #3 came Wednesday, and I thank you for them. I've managed to get another pipe and we've plenty of tobacco here. So, we live pretty well and are not too bored. The temperature for the most part is more like middle Europe than Russia. Recently I've been using foot powder against the lice and it works pretty well to relieve the itching and to heal the bites. Right now, I hold the initiative against them.

Greetings,
Reiner

23 February 1943

Dear Parents,

Today is the last day to write and then it might be a while before you hear from me again. You know how things are in the Army. And, there is so much I could tell you. But first let me thank you for letters #2 and #3, which I received on the 8th. The pocket book you sent I enjoyed, and the letter from Böhm. The call for total mobilization of the country sounds as serious as does the situation in the southern sector of the Eastern Front.[6] Strange that things here are relatively quiet and uneventful, almost as orderly as back in the barracks. Perhaps soon it will change. Sorry I can't finish the letter because our ration-carrier is going back and taking the mail with him.

Greetings to you all,
Your Reiner

There was a very good reason why Reiner could write no letters home for a while—the Germans were leaving Rzhev. For a year and a half, they had stubbornly clung to the Rzhev salient and to the hope that someday it would serve as the springboard for a renewed offensive towards Moscow. If ordered, they would hold it for another year and a half; if necessary, they would fight another four 'Battles for Rzhev'. However, events far to the south were forcing them to abandon that for which they had fought so long and so hard.

The Rzhev salient projected some 160 km deep into the Soviet central front. With a base of 200 km and a perimeter of 530 km, the Germans needed twenty-nine divisions to defend it. With the disaster at Stalingrad and the loss of the entire 6th Army, the Rzhev salient was a springboard to Moscow the Wehrmacht could no longer afford. The salient and the illusion of a renewed assault on Moscow had to be abandoned. A carefully planned withdrawal to straighten out the front line would reduce the front by over 300 km and require far fewer divisions to hold it. Those divisions, thus freed, could then be employed elsewhere or used to form a reserve.

Hitler, ever reluctant to take a step backwards, finally yielded to the new reality and the requests of his chief of staff and agreed on 6 February to allow a strategic withdrawal of the 9th and part of the 4th Army from the Rzhev salient. It would be a massive undertaking. With the codename of *Operation Büffel* (Buffalo), twenty-nine divisions with 250,000 men and all their equipment—nothing was to be left behind to the enemy—would have to be withdrawn over 100 km to the new front line. To do so would require the construction of successive lines of defensive positions to which the troops would withdraw as the sack was gradually collapsed in a phased withdrawal. Two hundred kilometers of new roads and 600 km of new paths for the sleds were required, while 1,000 km of railroad tracks would also have to be laid. All this had to happen in just four weeks, as X-day was set for 1 March; construction battalions, transport and supply troops worked feverishly throughout the month of February to meet the deadline. Staffs worked no less feverishly, working out timetables and routes for the withdrawal.

Nothing could go wrong. Withdrawing from prepared positions in the face of a numerically superior enemy is always a highly risky operation. If the enemy suspected anything and launched an attack, then the carefully planned withdrawal could turn into a disastrous rout. Security was of the utmost importance. Therefore there were no letters in, no letters out. The troops along the front were not informed of the withdrawal until 20 February and were not told of the actual date until the 27th.

However, a last-minute complication threatened to disrupt all the carefully laid plans; 60,000 Russian civilians demanded to be evacuated with the troops. Having worked for and cooperated with the Germans, they had little desire to remain behind and be 'liberated' by their countrymen. There was nothing for it; they would have to be taken along, otherwise they would simply leave on their own, clogging the roads with their wagons and sleds and dangerously upsetting the carefully laid-out time schedule of the withdrawal. Eventually all problems were worked out and *Operation Büffel* was set into motion as planned at 7 p.m. on 1 March.

The first units of Reiner's regiment began evacuating their positions in the Lepaticha bend of the Volga *Stellung*. Three squads were left behind as a rearguard under the command of *Leutnant* Hotzel of the 9th *Kompanie*. The first stage of the withdrawal was a non-stop 30-km march to the rear—no easy task for legs that had grown accustomed to defensive warfare over the past eighteen months. There was no motor transport either. All equipment had to either be dragged on sleds or carried by the men.

On 2 March, the withdrawing units reached the prepared positions at Stupino. A squad of six men was left to patrol the area near Okrokowa and to wait for the rear-guard units that were still in the old positions along the Volga. Earlier that morning, the Russians, sensing something was amiss had sent out a patrol across the Volga, which was turned back by the German rear-guard units. At noon, the Russians unleashed a heavy bombardment of the old position and a force of about 200 Russians leaped from a gorge on the north bank and stormed across the frozen Volga. The three rear-guard squads fought them off at times with hand grenades and hand-to-hand combat. The Russians left behind 110 men dead. It had cost the German rear guard four men. At around 2 a.m. on 3 March, the rear-guard units were ordered to pull out and rejoin the main body (they had been provided with motor transport).

Here follows a description of the fighting that occurred on 3 March from *The History of the 58th Regiment*.

Around two o'clock in the morning [Mar 3] the rear guard units were ordered to pull out without alerting the enemy. At 10 a.m., a Russian assault group attacked our patrol at Okrokowa. The attack was beaten back with a loss of 40 Russian dead. The enemy then tried to flank the patrol, which was forced to pull back. Around 5 p.m. 300 Russians attacked our position at Stupino. The enemy had heavy losses—100 dead and many wounded. Our own losses were 6 dead, among them Lt Kruse, 3rd *Kompanie* commander.[7] We were not able to properly bury our comrades. They were buried in a snowdrift since it was −5C. At 7.00 p.m. the regiment began its withdrawal to Ssytschwewka. The rear guards were under the command of Lt Lindemeyer of the 1st company. The Russians began shelling us heavily with mortars and attacked us with some two hundred men. This attack was fought off but cost us four dead, among them Lt Lindemeyer, Sergeant Rohde, and Sergeant Tieman. Several of our wounded were evacuated by our troops.

After March 3, *Operation Büffel* had to continue without Reiner.

Smolensk
6 March 1943

Dear Parents,

I have been wounded again and this time not so lightly as before. I have three shell fragments in my right backside and some unimportant fragments in the arm and head. I haven't spit up blood, so it looks as if the lungs aren't injured, although at first it was difficult to catch my breath. Nor does it seem as if I have any other internal injuries. I guess I am doing all right. It happened on March 3rd during a night rear-guard action. How I came back is not to be described. But last night I arrived here at the battalion hospital. And was put with nine other wounded, all with obvious lung injuries. Also, my KOB comrade from the course in Selenitschino was there. He's from the old 1st *Kompanie* and was shot through the lung three weeks ago. Soon enough I was on the leather table and the doctor concerned himself with removing the shell fragments. It didn't seem serious and I was declared 'Transportable'. I don't know when I'll leave from here. The main thing is that it's certain I'll be going to Germany. As a precaution, I didn't eat anything while I was being transported here. Neither did I smoke. You see, sometimes I can be careful. Here we eat a good though light diet. For breakfast: sweetened oatmeal, white bread with butter, red marmalade. And a half-cup of coffee. For brunch: millet with milk and lemon juice. For lunch: Rice soup with asparagus and bit of meat in it. We are served, fed, bathed, and shaved by Russians.[8] A couple of sturdy Red Cross nurses carry out the normal duties with a pair of hospital orderlies. Of my equipment and personal things, I have even less than last time. I'll write about that later. At least some of it didn't end up with Ivan. I'm getting tired now, so be good. When I scratch my bug bites now, I don't even bleed.

Your Reiner

Minsk
10 March 1943

Dear Parents,

I've been transported here and hope to be transported even farther. I've met a comrade from my labor service days and what's even crazier, an old school mate from my school days in Kassel. Despite his heavy head bandage and his banged-up face, I recognized him immediately. I'm doing better now, but not that great yet. I send you all my greetings and I'll write more later.

Your Reiner
I still have my watch and it runs fine and keeps perfect time.

Brest

13 March 1943

Dear Parents,

And so goes the endless, boring transport with its many stops: The Front–Smolensk–Minsk–Brest–Warsaw–Germany. I hope I can at least skip Warsaw. I will be here a week and I have no idea where I'll end up in Germany. They haven't done anything yet to my wounds. The fragments in my head, they simply pulled out with tweezers. The three fragments in my upper arm have healed over and lie beneath the skin. The three fragments in my back are not serious, although they do make lying in bed uncomfortable. I lie here in a small room with two other men, and all we do is sleep and talk and except for lunch we don't eat very much. The other two have received their '*Führer-Paket*'. I didn't get mine because all my papers including my *Soldbuch*[9] were left behind at the aid station in my field jacket. But I can always get my *Führer-Paket* later. It's not actually a package but a book of ration cards that are good for 2 lbs. of butter, 2 lbs. of sugar, 2lbs. of meat, 3 lbs. vegetables, 5 lbs. of wheat flour, and for a Sunday meal, one veal cutlet and a streusel cake. Unfortunately, the cards are only good for a certain time, otherwise they could be used for Christmas. Since I've been lying here in the hospital, it's been beautiful spring weather. I'm looking forward to cycling and the piano and all the books I got last Christmas. Here I'm reading a book *The Great Journey* by Blunck. It's not particularly exciting, but it's better than romances or detective novels. The radio plays all day, but otherwise things here are bearable. You might want to wait a bit before you write back. In the meantime, I send you my greetings.

From your Reiner

Brest

17 March 1943

Dear Parents,

I am still in Brest. Hopefully, I will soon get somewhere where something will be done for me, and hopefully that won't be in Poland but in Germany, preferably in southern Germany again. Here, out of sheer boredom, I have started studying astronomy. Among the 'knapsack reading' around here, I found a booklet that is interesting, and I'd like to know more. Perhaps when I have a firm address, Father could send me something about R. Henseling's study of the cosmos and some of the *Kosmos* magazines too. Perhaps Father could send some bread-wrapping paper or adding-machine paper in with it so I could draw and make schematic sketches on it. You know, I am lucky that I don't yield to anyone when it comes to knowledge—whether it be from classic antiquity or Albert Schweitzer's Johann Sebastian Bach or German Baroque music. Recently on the radio, they were playing a beautiful piece from Bach, one that I play on the piano. It was a worthy trio of stringed instruments. When I get home, I'll have to look up what they were playing. Otherwise, around here we swear a lot because everything goes so slowly. Recently it was announced that we would get five German cigarettes, two *cigarellos*, ten black Polish cigarettes, two envelopes, and a razor. There is little to read around here except stuff like Ernst Zahn or dime novels. The drivel on the radio is usually so boring, but it will all be better when we get on the train for Germany, compass setting 26, the same setting we used during our rear-guard action. So, I leave you now and hopefully for the last time from here.

From your old Reiner

In the Erzgebirge
21 March 1943

Dear Parents,

Today is the beginning of spring. We were transported here yesterday evening. I was able to travel sitting up, but I'll write more about that later. In 1938, I was here with Wolfgang and Uncle Friedrich in Oberschlema.[10] Where I am now is about 3 km from there.

Warm greetings from your Reiner

Neustädtel[11]
27 March 1943

Dear Parents,

I just now received your long letter, the first one in seven weeks. I thank you for it. The only letters I received from you in Russia were three long letters on the 8th and 9th of February, that was all. But that wasn't your fault. We were preparing for our withdrawal and so no post came through. That you didn't receive any mail from me for two weeks isn't my fault either, for the same reason. Before I was wounded, I wrote you every four to five days, if only a short letter. When I was wounded, I put my last letter, along with the letter of a fallen comrade, in my tunic, and I didn't get it back before I was transported out, so that letter and my *Soldbuch* are probably lost. Later I wrote you short, unnumbered letters from Smolensk (March 6th), from Minsk (March 10th), from Brest (March 13th & 17th) and then on the 21st the card from here. This letter would be #6.

My condition at present—the small wounds have at least healed on the outside. But I still have pain, either from the fragments or because they haven't healed on the inside. I can only lie on my back in bed and can smile but not laugh (don't worry, only on the outside). When I breathe deeply, I notice that something isn't right and if I am not careful when I move, I have a sharp pain in my right shoulder blade. Because of this I may be transported somewhere else because there is no x-ray machine here and they don't do operations here. It's only an auxiliary hospital. Due to the meager rations, and for various other reasons, Mother's intention to visit me here would be much more difficult than last year. Overall, everything is worse than a year ago. Our care is more limited. There is so little bread issued that I had to request more. Now I receive a double ration of butter in the evenings ($2 \times 0 = 0$), because we only receive margarine. In the morning, we only get skim milk. Work is required (but not for me since I'm mostly restricted to bed) and not just peeling potatoes but actual assembly work for the Army. For one thousand porcelain beads that are attached to the pull-strings of hand-grenades, you are paid seventy pfennigs. We are housed in a large assembly room of a factory where the inmates sleep on bunk beds of straw sacks, like in the barracks, but without lockers. Special cases like me are put in an extra room of the factory where the inventory is stored. The reception room is in the factory itself. There we have a radio, pool tables, and in the evening, a bar. In the upper hall is a two-lane bowling alley. In my ward itself, no radio noise reaches us from outside, which is worth a lot. One can rest in peace, that is unless the two sergeants here with me make an uproar.

At the moment, I am reading *Die Hosen des Herrn von Bredow*, *Pallieter*, and *Wind, Sand, und Sterne*. Earlier, I read *Die Preussische Novelle* by Beumelburg (very good), *Wenzel Tiegel* and *Das Hornunger Heimweh* by Bergengrün who writes with great empathy, and also, a short story by Storm, *Schweigen*. I'm allowed to go out, but I haven't managed it yet. I can't take any sudden jolts, so I walk like a nun, just not as fast. I walk so carefully that you can't hear me coming or going, and I have to laugh at myself how I shuffle around. I weighed myself, and I am down to 135 pounds in hospital clothing. But I do have an appetite, so I'm sure to gain it back.

I can't say much about how I was wounded. It was all primitive skirmishing full of confusion and missed opportunities. Ivan didn't fire much and cautiously followed us. My squad shot a great deal because at first we were the only ones there. A heavy machine gun had already pulled back but left ammunition behind, which we found. Later, another machine gun joined us for we were covering an important road. Ivan fired two mortar rounds, the second of which landed on my squad and swept us away. Later at the dressing station, I saw my entire squad, except for one man who had gone to fetch more ammunition and wasn't with us when the mortar round hit. When I regained my senses (after the blast), everyone had left so I ran after them. My hands wouldn't work. I had lost my gloves. I reported the mess at the company headquarters, then sat down and collapsed, mostly from the running and loss of blood. Everything else took place in a fog. I was only half-conscious and could hardly breathe. As always at such moments, I was thinking clearly: Get me out of here to the rear area, no matter how, so I can survive. So, that was it. And now my fingers have been blasted three times, but I have real feeling back in my hands.

I've seen a film by Schlüter. Don't know if I wrote you about it. My memory of it is not favorable. Mostly I found it ridiculous. Thank you for Mother's letter. Please don't send me cigarettes, just a pack of tobacco and pipe. Cigarette paper I have here. I inherited shaving things from an unknown comrade. He will probably miss them, but I don't know who he is.

For today, I send you warm greetings and thanks,

Your old Reiner

Neustädtel
30 March 1943

Dear Parents,

To put it simply: I am to be released from here April 2nd and will come home on leave. I was stunned to hear this and during the doctor's visit I asked how it was possible for me to be released when they didn't know where all the shell fragments were or what they have damaged. Wouldn't I have to at least be x-rayed to see if some of the fragments might be safely removed? The doctor only replied, 'You just let us do our job. We certainly wouldn't do anything that might be harmful, and anyway we will accept all responsibility.' I said this and that but finally realized there was nothing else I could say. Later as I looked around the hall, I could see many others in the same situation. I assumed this was all ordered from above. But, I don't know whether this was from a desire to avoid arousing more ill-will by keeping us here in these conditions or just to meet the goal of discharging people more quickly into the pool of usable manpower. No matter. I have my leave, and maybe there's a military hospital in Cologne where I can get more bread.

I received your letter #15 today, and I thank you for it. Looks like I might be able to catch the *Johannespassion*. It's a shame if both parents won't be able to come with me. I wonder if the *Matthäuspassion* will also be performed? I'm looking forward to it. This morning I listened to the 3rd Brandenburg concerto on the radio, which is in our room. The 3rd concerto begins with almost the same theme that Bach uses to begin one of his sonatas for strings, one that I played with Uncle Jörg. Yes, and I'm sure I'll get to see Brigitte[12] and Henseling.[13] That will be a good start, but I don't think I'll be able to travel to Trier. Nonetheless, I'll have a civilian travel permit. Otherwise, things are fine with me. I hardly have any more pain and tomorrow I go out for the first time here.

Greetings and a happy reunion,
Your Reiner

Büffel Aftermath

By the third week of March, Operation *Büffel* had ended successfully, with a minimal loss of men and materiel. The German Front was shortened by over 300 km. Twenty-two divisions were freed up for deployment elsewhere, including three of the indispensable Panzer divisions. Much was made of this withdrawal from the Rzhev salient, then and in later years. The Russians quite naturally hailed it as a great victory. Rzhev was Russian once more, and the fascist bandits had been driven back another 100 km and had suffered great losses in men and materiel. In truth, the Russian pursuit of the withdrawing German forces had been cautious at best. Any attempts to break up or to encircle the retreating units had been beaten back with heavy losses.

Likewise, the Germans proclaimed the operation a great success, as well it was, but from this point on in the war, the brilliant German military achievements seemed to have more and more to do with retreats, narrow escapes, and averting total disaster than they did with victorious advances.

Letters From The Barracks

The German Military Situation, 1943

For Germany, the year 1943 had gotten off to a dismal beginning. Less than a month after the *Weihnachtsbaum* had been taken down and the decorations put away for another year, the German populace was informed that the last defenders of Stalingrad were no more. They had fought heroically to the end for Führer and Fatherland. In reality, 107,000 starving skeletons clad in blankets and rags shuffled off to the prison camps in the east. A scant 5,000 would ever see Germany again.

Then the Americans arrived—not troops on the ground, but heavy fat bombers in the skies over Germany as they began their daylight bombing campaign against the German war industry. Now Germany would be bombed around the clock. The British were attacking by night, the Americans by day. The German day and night fighters were still a potent defensive force, but they couldn't be everywhere all the time. Between 24 July and 3 August, British and American bombers reduced the city of Hamburg to a smoldering ruin. Two hundred and fifty thousand houses were destroyed, and 1 million people were left homeless. The bombing killed 40,000 people, including 5,000 children.[1]

For Germany, things were no better elsewhere. Trapped in Tunisia by both the Anglo-American forces and the Führer's 'Victory or Death' order, the *Afrikakorps* chose neither. Out of fuel, ammunition, and hope, the Italo-Germany forces finally capitulated in May. Two hundred and fifty thousand Axis soldiers (of whom 13,000 were Germans) were marched into Allied captivity.

In July, the Western Allies landed in Sicily; Mussolini fell from power, and Italy dropped out of the war and joined the Allies against its former partner. In September, the Allies landed in Italy itself and began their long hard fight up the rocky peninsula.

In the east, however, there had been one brief period of hope. After the destruction of the German 6th Army at Stalingrad, Stalin and the Soviet High Command had become overconfident and recklessly sought to push their forces all the way to the Black Sea in order to trap the German forces in the Crimea and the Caucasus. *Feldmarschall* von Manstein allowed the Russians to plunge on ahead as far as they wanted, and then he cut them off and chewed them up, teaching Stalin and his high command that they still had much to learn when it came to modern armored warfare.

By the end of February, six Soviet tank corps, ten rifle divisions, and some half-dozen independent brigades had been destroyed, along with 615 tanks, 400 guns, and 600 anti-tank guns. Twenty-three thousand Russian dead were counted on the battlefield. Total losses were well over 100,000.

The Russians had stuck their noses out too far and Manstein had bloodied them. The Stalingrad disaster had been retrieved and the front had been stabilized for the time being. Did the opportunity exist for Germany to regain the initiative after freeing up many divisions through the withdrawal from the Rzhev salient? It did—but it was squandered.

The obvious target of a new German offensive was the Kursk salient, a westward projecting bulge in the German lines between Orel and Belgorod. A pincer attack from the north and the south at the base of the salient would cut off and trap the Russian forces within, which at the time represented some 40 percent of the Russian field forces.

Perhaps influenced by the disastrous results of his last grand strategy to seize the Caucasus, Hitler had become uncharacteristically indecisive and kept postponing the attack with one excuse or the other—more men, more tanks, or more artillery were needed. Meanwhile, the Russians (to whom the likely place of a German offensive was equally obvious) kept packing more men, more tanks, and more artillery into the Kursk salient and built what was the strongest defensive position that had ever been constructed in the war.

When Hitler finally gave the order to attack on 4 July, any chance of its success had long since passed. Two weeks later and after 55,000 casualties with minimal progress, Hitler called off the offensive. The excuse given was that the Western Allies had invaded Sicily and divisions had to be rushed west to stabilize the situation in Italy. The Soviets quickly launched a counter-attack that threatened the entire German central front.

The initiative had passed irretrievably to the Russians. Germany would never again mount a serious offensive in the east. Instead, its eastern armies would be subjected to successive, massive Soviet offensives forcing them into one withdrawal after the other for the rest of the war.

Münster

Reiner was away from the front for thirteen months, his wounds obviously more serious than one would gather from his letters. Unfit for active duty, he was classified GVH, (*Garnisonverwendungsfähig Heimat*), that is, fit only for garrison duty on the home front. He spent these months in hospitals, the *Landesschützen* convalescent companies, and in the barracks in Münster. For Reiner, it was a time of introspection and frustration. A veteran of two tours at the front, he could barely tolerate the unprofessional citizen-soldiers of the *Landesschützen* or the boredom and pettiness of the barracks. He was promoted to *Gefreiter* (lance-corporal), effective 3 March 1943, and awarded the Iron Cross Second Class on 12 March, but his career as an officer candidate seemed to be going nowhere because he was unfit for active duty.

To while away the boredom of barracks life, he often visited the Wolfs, close family friends who lived in Münster, with whom he enjoyed the one pleasure he had left—music.

Münster
19 April 1943

Dear Parents,

I arrived here all right, was back at the barracks around 2 a.m. and managed to sleep a little. Even though the train was over-crowded, I was able to find a seat. On the way, there was an air-raid alarm that lasted from 11.30 a.m. to around 12.15 p.m. Here there was no alarm. This afternoon I am going to the Wolfs, and then tomorrow begins the everyday grind of a soldier's life. I've already run into a number of familiar faces. I don't always know how to react. Some hesitantly address me as 'Herr *Gefreiter*', others slap me on the back like we've always been together. Sometimes I have to talk to one for a while before I can actually place him. I've met *Unteroffizier* Zehres, my squad leader from my days as a recruit, and another comrade of that squad. I've also seen others that I don't really speak to because I don't know if we were on good or bad terms back then. Even so, it seems to me I haven't forgotten anything. Anyway, I'm perfectly happy.

For today, warm greetings from your Reiner

Münster
20 April 1943

Dear Parents,

As you read in my postcard, I got back here all right even though I walked through the gates at 2 a.m. instead of 10 p.m. Monday I went to the doctor here and told him that the hospital from which I was released did not have an x-ray and that the doctor there told me that if I had any trouble I should get x-rayed here at the base hospital. He sent me for x-rays, which took the entire day. This is what they found: a bean-size metal fragment at the level of the 12th thoracic vertebra on the left half of my back near the bottom rib (but that doesn't hurt me); a pea-size fragment below the right diaphragm in the liver tissue that was causing the pain I was having in my right side. The doctor mentioned another fragment about 20 cm higher, which I could also sense, but he did not put it in the report. The doctor also found one small fragment just under the skin in the back of my upper right arm and a larger one on the inside of my upper arm. My lungs and heart are uninjured but he says there is some impairment of my diaphragm, which Dr Posth had suspected.

21 April 1943

At 11.00 a.m., I am to see the doctor to find out what he has decided to do.

Telegram
22 April 1943

Easter meeting possible. Can probably get leave. Wolf stays here with Heidi. Letter follows.

Reiner

22 April 1943

The doctor was unable to decide because he didn't show up, so I went ahead and sent off the telegram anyway in the evening. Today the doctor did decide: I am to be classified GVH until July 20th and transferred to the *Landesschützen*, but because I am a KOB, I might be transferred as an instructor for a training battalion in Denmark. It is not clear. Today I ran into a member of the squad I had in Russia. He had been wounded March 7th and was able to give me news about the company. He said I had been recommended for the Iron Cross. I hope my promotion to *Unteroffizier* comes with it. Several KOBs with whom I was in class or with whom I served as an auxiliary instructor are already *Leutnants*. And me? Tomorrow I have to collect, assemble, and distribute matchsticks or some other meaningless task. I won't report myself as sick because then I wouldn't get leave for Easter. I'm feeling pretty well now except for sore muscles. That comes from running around, which I'm still not used to. Have to close now. We have to be cleaned and polished for inspection. Because I'm not KV,[2] I probably won't be receiving any more leave. Perhaps I can apply for a work leave, but as what? A draughtsman?
    Take care for now.

Warm greetings from your Reiner

1 May 1943

Dear Parents,

Thanks for the letter of the 27th and for the Easter letter. Hopefully Bauwens knows, or Father has told him that the request has to go through the WBK.[3] In any event, the man here who handles all the matters concerning leaves told me that if I've already been transferred to the *Landeschützen*, then the application for leave will be forwarded to me there and will be handled by the *Landeschützen*, if everything is in order. The day after he told me this, I was informed that on next Monday or Tuesday I would be transferred to the *Landeschützen*. First, to the local Schlieffen Barracks, and then later somewhere else. You will have to wait for the address. Perhaps today or tomorrow will be the last time I can see the Wolfs or be in Münster. Here at the barracks I've been moved from cleaning potatoes to peeling them and work every day from 7.30 a.m. to 11.30 a.m. and from 1.30 p.m. to 6.00 p.m. Here in the cellar it's not as cold and drafty as the Riding Hall where the potatoes are cleaned and stored, but I have to work longer hours. I've run into old acquaintances who told me the latest news. For example, our old platoon leader at the KOB course was killed in action. My company commander in Russia, *Leutnant* Voss[4], has arrived here and has taken over a training course. I will show them in the office my record from the front whenever this matter of *Landesschützen* comes about. Maybe it will delay the transfer or at least be of some advantage in getting a work leave.

The daily peeling of potatoes brings one into contact with rather interesting people and likewise interesting conversation. It usually begins with the normal jokes, then it proceeds to politics, and finally they bring out the heavy artillery and begin talking about the war and anything to do with it. Recently a coal miner from the nearby mine was here and spoke of things that were rather eye-opening. Everyone listened attentively, and now and again, one would make a cautious remark. It was interesting to note who was influenced by the masses and who thought for himself. For the most part, they agreed on one point, that the Church was the most important thing—the stone on which they would break their necks. I didn't say anything during the whole debate and could only wonder what Möve [family friend] would have made of the discussion if she'd listened to it.

For now, warm greetings to you from all the Wolfs and from your Reiner.

Münster
4 May 1943

Dear Parents,

We've just arrived at the Schlieffen Barracks, the reception center for the
Landesschützen, and in the next few days, we'll be transferred somewhere else.
Every day they announce which groups will be sent where. However, one can
request to be sent to a certain area. I will probably be in your area. Any work
leave will then be granted by the *Landesschützen*. I wrote to Bauwens and gave
him my military district number: Cologne 22/14/1/1. Also, I've taken my Iron
Cross ribbon from my new *Soldbuch* and put it in the buttonhole of my tunic.[5]
I only wonder if my machine-gunner received one as well. Thanks for the letter.
This week has started out great. The weather is beautiful. Monday morning:
terrain duty (long walks in the green countryside with plenty of breaks). In
the afternoon, horseback riding to the butcher (to pick up sausage) and today
waiting around to be transferred and am enjoying milk-soup and a day without
work-duty.

Warm greetings from your Reiner.

Düsseldorf
7 May 1943

Dear Parents,

So now, I've landed here. On Tuesday, I returned to the Schlieffen barracks and
the next morning I was transferred here. There was no unit going to Cologne,
only Düren or Düsseldorf, so I chose Düsseldorf because it has better connections,
even without railroad, though I'll only be able to get home on Sundays every six
weeks because we have too few men for all the guard duties we have to perform.
Consequently, we won't get much sleep either. Otherwise, things are not so bad
here. The food is decent and we have fine quarters in the dance hall of a local
factory. As for other conditions, I'll have to get to know the place better before I
judge. Düsseldorf has made a rather favorable impression on me. With its broad
streets and large blocks of houses, it reminds me of Berlin. I haven't seen that
much of it yet because we don't get out that often. More soon.

Warm greetings,
Your Reiner

Address: *Gefreiter*, Reiner Niemann, Düsseldorf, *Landesschützen Bataillon* 478
1. *Kompanie*

Gefreiter Niemann
Düsseldorf-Westen
Landesschützen Bataillon 478
1. *Kompanie*

Düsseldorf
21 May 1943

To: Convalescent Company, Grenadier Replacement Battalion 58, Münster
Re: Work Furlough

On 5 May 1943, I was transferred here to the *Landesschützen*. As I had already applied for a work furlough through your company, I ask that said work furlough be forwarded directly to my present unit when it arrives at your company.

Heil Hitler!
R. Niemann, *Gefreiter*
Convalescent Company, Grenadier Replacement Battalion 58, Münster

24 May 1943

Re: Your correspondence from 11–21 May 1943

Gefreiter R. Niemann
Düsseldorf
Landesschützen Bataillon 478
1 Company

Regarding your correspondence, the company informs you that no such work furlough has arrived here. Should one arrive here, it will be forwarded immediately to you.

[Signature]
Oberleutnant and Company Commander

Thursday morning, 10 June 1943

Dear Parents,

I am coming for Pentecost holiday.[6] I arrive late Friday evening, and I must leave Tuesday morning. I'll bring two loaves of bread but nothing else, not even a bicycle, because I almost always use the train. Many thanks to Heidi for her postcard. Greetings to all, and wishing you a cheerful mood.

Your Reiner

Düsseldorf
19 June 1943

Dear Parents,

Once again, I made it back here fine. Actually, I was here too early. I could have waited until the noon watch had taken up duty. But better early than late. Yesterday I had guard duty in Nordfriedhof, which actually means guarding the garages there. Right now, it's being used to store the great part of the air raid victims awaiting burial.[7] New bodies arrive every day and others are hauled away. And every day people come to try to find family members or to see them again. That makes sentry duty here quite unpleasant. We have to check to see if they have permission to be here. We see a great deal of tears and suffering. It doesn't smell very nice here either, and how the dead look: mutilated, burned, bloated. I cannot write about it. It's like something you would read in Faust or The Bible. Nearby is the Cross of the Schlageter[8] monument that in connection with the cemetery in the bleak surroundings of a typical suburb— with trash heaps, overgrown weeds, bushes, and the small allotments of worker dwellings—makes a most peculiar impression. When one reads Faust and thinks about the war, one cannot help but become depressed.

22 June 1943

You must excuse me that I haven't written, but Uncle Fritz[9] has sent me a so-called 'Dagger of Honor' and such a humorous letter that I had to write him in turn. Among other things, he mentioned that he wanted to procure a work leave permit for me so that I could oversee the building of another factory for him in Breslau and thus free him for other business. I was honored but it was just another typical idea from 'Uncle Fietsche'. He also sends you his greetings. This morning as I was about to go on duty, I received your telegram. Tomorrow I will try to get a *Bombenurlaub* [bombing leave].[10] Several other guys have obtained leaves from Düsseldorf because of the attack here and one in Krefeld, which is said to have been as bad as the one in Düsseldorf. Let's hope I can get leave. I'm sure I can't get a Sunday pass from here. This past Sunday I was going to attend a concert for the first time. It was to be held at the Benrather Castle and to feature the works of Handel, Telemann, and Bach, but naturally, it didn't take place due to all the confusion here. So, instead I went on a stupid tour of the castle and whiled away a half-day in the castle gardens. I wasn't really feeling well, but it's too far to go to the doctor. And so, since my pen isn't working right and what I write depresses me, I'll close this letter. Soon I go on watch duty from where I can see the cathedral in Cologne. I'll take my compass with me.

I send you all my greetings, especially to Wolf, from your Reiner.

28 June 1943

Dear Parents,

Today the Captain was on a rampage and arranged more nonsense and aggravation for us to deal with. Every evening the blankets are to be passed out for bed and every morning collected again. In addition, name cards must be put on every locker and bed for better control. This is bad. It's high time I make myself scarce around here. I've had enough of this nonsense. I'm not doing anything of use around here, just writing letters and yesterday at this time I was on an excursion. It's hard to believe how different one is at home. It is really more like a dream than reality. Here I'd like to get drunk or smash everything to bits. You see, I am not in the mood to write much. The main thing, you know, everything worked out fine.

Warm greetings, your Reiner

Düsseldorf
29 June 1943

Dear Parents,

I hear that Cologne is now as distinguished as Düsseldorf.[11] Even the Cathedral wasn't spared. I suppose there is no purpose in writing this letter for I am sure that your postal service is no longer operating. Anyway, I need to let you know as soon as possible that for the time being there won't be any more 'Schwarzfahrten'.[12] The Captain smelled a rat and has thrown a fit. He caught a number of men here who had been staying out overnight and sometimes well into the morning without passes. I almost went with them but decided to stay here, which turned out to be a good thing. But now I have to be more careful. Our names are now posted on our lockers and beds, so that they can keep better track of us. Anyway, my last maneuver turned out fine even though I probably stayed at home too long. I made up the lost time by running to the station. When I got there, I asked a civilian in line at the ticket booth if I could go ahead of him. A *Stabsfeldwebel* [staff-sergeant] who was actually at the window asked me where I wanted to go. I guess my honest answer touched him and he let me go in his place. I have to admit though that this was more a matter of my good luck than my being able to read people. The train was scheduled to leave in two minutes but was actually five minutes late, but it made up the time on its way to Benrath. When I arrived, I made a few cautious inquiries as to what was going to happen on that day and what the password would be, and so at precisely 7.30 a.m. I went on guard duty. For two days now I've had guard duty at an Army detention center and it is planned that I will have this duty for six to eight more days. I hope it doesn't delay my convalescent leave. Right now, I have duty from eleven to one and just sit at an office desk. I've already slept some and have had time to read a short story by Stifter, *Das Alte Siegel*, which with its simple style and plot was effective, if you can relate the present cynicism to the main character. As I was reading, it struck me as being like a simple melody by Schumann, who seems to have much in common with Stifter.

Yesterday, I received Wolfgang's letter of the 9th in which he indicated when he would come. He's been on the road too long, eighteen days. Is that how long his mail takes; letters, cards, and packages? Today I got a short letter from Uncle Fritz, who isn't thinking just about me, but actually needs someone to help him out. I will send you his letter.

Because at this time I really don't know for sure if you have suffered serious damage from the bombing raid, though I know it is a possibility, I'm not going to let myself worry. But I do often think of your situation and what could happen. Until I actually get a telegram from you, I can't really apply for a *Bombenurlaub* [bombing leave].

Heartfelt greetings, your Reiner

Düsseldorf
17 July 1943

Dear Parents,

I'm back on guard duty at the Ulanen Barracks after three days and nights of duty at the detention center. I often think of the 'golden' days when I will no longer be with the *Landesschützen*. I know I curse and complain about the *Landesschützen*, but getting away from them will be better for me. Half the problem is the nonsense around here and the other half is about being jerked around and being classified as KVH or GVH. That will be decided by the Replacement Office. If I am classified KVH, that's not so bad. I wouldn't be sent to the front before early next year. But between now and then I see a whole range of options disappearing. In this time, I must find a way to combine the necessary with the useful; and the useful with the good, because I see the beginning of the ending of the war starting to come into play.

It does appear that the Captain is going on leave for three weeks. He is to leave tomorrow, so the heavy clouds have lifted and perhaps I can think again about slipping out of here to visit home. The only thing making that difficult is the rail line. Write me as soon as possible and let me know when and if the three stations, Mülheim, Deutz, and the main station are up and running again. Also how the tram in Mülheim is operating.

Recently I actually did some real duty for the first time. That is to say, I lay in the green grass for two hours and successfully defended my position with a bent-up piece of pipe against mock attacks of grenadiers wearing gasmasks. In the afternoon, I did live firing with a Czech machine gun, which I had never used before. However, my score—five shots, four hits—allowed me to denounce the assembled home guards as inept bunglers. Only the Company Sergeant did as well. The home guard couldn't hit a thing. Even the non-coms couldn't get a single hit, and they were familiar with the gun. In many respects, the home guards are worse than recruits. I've had my fill of them. Those who are temporarily classified GVH should be kept away from the *Landesschützen*. Otherwise, they will be spoiled by them. Like the way I spoil my letters when I write and am not in the mood for writing. Maybe things will get better.

Heartfelt greetings, your Reiner

Düsseldorf
18 July 1943

Dear Parents,

In Sicily and around Orel and Kuban, things seem rather serious.[13] Everywhere we are being forced back with heavy losses. The concentration of our forces, which in the early years of the war brought us great success, is no longer possible with us, and much more possible with our enemies. I am convinced that we stand before a great surprise that perhaps might create another *Blitzkrieg*. The situation has never been so tense and uncertain as now. Have you understood what it means to have a mobile artillery force of six battleships, thirty cruisers, and one hundred smaller warships along the entire Italian coast? That is some seventy 24-cm guns, five hundred 15-cm guns, seven hundred 10-cm guns, and one thousand guns of smaller caliber. Add to that their air superiority and not the worst weapons and soldiers on earth. We'll have to wait and see. But if we don't do something about their air superiority, Italy will be lost. True, we will still have the Alps between us and them.

I think it's ridiculous now that there is no direct way home since it reached the point that the family is scattered about for protection from air raids. Perhaps our company should give up all our watches and look after transportation, that is, the transport of supplies and provisions. It has been done before in individual cases. The Company Sergeant did it so that some men who live far from Düsseldorf could get home at times. If we had that duty, then it might not be so bad being GVH, even though I still want to get away from the *Landesschützen*. You can see that my situation here is still not clear. It's hard to tell who has the initiative. We will just have to wait and see. I am still hoping to get leave, still looking forward to two weeks of authorized existence. I think it will work out because the Captain is not here.

And now I send you my warm greetings. Has it rained through the window or roof yet? Here's wishing you good weather and good spirits.

From your 'job-hunting' son and brother, Reiner

Dear Parents,

Just as I was afraid of, my examination has put a wrench into my plans. I had just been to our present commander and had my leave all arranged, and now I am classified GV *Feld*.[14] and I will first be transferred to the Replacement Battalion, and I have no idea when I can get leave. I can't claim a KV leave since I am still GV. Recently I've heard talk that any soldier in the air raid district who hasn't already suffered bomb damage is to get seven days leave if they have proof from local authorities that they must vacate their homes and must move somewhere else. Perhaps Father can ask the Captain some time about this. Meanwhile I will try here in Münster to get a leave somehow. I'll either manage to get myself classified KV or try talking to the Company Sergeant Major of the Convalescent Company. My present address is: Grenadier Replacement Battalion 58. Münster, 13th Barracks.

Warm greetings,
Reiner

Münster
8 August 1943

Dear Parents,

Heidi has just called and says she and Knud will meet me this afternoon at the Café Middendorf. So, I will write you a quick letter during my noon break. In the past day and a half that I have been here, I've run into a number of old comrades, foremost of which, my machine gunner from my squad in Russia. He's a corporal and it was good to see his broad, smiling Westphalian face. He was the only one of us who wasn't wounded by the direct hit we took. He later became ill and came back here March 12th. Now, there is only one member of my old squad I haven't seen yet. This evening we intended to celebrate our reunion. I'll probably have to put it off though. But since our former commander Lt Voss is also here, we will have to go together some time to see him. I want to see that he gets the Iron Cross. He deserves it as much as I do, or as little. He himself never mentioned it. The day after tomorrow I have to report to the Battalion, maybe they want me to conduct the new recruits to Denmark, who are leaving today. They are almost all from the 1925 conscription class. I may take my convalescent leave there, but if I do, I'll have to convert my leave pay to Kroner in order to buy anything. I'll write you as soon as I know if I'm going to Denmark and send a telegram from there if I go. I received your letter of July 21st. The *Landesschützen* forwarded it. I thank you for it and send my greetings from your Reiner.

Münster
11 September 1943

As you can see, I only limit my writing when I am on leave. I am beginning this letter today but it might take a few days to finish and mail it off. My present situation is that I am to be transferred to the SE Company 58.[15] I've already received my drill clothes and equipment and in a few weeks will be ready to go to Russia. I don't know if the departure date has been fixed, but I have to admit that things are more interesting now. This morning when I showed my leave papers to the company clerk—one of those creatures of higher wisdom—he acted as though he'd been hit by thunder and lightning. I simply returned to my quarters, turned on the radio and pondered what steps I should take now and in which order. There's really not that much to think about. First, of course, a medical examination, since I really haven't been examined, and then we will see. If I am not classified GVH, then there is still a chance I will go to Poland. It may be that nothing definite has been decided, but I think one thing is clear—my being transferred to the base company has to do with my certification as a squad leader. I only completed five of the eight required weeks while in Russia. Of course, there may be other factors involved of which I am not aware.

14 September 1943

Again I am classified GVH [unfit for active duty], but I've had more or less a difficult struggle. First just to see a doctor for an exam, then to get an x-ray, and finally to object to being classified GVH. They tried to placate me with empty talk and generalities about similar cases. What is going to become of me now, I have no idea. Perhaps tomorrow I'll be going with the base company to Senne. How long I will remain classified GVH, they didn't say, and I assume that means

I'll be GVH for six months, that is, until my next six-month examination. The Company Sergeant here thinks that would make it is impossible for me to become an officer. I think I need to get into contact with someone at Battalion, but how? Oh well, things will work out somehow. Take care and now I can send this letter.

Warm greetings from your Reiner.
If possible, give my shaving brush to Knud.

[Undated]

Well, I won't be going to Senne with the company either. There wasn't anything there that I could do, nor is there much here that I can do. Presently I am lying around in a room full of Alsatians. They had served previously with the French Army and are frightfully unsoldierly, clumsy, and pretty dumb. And then there's their hopeless dialect and unclean demeanor, which is not pleasant. I'm really in need of a leave, but Christmas is a long way off. My address now is SE Company, GEB 58, 13th Barracks. Post number isn't yet determined. For now I send my warm greetings again,

Your Reiner

Münster
16 September 1943

Dear Father,

I had completely forgotten that today was your birthday, which is why I did not mention it in the letter that I mailed you yesterday, even though when I mailed it I had the feeling I had forgotten something. Anyway, I will make up for it now and offer you my heartfelt congratulations on your birthday and wish that it is your last wartime birthday. Will your first peacetime birthday be better? I can only wish it, and it doesn't hurt to wish. The Wolfs say that in times like these, one should hold onto what one has, but one could also say that in these times one might think about making a complete change. I hope that things change for you, Father, in the coming year.

For the moment, things here are going fine. The *Spiess* [slang for Company Sergeant Major] is with the company in Senne; the company commander is still on leave; and all that's left here are a half dozen NCOs and as many men. Since the NCOs go out for the whole day, there is hardly anything left for us to do. We sleep late, and in the morning, we sweep out a few of the NCOs quarters, then do almost nothing the rest of the day. We leave the base early to go into town and can stay out all night because no one bothers to check on us. Unfortunately, this won't last much longer because the company is returning on Saturday, and we'll be back to a typical military base. How much training and exercises I'll be allowed to do I don't know yet. Field maneuvers are unlikely. I hope they find something to do with me.

In Münster right now, like before in most other cities, they are preparing for concerts and other entertainment for winter. How it comes out is hard to say, but they are planning all the same. Chamber concerts, symphonies, poetry readings would all be nice, but I don't think it will happen. By the way, the Wolfs didn't stay on vacation for three weeks. I visited them Sunday evening. We spent the evening in the garden, which is where they like to be. In the evening when Suse [daughter] left again, things weren't as cheerful as usual, or perhaps it was just me. I couldn't take the conversation seriously because my mind was on the situation in Russia, but I went ahead and chattered anyway. It's probably better to seem like a lump of lead to those around you than a chatter box. I remember a passage from '*Schuss von der Kanzel*' that would have justified me.

Evening, 16 September 1943

Once again, I've just jogged back from town so that I could be through the barracks gate before ten. Earlier around four, I left the base with a medical student and we went into town. There we bought some things, went to Middendorf and had some cake, then to a movie *Der Ewige Klang*. It was a shocker as usual, and I had a lively discussion about it afterwards with the medical student. Then I went over to the Wolfs where we talked a bit and I played the piano. Gustav Wolf is for now no longer with the anti-aircraft. Peter [son] writes that one day the flak battery was locked up and they were all marched back to their quarters. Right now, there's an air-raid alarm. Again, I wish you a happy birthday and send you my warm greetings.

Your son, Reiner

Münster
23 September 1943

Dear Parents and Heidi,

I'm still not doing much here. After the seven fat years, actually three fat days while the company was away in Senne, now begin the lean days.

First, I had two straight days of quasi-voluntary garrison duty because the company was on field maneuvers, which I'm not allowed to do because I am restricted to no more than 5 km of marching. The maneuver was cut short because forty-three Polish officers had escaped from the prisoner of war camp in Warburg and had created a security problem in the area. Consequently, all available personnel, probably throughout Germany, were put on security duty or were to be employed in trying to catch them. Monday morning around 10 a.m., we were hauled out of bed and told to be ready for this assignment, then we went back to bed. However, on Tuesday we were awakened at 4.30 a.m. and at 6.30 a.m. we were marched off. By 8 a.m. I was standing at a crossroad somewhere in Münsterland, forgotten and alone. I was to check the papers of every soldier who walked by. There were hardly a dozen. The sentry I relieved had been there since midnight. It was like at the front where we were told nothing nor was anything explained. I didn't know if or when I would be fed, or when I might be relieved. It did finally happen, but not soon. Food arrived around 4 p.m. (cold, of course) and I was relieved around 8.30 by another sentry who, like me, had no overcoat and hadn't been fed. His unit had also been sent out without preparation and had stood guard duty for twelve hours until the next morning. I made my way, an hour and a half trip, back to the barracks where, at eleven, I dropped dead tired into bed.

Then the next morning, I was awakened before 5 a.m. and the whole game started over again except this time my post was at a highway intersection. Food didn't arrive until 5.30 p.m. and my return to the barracks was interrupted by an air raid alarm, so I didn't get into bed until 1 a.m. At 4.45 a.m., we were made to get up and I finally gave in and reported myself sick. I had gout or something wrong with my knee and couldn't make it work. The Army makes you old quickly, and the Russian swamps are to blame.[16]

I saw the doctor this morning and he gave my knee a ten-minute ultraviolet light treatment but overall listed me as fit for duty. I'll probably see him again tomorrow because this cold wind in Münsterland is sure to bring on a cough and a cold. It's ridiculous to be standing around in the wind and the cold. When the sun doesn't shine, you freeze like a tailor; your teeth chatter and your knees shake like an Affenpinscher, Lütte's favorite dog. If this standing around didn't last for twelve hours, there might be a good side to all this. The first day I was stationed not far from a farm, and after carefully scouting it out, it seemed a promising prospect for the next day. Fate, however, intervened, and as I mentioned, I was stationed at a different crossroad not far from a newly built air radio base. I ate there at noon and the food put our usual meals to shame. I got plenty of apples there, and far better than I would have the day before at the farm. There were quite a few trucks hauling their produce to market and they pay their 'toll' here. At dinner there, I allowed myself to be warmed up with *Schmalz*, meal, bacon, and sugar because there was also red cabbage. I was also amused by a picture there with the caption: *Zum Reisen braucht man Schuhe; zum Scheissen braucht man Ruhe* [to travel one needs shoes; to shit one needs peace].

And so, that is how things are going with my life. I know Father will probably grumble quietly and say: 'Why is he doing this and not that?' I am doing what I have to do under these circumstances. First, Father doesn't know the circumstances, and second, Father isn't me. I am in many ways a real *Hans im Glück* [Lucky Hans]. I deeply trust my innate fortune and intuition in minor affairs—often, I admit, to my disadvantage, so that in important matters it does not desert me. Like most people, I trust that my good fortune will make up for my deficiencies and allow me to attain that which, by right, I should have. Perhaps it is a deficiency on my part that I haven't progressed and am content to sweep out the NCOs quarters, but bitterness distorts both the world and the individual. Many times, I tell myself that I am only average, that I belong to the class of ordinary, the mediocre. True, I was formed at home not to be so, but now the form contains nothing, has become empty. There is no hint as to what is to be done with it. But then I conclude that I would much rather be common and true than noble and untrue. I had always wanted to enter a sphere in which I could develop not just a craftsman's ability but also a technical understanding and mastery. I was afraid that as a recruit in the army, I would be pulled from this sphere. It has reached a level now that I no longer wish to be an officer. I'm just waiting for the situation to play itself out.

24 September 1943

Today my company commander Lt Voss has come back from leave, and I am now being used as an instructor for the new recruits. Nothing is right. The recruits are reluctant Alsatians, formerly French soldiers, transfers from the Luftwaffe, or older reservists taking refresher courses. These training replacement units are nothing more than *ad hoc* formations that have been thrown together and which lack cohesion or unity of goal or spirit. But I guess they do serve as a beginning point for KOBs who have nothing to do.

Anyway, after three days of twelve-hour watch duty at crossroads and street crossings, the whole search was suddenly cancelled this morning. Thirty-five of the forty-three escaped prisoners of war have been caught.[17]

I have received Father's letter of the 22nd. And I thank you for it. I have one request before I close. Mother, could you send me two pairs of socks, if they haven't already been packed up and sent off? I send you my warm greetings and I will write again soon.

Your Reiner

Hagen
2 October 1943

Dear Parents,

Two years ago today, I was sitting in a train, still wearing my civilian clothes on my way to my new garrison in Osnabrück. Once again, I am sitting in a train, but this time I am on my way to Hagen as part of a *Katastropheneinzatz*[18] I don't think I'll have to do any work myself. Last night Tommy[19] hit Hagen but how much damage was done is unclear, as is how long we will be here. One thing is clear; our much appreciated Saturday evenings and free Sundays are over. Sunday I wanted to go to a concert, a cello solo featuring music of Cassado, von Jeger, Dvorak, and Schumann. My new companion here had already gotten tickets. I often go with him to the finest hotels in Münster where he has connections and play the piano. If you can, please send me the last pack of tobacco and the gray knit gloves. They were last in the top drawer of the cabinet. Forgive me if I don't write you very often from here. I send you my warm greetings from

Your Reiner

6 November 1943

Dear Parents,

I have garrison duty again but I want to write you a short letter to tell you that I assume I will have my short leave on the 12th through the 14th of November. Yesterday during the day between 1.10 p.m. and 3.00 p.m., a large number of English bombers flew over Münster[20] and dropped their bombs on the western side of the city. Nothing happened to us here and overall it doesn't seem to have been that bad for Münster, but it was impressive. It was like a great plain of well-ordered crosses that slowly moved like a great wave across the slightly overcast sky. And just as well ordered was the broad stretch of the black puffs of smoke from the explosion of the anti-aircraft shells that drifted away like swirls in the great wave. I don't know if anything happened to the Wolfs. I'll write more tomorrow, so for now I send my greetings.

Your Reiner

Wiedenbrück
21 November 1943

Dear Parents,

I am once again on my way to Senne. Unfortunately, I forgot to mail the letter that I wrote at the Wolfs. Therefore, I'm trying to write you a replacement letter quickly, here at the train station, so you won't think that something unusual has happened. Everything here is the same as before. The only special times are when we go to Senne, change quarters, or when there is no evening air raid alarm. This is how it will be for a good month. My physical examination is on December 15th. If I am classified GVH[21] again, then I will give up my KOB status so that I can be promoted to *Obergefreiter* [Corporal] on 1 January 1944. If I am classified KV[22], which seems to me improbable, I will talk to the company commander about how things stand for an officer training course. There is the danger that too much time has passed since I did my term as squad leader at the front and that it is no longer valid.

Münster
24 November 1943

Dear Parents,

Earlier I mailed the letter I had forgotten to mail because we were on our way to Senne. It's not a good letter but better than nothing. In any case, it will have to suffice, as I don't write often enough. I wanted to go to the Wolfs this evening, but the Company Sergeant Major's newest fad is singing, and often it lasts so long that it's not worth the half-hour trip to the Wolfs and the half-hour trip back. In addition we have to get up tomorrow at 3.15 a.m. for a 30 km march. True, I don't have to participate, but I have to get up nonetheless.

Yesterday we returned from Senne (and right now I'm returning from a forty-minute stay in the air raid shelter). It was more than a twenty-five-hour trip from Senne in a freight train. At Senne, I was given the task of carrying out a rather difficult assault drill with a squad, and in addition, it was over unfamiliar land. We were to take and occupy a village, assault-group style. The main criticism was that my voice wasn't loud enough as we took up our jump-off positions. So then, I bellowed like a bull as we went through the woods, and nobody said a word about that. (Everyone knows you move through a wooded area in total silence). Anyway, I am satisfied with my performance.

Today Kumpel, another KOB, was promoted to Sergeant. My other KOB comrade, with whom I traveled to Russia and who was wounded after having been there only three days as a squad leader, has arrived here from war-school as a *Leutnant*. I haven't seen him yet, and I am sure he could tell me some things. He too was pretty well shot up, but somehow he has managed. Sometimes I think I would like to be a *Leutnant*, but then when you think about it further, I would be one of those who'd administer all this crap, and wanting to do so is hardly an act of camaraderie with the other men. However, if you want to ruin your life with such considerations, because the Army is not the only place that it's like this, then one is going too far.

Also, it would be foolish not to make an exception for those who because of their background rise to a higher position in life. It is sad that in the Army, particularly the infantry, the path to becoming an officer, a position that demands the greatest self-control and responsibility, is open to almost anyone who isn't entirely worthless. Anyone who can fulfill a certain set of requirements—many of which have nothing to do with being a true officer—is accepted. For most, becoming an officer is a matter of calculation. However, these reproaches I must also level at myself for if the opportunity arose to be an officer, I, like the others, would not refuse. I could only hope to maintain the illusion that my motives are more honorable than those of the others. It is the Army that has made me this way, or is something else the cause, something other than myself? That is the first dent in a life that was once full but has now become hollow. But I should leave Reiner alone now and move on to the next theme.

Münster
1 December 1943

Dear Parents,

A quick letter to answer your letter (#59) that arrived here today. Yesterday I sent a birthday letter to Wolfgang, obviously already late, to his old *Feldpost* number because I didn't know his new one. When I have time, I'll write him a new letter. They have decided about Christmas leaves and it doesn't look good for me. There are too many married men in the company, which outnumbers the allotment of holiday leaves. I don't have a chance at one. All I can do is apply for a short forty-eight-hour leave before Christmas. Please let me know when the Christmas oratorio is or some concert in case my leave comes through. Right now, the only times available are between December 12th and 21st. The sooner I apply for leave, the more certain I will get the dates I request. Also, let me know when you are planning to travel to the east. I hope to have a couple of days off at Christmas here in the barracks to stay at the Wolfs. That Wolfgang's leave didn't come through is bad for us all. Seems the choice of where you have Christmas has been simplified. Yes, war is the father of all things and the root of all evil.

Warm greetings from me, *Reinerleinkeinrein*

Sennelager
15 December 1943

Dear Parents,

I have just received your card and a few days ago your letter #61, and I thank you for both of them. It looks like Flinsberg is out, and I am once again in Senne. On Monday, I will have my medical exam. If I am classified GVF or KV and have luck, then maybe I can get sixteen days' leave. I doubt it, but I will try because it would be a shame if only three of our family were able to be together at Christmas. Today at noon, we left for Senne via Paderborn in a passenger train that is much faster than a freight train. Tomorrow we have target practice and in the evening, we head back to Münster, so no big deal. The rest I'll write later. Now I need to get to bed. Good night.

17 December 1943

Now I'm back from Senne. That was no small feat. Today I was at my follow-up visit. It was like the doctor knew what I wanted. He wrote me down as GVH and thereby destroyed my last hope for a Christmas leave. Otherwise, it's not terrible. If I still think it worthwhile to become an officer, I will just wait for the right time to have myself classified GVF. That, they would do some other time. Anyway, we're expecting a large number of recruits to arrive so that anyone with some service time here will be needed for training. Right now we have twenty assistant instructors and as many NCOs who are waiting for something to do.

For the time being, we have fairly decent duties. The *Leutnant* with whom I was in bivouac is holding instructor classes, which are interesting. Next week the recruits arrive. I have applied for a local pass at Christmas, which I will probably get. I'll stay with the Wolfs, as we have already discussed this. Have you received my letter with ration cards? They are still good even though they are dated November 14th. Things are now going somewhat better with me. Now and then, I have brighter periods when I feel as if I don't need to be so stubborn. But then when I have time to write a letter, I am often too tired to write. And during my lucid moments, I can't think of anything to say. And now warm greetings to you and Heidi, and also to Wawi [unknown], if they come.

From your Reiner

Münster
26 December 1943

Dear Ones at home,

A strange thing happened to me earlier as I was playing the piano. I was playing quite well and was rather satisfied with myself. Seldom before had I managed so well the runs of Mozart, the single-toned bass of Brahms, the rising and falling melodies. But the more I immersed myself into this unexpected success, the more there arose in me a warning voice that said, 'Stop and go no further because beyond this there will only be disappointment when you realize that you have reached the limits of your ability,' or it said, 'Stop, do not plunge too deeply into this for after this lies the return of the despised everyday life of the barracks grounds. The more you enjoy this, the more difficult and painful the return will be.' In any case, It was one of those moments when one is shocked to realize that for one to do anything more than superficially enjoy things only makes life more difficult when you have to deal with the countless unhappy experiences. How can one strive for beauty, feeling, or dreams when one must live with the ugliness, the dullness, and the superficiality of this earthly life? Music is the most powerful art form.

But once again, I'm writing rubbish. Indeed though, I actually feel that way about all forms of art, not just music. Nowadays one dares not do more than superficially enjoy photos, models, architectural reproductions in plaster, but I look forward to the time when one can do more than that, when one can combine beauty and soul with development and expression, as I have always intended to do. However, I no longer nurse the hope that it will happen immediately after I am no longer in the Army. I do keep plenty of material on hand; particularly impressive is the *Olympian Art* by Hamann.

Anyway, I am in a better mood than I was Christmas Eve. I was feverish and locked away deep inside myself and probably made the Wolfs a bit uncomfortable as I sat with them for coffee and cake. I was also down because I didn't have anything nice to bring them for Christmas and that I had so few people I could write to. I just couldn't get into the Christmas spirit either Christmas Eve or Christmas day. It was only this afternoon that the heavy veil lifted and allowed me to be a bit less melancholy. It would have been different had I been at home, sitting around the Christmas tree with you all near me. The Wolfs, as well meaning as they are, are no substitute for that. They are so charming, so polite, so correct because they never say what they mean. They are so considerate that they probably thought it was some fault of their own that I could not be lifted out of my depressed mood. Only Regine [daughter, perhaps] is somewhat more free, more humorous, indeed fresher, but too sensitive all the same. They are so innocent that often they do not realize that they are sometimes insensitive. But enough of this. The important news is that Peter is back from Russia. Most of the time here, he sat quietly in the background.

Friday, 7 January 1944

Dear Parents,

I had just reached the Sülzburgstrasse when the air raid started. Ten minutes later, I was sitting in the streetcar and arrived at the train station thirteen minutes before nine. The train was only a little late, but all the more full because of that. Despite that, from the beginning I had a seat in a heated coach and everything went fine. This morning I was sent along with the rest of the instructors to the Boelcke Barracks where four hundred home guardsmen were to be trained. All of them were either *Obergefreiter* or *Stabsgefreiter*, and most are over forty years old and they don't have any idea of what to do unless they are told constantly. I have a group of twenty-three men without sergeants because they couldn't come up with another instructor. It's a situation in which I can learn a great deal, but it's not particularly enjoyable because even the newest recruits don't behave this stupidly. But this command will only last until January 12th.

Münster
20 January 1944

Dear Parents,

Yesterday I finally did something about my situation. I submitted a request for a transfer to Denmark. I wrote it in a most definite albeit correct form and now I must wait and see how the company commander and the Sergeant Major react to it. The request was as follows: I request that the company transfer me as an instructor to the grenadier training Battalion 58 in Denmark for the following reasons: 1) I have been classified by the doctor as GVH[23] for an undetermined period of time, but I expect that at some time I will be considered recovered and fully fit for active duty. 2) As an officer trainee, I would best be used as an instructor where young recruits are receiving their basic training.

The CO will probably call me in to discuss my request and then I can further explain my reasons that I couldn't explain in the request. I hope that the matter does not go badly due to some fault of mine or to the commander's stubbornness. In any case, I would not be transferred until the next group of recruits is sent off.

Münster
29 January 1944

Dear Parents,

I've just received a copy of a Russian map from the graphic artist with whom I spent some time here three days ago. He had traced a copy for the company showing the area around Rzhev where I was at the front a year ago. Looking at it brought back a great deal of detailed memories. Ivan was on the north side of the Volga, and our company was in the middle of the line between the two places named Suamenskoje. My platoon was holding a strong point with all around defense in the square opposite the convalescent center. When the company withdrew on 1 March, I had to take over the sector for thirty hours with my squad of six men. The following night we pulled out in a southwesterly direction along marked paths through the village of Burmussowo. Compass setting twenty-six was announced for the withdrawal. The regimental staff was in Pelenitschino and the staff units were in Potschigajewo, where we had once taken our KOB exams. That was a year ago, and I had only been back up to the front for three days. I considered the rumor that we were going to evacuate Rzhev and make a large-scale withdrawal total nonsense. A year ago, I felt myself useful. Now I belong on the scrapheap and am more than superfluous.

At the moment, I am on sick leave and lie in bed all day, writing, reading, and trying to figure out how to pass the time. I caught a cold during the Battalion exercise, and I had to get caught up on my rest. Tomorrow, I will be going out, at least to the Wolfs. Otherwise, nothing important has taken place. The barracks are filling up again with civilians, mostly coal miners who had previously been exempt as well as those in the youngest age group. I think there will soon be a great deal of work for instructors.

30 January 1944

I am at the Wolfs' again. Next to me is a thin book about Käthe Kollwitz with numerous illustrations of her works. It also contains an interesting quote from a Count Coudenhove-Kalergi, "War breeds slaves, kills heroes, rewards parasites. Therefore the struggle against war is one of the most honorable tasks of Mankind.' There is truth in that.

Today, Tommy noted the 11th anniversary of the National Rebirth.[24] During the day, we had a full air raid alert for two hours and then one for a half hour. We also had a rather prolonged pre-alert. There was to have been a community reception of the Führer's speech and a military parade through the city. Because of the alerts, both of the plans were a wash. In addition, the entire company was restricted to the barracks today. Why? I don't know. I couldn't stand it in the barracks, so I went out anyway, even though I was also restricted by sick bay. It's all the same crap to me, as it is to the other men. They're incensed at having our leaves curtailed by the CO as punishment, and we weren't responsible for any of the mischief. They all say the CO is doing this because of the reprimand he received at the Battalion exercise. I don't think he would do that, but the rest of the company agrees that he would. I need to close for now. I thank you for your last letters, and I send you my greetings.

Your Reiner
I can't count on a short leave before February 10th.

Münster
1 February 1944

What has the State paid for all this burnt fiction? I find that every centralized state is a sorry creature: dead, bleak. They only seem to have a purpose when through some personality a face appears. I almost believe that we don't have any statesmen in these modern times. The type of leader with sufficient substance has not yet appeared. And so the war continues and when we lose this war, and the best of this type appears, that will be sufficient and far better than if we win this war under the present circumstances. Enough for now, and warm greetings.

Reiner, who is taking it easy now

Münster
7 February 1944

Dear Parents,

Yesterday I didn't write, and today I am sick again. That will delay my short leave that I would have had. The restriction on leaves was lifted on the 4th. Yesterday *Oberleutnant* Voss [1st Lieutenant] took his leave of us. He will be going back to Russia. Yesterday I talked with a KOB who is also going to the front. He is a sergeant and had been certified as a squad leader a long time ago, but since he became KOB after that, he thinks the certification won't count. I will probably have to do mine over again because if I go to officer's school in April, it will be a year since I was at the front.

Münster
13 February 1944

I have my hands full with new recruits, and I must admit I'm not enthusiastic about it, even though it's the best activity I could ask for. Most of the recruits are between thirty-eight and forty-three years old. All Westphalians without initiative or imagination. They are coal miners, iron workers, office clerks, not the most interesting people, and I have no use for them. As a soldier I ask myself, 'Is this what it has come to? Does the future depend on these military cripples?' As a civilian, I find it sad that another batch of men are being pressed into the form of a soldier, making them otherwise useless for any constructive purpose. Because of these near-civilians, fifteen of whom are under my command as the senior soldier in our barrack, I haven't been able to visit the Wolfs once in the past week nor go outside the barrack for any other reason. That has got to change. I still keep thinking about a sixteen-day leave. I know I wanted to write you more about something, but in these late evening hours, it escapes me.

Yesterday we were given mulled wine to celebrate the installation of a new radio, and today I received a letter from an old teacher at Riedwiesen with sketches of his work concerning the pentagon and other projects. Otherwise, there is nothing new that I know about. Just be patient a while longer. Stay well and I thank you for the letters and the call today, which really lightened my mood. I send you my greetings and greetings from the Wolfs.

From your Reiner

Münster
22 February 1944

Dear Parents,

Often in the course of time, I realize that I ought to be writing you a letter, but everything comes to nothing because of my duty here whose dullness was made ever so clear to me during my leave. It would be laudable to be able to do both and to do them both sufficiently. At the concert, I realized how far I have strayed from the well-mannered, educated stratum, and within the first hours of duty here, I knew how unsuited I am for army life, especially when I am supposed to be busy. And so one is forced to compromise and will not be free from the fear that he has become a compromised person, unless one finds the strength to prevent it.

Münster
27 February 1944

Dear Parents,

It is Sunday and I have duty again today. I have to spend the entire afternoon in the office sitting with the squawking radio, the ringing telephone, and the constant coming and going, which is hardly a suitable backdrop for reading or writing. It scatters the mind and makes it impossible to have a coherent thought. But a coherent, rational thought is obviously what people around here don't want, and that is understandable. They don't want to have to find themselves. They want to uproot themselves and dissolve into the masses, which gives them comfort doing only what they are accustomed to doing, doing only that which concerns themselves, without interest in anything else. Lately it seems that every occupation demands this of a person. But even clerks and bureaucrats do not have their personalities eliminated as much as we in the military do. No matter what your perspective, you can always come to that conclusion. As long as you're a common soldier, you'll experience this and suffer from it. As an officer, though, this malady may seem less unpleasant. It may actually be more dangerous in the gradual and insidious way it progresses, unless you're constantly on guard and defend yourself against it.

11 March 1944

Dear Parents,

Today I drew maps for the company, which otherwise would have been made by the artist I mentioned who was transferred to an artillery training regiment. Three of us were detailed to make a number of maps for a training exercise at Senne. We had to make five copies of each and although the other two men were not keen on it, I carried out my task with great pleasure. I really enjoyed it and it put me in a good mood. Afterwards, I went over to the Wolfs where I am now, sitting around, reading Father's letter again, and the collection of Eichendorff's poems.

Right now, outside, they are having a memorial service for the fallen, with music and the other comforts. I don't have to take part because I have an ear infection and am restricted to inside duty. I have opened a shutter that faces the parade ground to let the sun shine in on the table. I am listening to the sparrows and starlings singing happily as they sit along the gutter, knowing that a better time for them has come.

Once again, I looked at the developments in Russia with special concern. I must say it doesn't look good. *Panje* [the Russians] has already reached Tarnopol, Jampal, and Luck, and it is not likely that the front can hold. Hopefully it won't become another Stalingrad. And in the north, it will be the same if things continue. I will write you as soon as possible and let you know how my medical exam turns out. For today, I will close now. I thank you for all your letters. The poem by Eichendorff and Father's last letter have made the rounds at the Wolfs, who of course send you their greetings.

13 March 1944

Dear Parents,

It has been decided. I am again classified as conditionally fit for active duty, which nowadays is what GVH is called. However, what is important is that I am classified for duty at the front. I found this out after further questioning. I didn't expect it, but it suits me. I hope now that I can get a sixteen-day leave at the right time. That is so that I can go with you to Breslau at Easter. I would submit a request to go to both Breslau and Cologne. From Breslau I could then try to get permission to go to Bad Flinsberg. In the meantime, we can discuss it among ourselves when I get home for a short leave some time between the 20th and the 25th of March. I'll see what happens here.

Otherwise, things are routine around here. Every evening is the same. One has time to write in the evening but has neither the peace and quiet nor the energy. The young recruits are lively and energetic enough in their training, but after hours, they allow no peace and can't be left unsupervised. They are still children and quickly argue with one another and turn everything upside down. However, they are easy to motivate and it's easy to gain their trust. A whole group of them are from the outskirts of Cologne, but none of them have advanced education. But enough of that. I send my greetings and thank you for letter #83 with the money.

Your Reiner

Münster
5 April 1944

Dear Parents,

Now the time has come. I have already been issued my equipment and some time tomorrow I will begin my trip to the east. Initial destination will be Minsk. What I hadn't written you is that I found my gasmask safe and sound at the Wolfs' when I visited them the evening I returned from leave.

Now I have definite orders: tomorrow at 11.47, I depart here for a key position at the front, which is in the introduction of this letter. I send you my greetings and hopes for a happy reunion.

Your Reiner
Punktiert: Babruysk

Third Time Out:
Letters From Babruysk

The German Military Situation Spring 1944

The year 1944 would prove to be the decisive year of the war; it was when the iron ring encircling Germany would finally be closed, setting the stage for the inevitable destruction of Hitler's Third Reich. In the west, the Americans restarted their daylight bombing campaign—this time with massive fighter protection made possible by the new long-range fighter, the American P-51. For the first time, the American bomber squadrons targeted Berlin—not for any immediate military result, but rather to force the German fighters to defend the capital of the Reich. The bombers were the bait, the German fighters the prey. True, the American bombers would suffer heavy casualties, but so too would the Germans. The German armament industry might be able to replace the aircraft but not the adequately trained pilots and skilled and experienced squadron leaders. By April, the German day fighters had lost 1,000 pilots, including a large number of those irreplaceable squadron leaders.[1] This strategy ensured that the once-powerful Luftwaffe would not be a factor during the coming invasion of northern France.

Meanwhile, the Western Allies were making the final preparations for the cross-channel assault. Eventually they amassed a force of thirty-nine divisions with 2.8 million men, 6,000 naval vessels, and over 13,000 aircraft. Another forty-one divisions stood by in America, waiting to be transported to Britain once the invasion had succeeded. Even Stalin could appreciate these numbers.

On the Southern Front, in Italy, the Germans were enjoying some measure of success. Although Italy had dropped out of the war the previous year, the Germans were doing quite well in holding the Italian Front without their former allies. Having made only slow progress fighting their way up the Italian peninsula, in January, the Anglo-American forces found themselves confronting the 'Gustav Line' in the Volturo Valley, some 150 km south of Rome, and here their advance stopped. In three costly battles, the Allies attempted to take the

Germans' anchor position of Monte Cassino. They all failed. Even bombing the Benedictine monastery that sat atop its peak to rubble did not drive the Germans from their positions. An attempt to outflank the Gustav Line by a sea landing behind it at Anzio likewise failed as the Germans were able to contain the beachhead and bottle up the Allied forces within. The Gustav Line would hold until May.

However, in the east, the Germans were enjoying no such success. When 1944 began, the Eastern Front was still deep in Russia. All that would change over the course of the year. After the attempt by the Germans to regain the initiative had failed the previous year at Kursk, the German armies in the east had been forced by relentless Russian offensives into one retreat after another—masterfully conducted retreats that would be much studied in later years, but retreats all the same, leaving German generals unable to do little more than to congratulate themselves on narrow escapes and the averting of complete disasters.

Throughout the first half of 1944, the Russians, with a striking force of 300 divisions totaling 4.5 million men, launched a series of offensives along the front, concentrating mostly on the northern and southern sectors. In the north, Russian attacks in January and February finally broke the 900-day siege of Leningrad and pushed the German armies of *Heeresgruppe Nord* back to the Estonian and Latvian borders. Leningrad would never again be threatened by the Germans.

In the south, the Russians kept up their pressure on the Germans with one massive offensive after the other, forcing the Germans to retreat from one river to the next: the Dnieper, the Bug, the Dniester, and the Prut. The German and Romanian forces in the Crimea were completely cut off and destroyed in May. By June, the Soviet armies had driven the Germans out of the Ukraine and had reached the Carpathian Mountains and the border of Romania.

The extensive Soviet gains on the southern flank had essentially created two eastern fronts—one north of the Pripet marshes and one south—consequently greatly complicating the German defense strategy. The front lines of *Heeresgruppen Nord* and *Mitte* ran in a generally north–south direction some 800 km from the Gulf of Finland to the Pripet Marshes, but then the German front line bent sharply back to the west some 400 km before connecting with *Heeresgruppe Süd*, where the front followed along the Carpathians and Romanian border. Not only did this westward bend in the line give the Germans another 400 km of front to man, it also left *Heeresgruppe Mitte* with a long, vulnerable southern flank. It was like a jaw jutting out, begging to be hit with an uppercut.

During the first half of 1944, as the Soviet offensives were hammering the German armies on the northern and southern sectors of the front, *Heeresgruppe Mitte* was left in relative peace; that would soon change, however, as Stalin and his High Command were laying the plans for its total destruction.

The 6th Grenadier Division at Babruysk

After having been engaged in constant combat since the beginning of the Kursk offensive in July 1943 and the subsequent withdrawals to the northwest, the 6th Grenadier Division reached what would prove to be its final destination. On 3–4 December, they were assigned the forward positions on the east bank of the Dnieper River, near Zlobin, in the southeast corner of *Heeresgruppe Mitte*, at the very bend of the German front line. They were the chin of the projecting jaw.

Although *Heeresgruppe Mitte* would be spared the heavy Soviet assaults during the first half of 1944, that did not mean there would not be considerable fighting along its front. At 9 p.m. on 4 December, the very night that the 6th Grenadier Division took up its new positions in the swampy lowlands of the *Dnieper*, the right flank of its 18th Regiment was broken into by an attacking force of 400 Russians. The flanks of the break-in were immediately secured, but it was not until dawn and after three counter-attacks that the Germans were able to throw the Russians out and reestablish the original battle line. The Russians left behind eighteen prisoners (five of whom were officers) and 250 dead. Such was the welcome the 6th Grenadiers received in their new home.

They spent the next several weeks improving their positions, laying minefields, stringing barbed wire, and engaging in deadly trench raids of their own, which developed into a front-line sport similar to that in the First World War. One such raid conducted by the 10th *Kompanie* of the 58th Regiment (Reiner's future company), under the leadership of *Oberfeldwebel* Wunderlich, broke into the Russian lines, destroyed several bunkers, killed twenty Russians, and brought back three prisoners. The raid cost them three dead.

In addition to carrying out these trench raids, the men also prepared for the upcoming Christmas. Heinz Löhdorf described the 58th's celebration of their third Christmas in Russia:

> Not one bunker lacked a Christmas tree for Christmas Eve. Tobacco, alcohol, and other specialties had been richly provided. A brass quartet from the Musik Korps under the leadership of Obermusikmeister Ertl, nicknamed 'Beethoven', performed Christmas carols in the front trenches. At first this caused much consternation among the Russians, but then they quieted down and became peaceful.

Unfortunately, not all members of the regiment were able to enjoy the Christmas festivities. Reiner's future company, the 10th, and his former company, the 3rd, were loaded onto trucks on Christmas Eve and rushed north to deal with a Russian incursion. That night, while their comrades were singing *O, Tannenbaum* and *Es ist ein Ros Entsprungen*, they were retaking the German positions with hand grenades and spades to the shouts of '*Hurra*!' The German lines were restored, and in a few days the men of the 10th and 3rd *Kompanie* returned to the regiment, bringing back ten heavy machine guns, twenty light machine guns, and eighty rifles as war booty. There they celebrated a belated Christmas.

The losses of the regiment for December were cryptically noted as thirty-two dead and twelve missing.

In mid-January, Reiner's regiment was pulled out of the forward positions and sent back across the Dnieper, where it was placed in 9th Army Reserve. It was no vacation or rest cure. As Army Reserve, they were rushed from one hotspot to another all along the 9th Army's front to a list of unpronounceable Russian towns and villages—Russowa, Paritschi, Preschinitschi, Petrowitschi. By the time they returned to their division two weeks later, they had lost 632 officers and men, of whom eight officers and 119 men had been killed.[2]

At the end of February, the Germans evacuated the vulnerable forward positions easts of the Dnieper and withdrew their units to the west bank to establish the new *Hauptkampflinie* (HKL) or main combat line. The 6th Grenadiers were pulled back due west where they were deployed in their new positions, a 50-km-long front with the 37th Regiment north of Zlobin, the 18th Regiment in Zlobin, and the 58th Regiment south of the city, in the southwest corner of the 9th Army.

After taking up their new positions, the men used the period of quiet to improve their defenses by laying out mine fields, stringing barbed wire entanglements, and continually clearing their trenches of snow. To protect against deep Russian incursions, all positions were designed to be capable of all-round defense.

For the well-being of the troops, the Germans established an *Erholungsheim* in Babruysk, maintained by the medical staff and two nurses from the German Red Cross. In a simple house, converted to a more German style, forty-six men at a time could be rotated off the front line for seven days of rest and relaxation. Here they could enjoy warm food, clean beds, movies, performances by the divisional variety troop, '*die Kuriere aus Rzhev*', or read the latest edition of the divisional newspaper, the *Lückenbüßer* (by the time Reiner arrived, *Erholung* (rest and recuperation) had been reduced to one day).

The 6th Division changed both its position and its command structure. In April, *Oberstleutnant* von Issendorf, the commander of the 58th Regiment, was transferred to the General *Kommando* of the VI *Wehrkreis* in Münster. His replacement was *Oberst* Wodtke. In May, the well-respected *Generalleutnant* Grossman, who had commanded the 6th division since December 1941 and had seen them through all the bloody battles of Rzhev, left to take over command of an Army *Korps*. The new divisional chief was *Generalmajor* Heyne.

When Reiner finally returned to the front after having been away for thirteen months, he found that much had changed. His division was no longer on the Volga, 1,000 km deep in Russia; they were on the Dnieper, 350 km from the Polish border. The trusted division and regiment commanders were gone, replaced by strangers. Reiner did not return to either of his old companies. Instead, he was assigned to the 10th *Kompanie* (*Oberleutnant* Kurt Haas)[3] of the III *Bataillon* (*Hauptmann* Kurt Ohms[4]), and he found no familiar faces.

On the March
9 April 1944

Dear Parents,

It is already Easter Sunday but there isn't much evidence of it here other than the pudding we were given as dessert, and I had a barber cut my hair and shave my beard. The Easter mood is barely noticeable, but then again we are finally out of the German area and must now deal with the Russian conditions. I'm feeling rather tired and lazy for no real reason. It's only the first night that I've spent on a rolling train. There's no hint of spring here. The ground is still frozen as are all the edges of the rivers and ponds, and there are patches of snow everywhere. But the weather is clear and sunny and promises that the conditions will soon change.

I send my greetings,

From your Reiner

On the March
10 April 1944

Dear Parents,

Right now, I have just a little time. This morning I arrived in the second designated destination and tomorrow I depart for the division. I washed myself thoroughly and shaved, and will be off to catch a movie. It will be my last chance to make use of this cultural offering. The weigh-station master has benevolently provided me with a perspective on the food supply with regard to the continuing war. An example: The Ukraine only provided us with 1.6 million tons of grain in the previous year whereas our own harvest amounted to twenty-six million tons as compared to a normal harvest of twenty-one million tons.

Otherwise, there is not too much to report except that one third of the land is still covered with snow and at least as much covered with wide stretches of water. It hasn't warmed up yet. But if the weather stays as it is, it will soon be better with both. For now, be well. I think tomorrow I will be getting my field post number and my mail. I send you my greetings, especially to Wolf, who I hope is already there.

Your Reiner

12 April 1944

Dear Parents,

It's the afternoon now, and we three KOBs went through the water and the damp to report to the regimental commander, but he kept us waiting and so we had to find our way back in the dark, which was bad because you can't see to avoid the water. We've been sitting here three hours waiting to be called. I've been able to read a nice, small book, unremarkable but it contained fine and tender stories from Flanders during the previous world war. Until later—we are being called now.

12 April 1944

Dear Parents,

Now I've gone as far forward as the supply depot, and I think I'll be assigned to a company today, but that has to be decided by the regiment. However, I won't be going to the front before tomorrow. It's supposed to be quiet here, but it is not that pleasant due to all the water around. I can't imagine why they wanted to build bunkers here. The streets and roads are nothing but mud, much like those you see in the newsreels. But I can get used to anything. We arrived here yesterday evening and were put up in an empty Russian house. And then things were familiar again. We got a fire going, scrounged up some leftover goulash from the kitchen, which we warmed up, lit two candles and sat down to eat. Needless to say, the smell of food enticed a guy from the supply troop to come sniffing around. He told us all his woes and troubles, truly sorrowful stories. And one can understand him. They are always stuck in the rear area, never left alone or allowed free time. They just sit around in Russia, waiting for a leave. And so it was there, once again, the camaraderie of the Russian Front. Besides me, there are two other KOB *Unteroffiziere* [sergeants] with one year of service, coming out of Denmark. There is also a medic lance-corporal from the military hospital in Wilna.

13 April 1944

And now it's one evening later. After marching nine kilometers back here yesterday in the darkness, this afternoon we had to make the same trip for the third time, with the necessary equipment, of course. We still don't have a regular, permanent *Feldpost* number. We still have to remain here in the rear with a temporary unit, so don't write me yet. Right now we are sitting in an empty bunker and whose wall-oven we had to seal up. Otherwise, it is all right in here—plenty of room and independence. Our superiors haven't made a bad impression. There's constant rumbling in the distance, but that doesn't mean anything.

Greetings from your Reiner
Punktiert: 10 km south of Zlobin

16 April 1944

Dear Parents,

First thing, I'm sending you this piece of a letter I already started, and second: Today is Sunday. The weather is outstanding and we KOBs are still sitting around in the rear area of the Regiment, still waiting to be sent forward and now and again kept busy with written exercises about combat positions and so forth. Yesterday we started building a sandbox[5] and it looks just like one that children would use—four planks and a heap of beautiful white sand in the middle. Thank God, we have plenty of it around here, otherwise our bunkers wouldn't be so dry. We really don't have to bail out our bunkers, and it's quite comfortable for five men. A nice-sized bunker isn't so cramped, and I haven't banged my head on the ceiling once. Unfortunately, we three KOBs will have to move because the *Oberst* [Colonel][6] wants us nearer to him. And things were so peaceful here. Yesterday we lay about in just our shirt sleeves in the sun for two hours in a thicket of cattails. Of course, we had our trousers on as well. One could just see the knots from which the buds and leaves would bloom even though the snow will be here a while longer. But on nice days, you can tell spring is coming. It snowed the day before yesterday and the ground froze, and today you can work without a shirt.

Yesterday I saw the first bullfinch in the wild, a remarkable bird in form and color. Instead of sparrows, around here we have perky robins which make you laugh with their lively ways. In the swamps, there is a large, black and white bird that flies in a curious zigzag pattern. I believe they are called kibitzer. You hear their strange call at night. Father should look them up in the bird album of the Ovaschecks. There are, of course, magpies here, and larks fly about in the blue sky, announcing the coming of spring. You can often see doves, crows, and many birds of prey: vultures and small hawks.

Now we have moved to our new quarters and have spent the whole afternoon building tables and benches. We have to wait and see what they intend to do with us tomorrow. So far, it's been like a summer health resort for us.

There is always a little outdoor work: chopping wood, fetching water, organizing things, but little of any duty. And we get plenty of food. At noon, thick, heavy soup with plenty of canned meat, or we get horsemeat and extra potatoes and goulash as well. We get two to three times as much butter, twice as much sausage, cheese, or honey. Today we even got a mess-tin lid full of applesauce. We get an average of seven cigarettes and a roll of tobacco almost every day. In addition, up until today I still had some leftover rations that I was given for my trip out here. The bread is good; well baked and practically as much as one needs—at least a half loaf. We also have plenty of candles and Hindenburg lamps, and actually for the time being, we have it better than we deserve. In the evening, the so-called 'Coffee-Grinders'[7] fly over. They are primitive, single engine Russian aircraft whose engines make a monotonous—though somewhat pleasant—droning noise. They toss out individual bombs, hand-grenades with pulled pins, and pieces of train track rails, and they scatter the newest surrender leaflets all over.

What is also nice around here is that we get to sleep through the night without having to stand watch duty, and that is the most important factor for our general well-being. When I say 'we', I mean the two other KOB *Unteroffiziere*—eighteen- and nineteen-years-old—and myself. One is an efficient jurist, with all the advantages and disadvantages of the profession. The other, Andreas, is our 'Benjamin' who has such a hesitant and weak character with no self-confidence or talents, nor does he ever step in to lend a hand. But they are both good comrades. And here comes the other of our group, whom we call 'the Fourth One'. He brings plenty of liveliness and stories to our quarters, as he seems to have experienced everything. So, I will close now. I will send along my leftover bread coupons. Be well, and I send my greetings.

Your Reiner

18 April 1944

Dear Parents,

We are still here in the rear area of the Regiment in a four-man bunker with four KOBs and two corporals. They have already left and we KOBs are still lazing around. We go to bed early in the evening and have to eat in two shifts, and since the early bird gets the worm, I'm already up, have started a fire in the stove, lit a big cigar, read a couple of nice poems by Eichendorff, and have sat down to write because I am thinking of you and dreamed of you. I am thinking about how I spent my thousand marks in an art and antiques shop. I picked up an antique silver ring, two colorful reproductions in delicate colors with soft, silken undertones, and a beautiful, delicately carved ivory cross in the south German style—like Böhm once had. I'm looking forward to bringing these things home. Otherwise, I think of Father because yesterday we were able to get plenty of tobacco from the commissary. You would be astonished: 180 German and 150 French black cigarettes, fifteen cigars, and fifteen cigarillos of good quality, and three pouches of tobacco as well. In addition to that, we were able to get some schnapps, and on the 20th, we are supposed to be issued a liter of schnapps each—if that is true! So that's how we live here. We sleep through the night, get plenty of food, and in the course of the day, lie in the sun for three to four hours. When I think back on Münster!

A month ago today, I was supposed to be going on leave. Well, now you probably have Wolf with you, whom I'm certain will be able to deliver all kinds of good things to you.

21 April 1944

Yesterday, after being supplied with far too little *Sekt* [sparkling wine], and far too much schnapps and beer, we are finally going up to the front line this evening. We are assigned to a *Feste Kompanie*[8] and have finally received our field post number, so that you can now write to me.

I send you my greetings,
Your Reiner

22 April 1944

Dear Parents,

In front of me sits a nice package. I'll have to come up with the packaging myself because we have no packing material. But somehow, I'll send off the contents because we can only take our bread bag and assault packs with us to the front line, and they don't hold very much. I'm assigned to a new company and will be in a new battalion as well.[9] Hopefully this package will soon sit undamaged on your table. The contents are not intended for Tommy, who I hope, despite the military reports, hasn't caused you any damage. Father should have plenty to smoke, as I do. In fact, I have manure, as we say around here, which means enormous amounts. My company commander has the same name as my previous commander[10] and is actually the third of that name that I have had in Russia. I hope to be able to write you more soon. For now, I send greetings from your old Reiner.

23 April 1944

Dear Parents,

And now at the last minute, I've been assigned to another company.[11] So, instead of a D, I will have a C in my *FPNr* [field post number, 21199C]. I hope you haven't already sent off a letter because with the local post service, it is easily possible that they will send it back stamped 'waiting for a new address'. But I hardly need to tell you that. As for all the rest, I believe that what I can hope for here at the front is to know what I am here for and that I won't be unneeded or superfluous for too long. True, I won't be assigned a squad because there are almost twice as many sergeants as are needed. But the mood here is good, and I am satisfied—just the opposite of my time as *zbV* [*zur besonderen Verwendung*—special employment] in Münster.

Greetings,
Reiner

26 April 1944

Dear Parents,

I've been here on the front line for four or five days. I don't exactly know the day or date. One hardly knows the day or date because there is no Sunday here. One day pretty much passes like the next. Some days are better, some worse than what I've experienced before. The food is better. Heavy portions that almost fill your mess kit. We don't have to share our bread because there is plenty of it. Smokes are sufficient because we hardly have time to smoke. We are outside all night, and we do some entrenching during which we eat our hot meals that are usually cold by the time we eat them. But at night, things happen; either patrols or assault parties. But those don't happen very often, and so are not important. During the day, military action would be impossible because Ivan would have to cross a wide-open area. We sleep between 5 a.m. and 1 p.m., and then it's back to work. One has little time to write. I have to depend on stealing away some time to write. We can't wash because there is no water. As for lice—they simply don't exist ever since I. G. Farben invented a solution that you wash your clothes in to make them lice-proof. I've not been assigned a squad because there are so many sergeants that some of them don't even have squads. Our company commander is good but he sometimes gives the men too much to do, though it is definitely necessary because many things here are obsolete and old-fashioned in our positions and in our company. The soil around here is almost completely sand, which is good for digging because we can do it quickly and we don't run into water. On the other hand, our trenches fall in easily. The bunkers are dry and most are rather narrow. Ours, however, is a famous exception. It is roomy and light. Such are the conditions here. The region is desolate, devoid of woods. Some of the positions are swampy. The weather is inconsistent. The snow is gone, but the landscape isn't green yet. Above all, it is very windy, which causes your eyes to water. So far, my eyes have not become inflamed. Actually, I am completely healthy, and for the time being, I'm getting enough sleep.

I've just read your last three letters that I brought with me. I can't get reasonably priced postcards for Wolf any more. You'll have to ask me in a letter anything more you wish to know about the conditions here, but I'm not allowed to tell you everything. Despite all the smoking, I don't have a sore throat, and my occasional wet feet don't bother me either. I'm hardened to it. I don't see any old comrades here because I'm in a completely different battalion from before. I occasionally see a familiar face from Senne who was also running around in Münster.

I need to close now for it's high time I let myself be seen outside. Due to the shortage of space, I'm actually in a bunker with a different squad.

Greetings from your Reiner son, who feels much better here than with the replacement unit and with all that training and drilling, which was worse than physically killing someone. (Not really).

29 April 1944

Dear Parents,

Gradually, I am finding that I need mail from you. One gets hungry for it after a while, especially when one is in a foreign land and a desolate region. In comparison, Italy is certainly better, even if one is bothered more by artillery and aircraft. Also, there one has a more fair opponent who is less cunning and less unpredictable, and not as despised as the Russians. Now I have been here a week, and I am in a squad with an idiot for a sergeant. He has no idea of the situation and the men dance circles around him. Consequently, there is no cohesion in the group and no camaraderie. Each guy sneaks off or shirks his duty whenever he can. One is from Luxembourg and is untrustworthy in all respects; he does nothing but complain about everything in his poor, crude German.[12] Another is from Austria and is both dull and nervous at the same time. The third is quite young, wants to be a KOB, and opens up his scandal-mongering, East Prussian mouth to anyone who will listen. Then we have a street-worker from Thuringia who has a weak character, and a Rhinelander of the indolent, uninteresting type who hangs back and is just marking time here. And then there is the Sergeant; a rather dull representation of the *Niederlausitz*: tall, blustering, clumsy, and at a total loss. He doesn't understand that nothing is going to get done. And by the way, he is a former *Landesschütze* and that says it all. The company commander certainly had a reason for sticking me in this group, and I have often offered the Sergeant my opinions in private.

1 May 1944

Right now, we are busy baking, roasting, and grilling. We have eggs and have received flour as well, so we are making crispy omelettes. We only lack salt, and it's a lot of work, for which we don't really have the time.

Yesterday, for Sunday, we were given beer again, and it was of pre-war quality. But we couldn't get drunk because there wasn't enough of it. There are frequent changes on the menu. Our position lies in a large potato field, so everywhere there are stacks of potatoes. But we don't make use of them because the few full helmets that we fetch occasionally were nothing compared to the ones that we already had or the ones that were dug up while we were digging trenches. The supply depot still has plenty of frozen potatoes, which make all the soups somewhat sweet, which we don't like. We don't have time to clear the potatoes out, and it would have to be done at night. And we have no vehicle to transport them.

Elsewhere and in the homeland, there is a potato shortage. But that's war for you. One thing is lacking; and there isn't any of the other thing. This would be avoided if there were any organization from the top down. Even in our squad, there is no organization. Everyone does what he thinks is right, and that's a bunch of crap. And now I belong to a batch like this and can't do anything about it because the squad leader is so dull that he can't grasp anything. He lets the men say anything to him and he puts up with it. And even if I were to try and explain it to him, he still wouldn't comprehend it. I won't put up with this for long. I came out here determined to be positive and active—the opposite of what I was with the replacement battalion where I looked at everything negatively and indifferently accepted the situation without rebelling because I considered what we were doing as pointless. But here there is a point; it has to do with life and death, and when it finally comes to combat, this group will be bankrupt, completely different from the squad I had in February and March last year, a squad on whom I could rely completely.

Last night I went out on my third patrol here. Now that's a story. First, it was a clear, moonlit night, so we couldn't get too close to the enemy because the moon was on our back. Second, we had to lie out there from nine at night until three in the morning without our jackets in freezing temperature. Third, as we came through the barbed wire entanglements, we encountered a Russian troop of which we could see six to ten men, and we were seven men without automatic weapons. What our leader did afterwards, I'm not free to say, but in any case, he was right and later put one over on the company commander.[13] In many ways, it's not like 1942. As many a common soldier says sarcastically; the situation is serious but not hopeless. Anyway, I need to close now. The dung beetles are starting to buzz around, which usually begins right before nightfall, just like the larks that in the night announce the coming day. Don't think we'll have a peaceful night. We have to go out again, and on May first, Ivan usually does something. We've already seen some signaling on the horizon.

Greetings from your old boy, Reiner.

6 May 1944

Dear Parents,

Tomorrow I will have been in this position for two weeks. Gradually we're building it up. Today we have begun to widen it. Of course, nothing is logical because the Sergeant can't seem to plan anything. I've gradually become the mediator for the Sergeant with the men for whom I try to translate the incomprehensible and mumbled orders of our squad leader, so that they can understand them and know what is going on and what they need to do. I've practically become the squad leader and the Sergeant, a mere puppet. But this won't work in the long run, and I need to get my own squad soon. Otherwise, life is bearable, though one has little time to oneself. Recently I had to write a report for the company for the 1st of May, and although the CO was pleased with it, he wants me to write a more extensive one. I'll have to see where I can find the time for this new assignment. I'll close for today and write more soon.

Greetings from your Reiner

10 May 1944

Dear Parents,

I've just come in from the morning digging. True, the mornings are usually used for sleeping, but the soldier is not spared the ceremony of standing at post when morning arrives. One man from each squad must be in the trenches in addition to the observation post, which the squads take turns manning. So, I came back in and really needed to use the time to sleep, or to revise my report of May 1, which I had to write for our company commander—my report was still too detailed and polished. Either that or use the time to write out my curriculum for my second OB [*Offizier Bewerber*, officer-in-training] course, which I have to bring with me to Battalion. But what will be, will be.

   Today at daybreak, I received your first mail—four long letters. And in the dawn's light, while I was at my post, I totally forgot about the cold, the sharp wind, Ivan, our raiding parties, their attacks, everything as I buried myself in your letters, carefully reading every sentence, every word. I remained there, isolated and absorbed in your letters until the first day-sentry arrived and broke the spell, destroying the kaleidoscopic images of my imagination. Then suddenly, I was back in Russia. I continued reading your letters during breakfast, which otherwise I would have skipped in favor of sleeping. Then while we were further widening our small bunker, I would work until I was warm and then I would rest and read your letters until I got cold and I went back to digging. I got a lot done, actually more than I would have without your letters. Even so, I'm still not done.

I have read through Father's and Wolf's letters and could write many pages in reply. I'm reading Heidi's letters now, and I'm able to understand them better since I have some insight now into her life, especially when she wrote of her birthday [March 31], which genuinely touched me. On that day, I was completely bottled up inside myself, hardly the happy Reiner. I was in one of my moods during which I just couldn't get out of myself. Instead of improving, I just plunged deeper inside. The night before, I had stayed up until two in the morning, working in vain on a humorous poem that I could give her, so that I would not stand empty-handed at the birthday table. Despite my best efforts, I couldn't come up with anything that satisfied me that didn't appear as something banal, so I didn't present it to her in lieu of a gift. The next morning, I was the last to appear at breakfast as though I had overslept even though I had hardly closed my eyes the night before, tormented as I had been. And so, there I was, one of the main characters of the day, standing helpless and empty handed with the two ladies at the birthday table. I tried in vain to celebrate with them and to put on a good face. Even walking later with Heidi and Reinhold [his cousin Resi's son] in the zoo could not bring me out of my mood. There was simply nothing I could do. Instead of brightening the day with my presence, I simply darkened it. But birthday celebrations have never been my strong point.

13 May 1944

This evening a fellow is going on leave and will take this letter with him, so I'll have to close already. I thank you for your four letters. Number 1 arrived intact, and letter #2 arrived with one from Heidi two days later on May 12th. Excuse my briefness. I hope to write more later. I send my greetings, especially to Wolf, who must be there now.

Your son,
Reiner

14 May 1944

Dear Parents,

Yesterday I sent off a letter (#14) with one of our squad members who is going to Allenstein, East Prussia. I hope it catches up with the other letters (#13), which I sent off two days earlier, though I wrote it on the 6th. That came about because with all the activity in our crowded bunker, the letter to Mother was mislaid and only by chance did it reappear five days later. I did a lot of swearing, but you are the ones who must suffer. I hope it doesn't cause you too much concern, for it is easily possible for there to be a two-to-three-week gap in my letters, even from this quiet part of the front where most of the mail is carried out by people going on leave.

Two years ago yesterday was my first time at the front in Russia, and as of today, I have been here three weeks. In this time, I have been on seven patrols, which is the only time to get a *Heimatschuss*,[14] and probably not by the Russians. Since the company has been here, we haven't suffered a single casualty from enemy action. However, once an assault party of the neighboring company fired on our patrol, the bloody fools. We immediately recognized what was happening and began firing off recognition flares, but they kept blasting away at us with rifles, machine guns, sub-machine guns, rifle grenades, and hand grenades. We were unharmed, but they wounded two of their own men. Twice now, patrols have stepped on our own mines. Recently one of the squad members came running up to me saying, 'Ivan is in our wire.' It was night, and I went out but our squad leader wasn't around, as usual. It turned out to be one of those birds, which I thought were kibitzer. They often make a noise like a rusty wire being stretched. Usually they aren't that close to us because there is no swamp near here. I recognize them because our patrols often have to go through swampy areas, and those birds can become unpleasant. If when crawling around on patrol you disturb their nest, they leap up crying and circling around, and you have to get away quickly. Once these birds betrayed our presence, and Ivan began firing on us with machine guns and mortars.

I'll describe these gull-like birds again: They are not all that large and are black and white, especially on the wings, which are black on the outer side and bright white at the base and on the underside. The shape of the wing is also distinctive. They look like wide rags. Their flight is bat-like, but not as angular. There are kibitzers here too, but they are smaller and more rare. They are gray brown with slender wings that have a bright underside. Like doves, they fly about, throwing themselves from one side to another in a broad, zig-zag pattern.

16 May 1944

Dear Parents,

For several days now we've had beautiful May weather, warm and sunny. I'm sitting outside in the trench sentry post, writing. Now I have my peace and quiet, and the sun as well. Last night your letter #3 arrived, and I thank you. You praise me for writing so often, but soon you will have to take back your praise because from the first of May until the eleventh, no mail left here. Has my 22 April package with 200 gr. of fine-cut tobacco and 228 cigarettes arrived? I can probably send you another soon, mostly of tobacco. There's much I could write about from here, but writing without a plan, as I often do, leaves many things unsaid. For example, since May 4th, we have been having KOB instruction in the rear of the battalion. One could call these 'history classes' if they were done better. We would also have field exercises, if the difficult terrain didn't make every effort ridiculous. Instructions are conducted in a low-lying area, four hundred meters behind the front lines. We've even been instructed in patrols back here. The day before yesterday, we buried one of the KOBs. There are about a dozen of us here. We were traveling the whole day with only two hours of sleep. It wasn't a large ceremony and was almost too modest. It might have been bearable if the chaplain had come up with a few good words to say. What he said was wretched in the extreme, sounding sometimes like a newspaper, sometimes melodramatic, and sometimes detached and professional like a lawyer or statistician. This weighed on me the rest of the day—this bleak and insensitive tone, even at the grave of a hero, according to popular sentiment. This sergeant had fallen under conditions that automatically assumed courage: 1,400 rounds of artillery, forty-eight rockets [*Stuka zu Fuss*][15] and then assault with four men and two combat engineers because there were no more men available. And all this at night. That pretty much says it all.

Once we had coffee and cake with the officers of the battalion, and that will be repeated on a weekly basis. On these afternoons, we will have written assignments. For example, tomorrow I have to write why I want to be an officer. But as the common soldier says: you are interrogated only if you blab.

I could write of another thing, though it was some time ago, back during the pleasant days we had to spend at regiment, waiting for the battalion to take over the new position. During that time, we KOBs enlarged and improved the trench. The battalion had drawn up a duty schedule that partly made no sense and did not leave us enough time for writing and sleeping. Theoretically we could sleep five hours, but because of the faulty use of the squad leaders and other conditions, we got at most four hours, and often only three and sometimes two or one hour of sleep per day. That won't work in the long run. On birthdays, men are sent far to the rear to a 'resort' where there is plenty to be had: good food, even better schnapps, movies, and stage shows, but not one hour of sleep either before or after, so that one goes forty to fifty hours without being able to shut one's eyes. You leave for the rear area in the morning while the others sleep and come back just in time to go on duty again. And that's how I'll be celebrating my birthday. I'm looking forward to the food, which I can't complain about, and I'll slowly work on writing my essay.

See if you can still find my green mosquito net that I brought back from Russia. I can already notice these tormentors in the mornings and evenings.

Be well and I send my greetings from your Reiner son.

21 May 1944

Dear Parents,

I need to tell you that I haven't received your birthday letter, but I did get Heidi's and Lütte's. I hope it's the fault of our field post and not because of Tommy.[16]

Be that as it may, I will write my main letter later. I haven't celebrated my birthday yet—or what we call a celebration here—that is, spending the day back at the 'resort' with good food, drink, movies, and stage performances. I'll do that later. In the meantime, we have finished widening our bunker, and now I live in the best bunker of the company's sector. We have received mosquito nets, although these pests aren't as bad as they were in June 1942. Otherwise, things are fine here. The duty schedule has improved considerably. We get more sleep and have less work.

I send my greetings,
Your Reiner

23 May 1944

Dear Parents,

Last night your birthday letter arrived for which I heartily thank you. I also got another short letter from Heidi, which was nice of her and greatly valued considering her workload. Just think, I have something very nice coming up that I can add to my birthday ledger. That is a chamber concert, which sounds strange coming out of the mouth of a common soldier. I was asked if anyone had interest in a concert, and I volunteered, of course. So tomorrow morning at a quarter to four, I'll be marching off while the others are sleeping.

25 May 1944

Once again, something came up in the meantime. I had to go over to the neighboring company as a witness to an incident that happened during the last trench raid. I didn't take part in it, but unfortunately I was present when during the evacuation of the wounded, a brawl almost broke out 500 meters in front of our front lines. Ivan remained lively for he must have heard all the shouting and bellowing. The assault party—of which I was not a part—was the first group to engage in combat. I was the only one who came out of our trenches and ran forward almost to the area where the assault party had broken into the Russian position and there helped a sergeant drag off one of our dead. I only had a couple of hand grenades but no rifle. It was really a shame to watch from the trenches as the assault party came back in small groups and to see how long it took before others finally went out and helped them back in through the mine field. Many of the assault party were so angry that one of them, who had been drinking schnapps, hit the first sergeant he saw in the face with a hand grenade. Well, things like that happen at night. Afterward there was an investigation, and everything about the incident was written down.

There is more time for writing and sleeping now, but not for me. Every two days I have to spend the afternoon back at battalion for officer training, coffee, cake (once a week), and recently, riding instruction—only theoretical for the time being. I'll write about it more extensively later, but once again I must close.

By the way, one of us four who lazed about back at regiment for those five days was wounded in the assault party action and will get a crippled right hand out of it. The medical officer cadet will be leaving June 10th to go back to Germany in order to be there for the beginning of the semester. And then there's me—the only one left, and I still haven't been given a squad. And I was the oldest soldier in the group. For now, I can't say that I am satisfied, but I can put up with it for a while longer. I get along with everyone, although at times the squad leader and I have differences. One can get sick of him after a while. Yesterday I received a letter from Wolf and one from the Wolfs as well. So long, and I send you my greetings.

Your old Reiner, who is gradually finding his place in the company again.

28 May 1944

Dear Parents,

This morning when I awoke after several hours of uninterrupted sleep, it was *Pfingsten* [Pentecost]. For once, we were allowed to lie in bed and not go out on work detail. I grabbed a cigar from the shelf next to my sleeping place and fetched a bar of crème chocolate from my bread bag that they gave us yesterday. And that is how I enjoyed *Pfingsten* morning. Then I read a few of Hölderlin's poems and some of the enjoyable *Schulmeisterlein Wutz*, which I picked up around here, thoroughly rain-soaked. When I finally got up, I found a serving of pre-war quality cake and a quarter bottle of *Sekt* waiting for me, which was unfortunately a bit warm because today is a warm, beautiful, sunny day. After this festive breakfast, my cigar was glowing again as it usually does when I sit down in peace and write letters.

Last night I received two letters from you (#5 and #6) and one from Heidi with three pictures of Lütte's visit to Breslau, which are very nice. I am glad that the package of tobacco wares that I sent from Russia has arrived. I could send you another and even larger package—mostly tobacco—if I had some packing material. The twenty cigars you sent from Berlin were of the best quality, but after ten days, there are only six left. That though is only a trifle when one considers the great losses that the war has caused. I heartily thank you for your letters. It is a special feeling to know that my parents put a lighted candle on the table for my birthday because I could not be there. I thank you for your gifts. I enjoyed reading *Till Ulenspiegel* by de Coster whose version all others tend

to follow. I enjoyed the pictures that Father put in the folder and look forward
to when we can look at them together. When will that be? Once again, I've
completely settled in here at the front and find it bearable, even if I have to put up
with a lot of shit and have almost no free time. The duty schedule is back again,
and I'll gradually become a machine, lose all individualism, and unfortunately
all desire to change things, a desire I had when I was a new arrival here. One will
simply be waltzed to death by the all-too-deeply ingrained dullness of everyday
routine. And those above us, our company commander, considers this a good
thing! What is one to do?

Recently, I had a lively discussion about this with our CO and was told that
our squad leader is one of the best in the company. I was dumbfounded that
an officer could say that about such a limp rag who allows everything in the
squad to go on and then complains and grumbles when something goes wrong.
That was the first and only serious discussion I've ever had with him. It took
place after an incident that occurred while I was on sentry duty. I had the first
watch—after an entire night of sentry duty—in an observer's post for which I
was too tall. Consequently, I had to half-squat and lean against the wall, and
the moment the company commander showed up, my knees suddenly buckled.
That's the first time it ever happened to me. This 'falling out of the tree' as the
soldiers call it, often happens at night when one loses his equilibrium or the
knees suddenly buckle from fatigue. If one isn't leaning, then nothing happens.
But when one is dead tired—well, it happened. In the course of the following
discussion, which was conducted quietly and calmly, I openly expressed my
opinions and then requested that I be cancelled as an officer cadet. I eventually
submitted my request in writing. That will probably take place in the next few
days. The incident itself is of less importance than one would think because
I know that the Sergeant Major's report of me in Münster, which he wrote
at the last minute and which I copied down, is highly unusual but seems to
have been of importance to the company commander or he wouldn't have had
concerns. When I learned of that, my mind was made up, and so now, we have
an understanding. I now look forward to a future with trust and can stand
before my comrades free of doubt. The last assault party had especially shaken
my belief. In the end, the two dead and the six wounded—some of whom will
remain cripples—were not sacrificed for the success of the mission but for the
'Officer's Honor' of the assault group leader. This was confirmed by what the
company commander said against which I clearly expressed myself.

Well, enough of this story, which is unpleasant and painful for me. I won't
let the accusation of sleeping on duty pass lightly. Anyway, in the next action,
everything will be made good again, and I'll show what I'm made of. The laurels
of course will go to the company commander who is in line for a German Cross.
But stop, says the soldier, I should not talk like this because it's spiteful.

Now *Pfingsten* has passed, and it is evening. The May beetles are already buzzing about. They seem to have replaced the dung beetles around here since it warmed up. The evenings here are especially beautiful because of the splendid sunsets and the impressive clouds.

About the film, *Reise in die Vergangenheit*, which I saw in Münster and wrote to you about, at least we agree. Now I must close. Please send me stationery with your letters, but nothing too good. As for package stamps, it's best if you only send them if I ask you for them and put them in a durable container.

I send greetings from your Reiner who would rather be a *Schlot* [loser] than a KOB.

Summer 1944

With the Soviet offensives of the winter and spring beginning to die down, or rather beginning to bog down in the Russian mud, the German fronts were granted a brief breathing spell to consider what to do next—or, more correctly, what the Russians were planning to do next. In 1941, 1942, and 1943, Soviet winter and spring offensives had been followed by German summer offensives, but not this year. Germany's war situation had changed drastically in that rather than making their own plans, the Führer's headquarters were seeking to divine the intentions of their enemy and how best to thwart them. Truly, the initiative had been surrendered for good.

The Germans understood that the cross-channel invasion by the Anglo-Americans—that long-awaited opening of the second front—was coming that summer, most likely in June. Forces had already been deployed in the west to counter it, unfortunately by weakening the already inadequate Eastern armies. Ten Panzer divisions now sat far away in northern France; the divisions included six of the excellently equipped *Waffen SS Panzer* and *Panzergrenadier* divisions, which had on so many occasions intervened so effectively in the east.

Although the precise strategy for defeating the western invasion was still a matter of debate among the German commanders in the west, the overall German strategy was to hold on in the east, repel the Allied invasion of France, and then rush the available forces back to the east to deal with the situation there.

However, the question remained: what was Stalin going to do? A study of the situation map of the Eastern Front told the Führer all he thought he needed to know. The extensive Soviet advances on the southern flank had brought them to the borders of the Eastern Europe, but they had also left the northern and central fronts some 320 km behind to the east. Stalin would have to even up the fronts, which ruled out any major drive in the south. *Heeresgruppen Nord* and *Mitte* would have to be his next target—but where would Stalin strike? The obvious answer was at the extended southern flank of *Heeresgruppe Mitte*, at its juncture with the southern German armies. It was a bold, massive thrust northwards, all the way to the Baltic Sea, which would cut off two entire *Heeresgruppen*. That is what Hitler would do if he were Stalin; he had done it in France in 1940 and he would attempt it again in the Ardennes, against the Anglo-American forces. With the surety that Stalin would opt for just such a bold plan, the German High Command began moving all available forces—especially the indispensable Panzer forces (all at the expense of the already overextended *Heeresgruppe Mitte*)—to the southwest, near Kowel, to counter the expected Soviet offensive. The result was that *Heeresgruppe Mitte* was left with only thirty-four divisions to man its 1,100-km front and, most critically, could place only five of these in reserve. It had but one Panzer division for the entire front.

Stalin, however, was not Hitler. He envisioned an entirely different plan for the annihilation of *Heeresgruppe Mitte*. Through bitter and bloody experience, the Russians had learned that bold and overambitious operations rarely turned out well against the Germans (something the British would learn later in Holland). Deep, overreaching thrusts were all too fraught with risks, particularly against an enemy whose tactical abilities to deliver rapier-like counter-thrusts still deserved high respect. With an overwhelming superiority in men and materiel, there was no need for the Russians to take such a risk. Rather than striking from the south, along the vulnerable flank of *Heeresgruppe Mitte*, Stalin and the Soviet High Command opted for what the Germans were not expecting—an outright frontal assault against *Heeresgruppe Mitte*. It would not be outflanked and cut off; it would be destroyed in place by numerous thrusts carving up the German forces into many pockets and then grinding them to pieces. The date for their destruction was set for 22 June—the third anniversary of the German invasion of Russia.

1 June 1944

Dear Parents,

Today I finally went back to 'resort', which I should have done on my birthday or at least shortly after. In many respects, it's a double-edged sword because the chamber orchestra is no longer there. Even so, I have once again been led back to myself and away from all the difficulties of life's problems that we all sink into nowadays. Sometimes it's painful to reflect on things, but there is also the consolation of reflection: you have affirmed yourself and found no weakness. When I look at these strange people who indulge in this degenerate jazz, pop music, and such things with such obvious enjoyment, I do not envy them. In my opinion, they couldn't be working more against themselves. I am often interested in the faces of the players and soloists during these self-deceiving performances and find that it is only an act, a pose, even by the so-called actors and artists who have chosen a career to practice this so-called art. But enough of this. The house band is playing and they give me no peace because I am sitting up front.

As I said before, a break from the front back here is a double-edged sword, especially with regard to sleep. After a night of sentry duty, you leave the front lines early in the morning and come back here on foot for 5 km or 10 km by auto or rail so that you are here by 9 a.m. Then things begin immediately: music, theater, the band, then a movie—*The Swedish Nightingale*—and then more music, all of this with only pauses for eating. At five in the evening, the fun is over and you are back at the front on duty, bone-tired and fighting the temptation to fall asleep. I hope I won't have to go out on a patrol as a conclusion to all of this. But as a change, it is good and has its value, even if it can awaken some unpleasant things at times.

And now I'll close for today.

Your Reiner son

3 June 1944

Dear Parents,

Before I forget, first an address: Johann Fuchs, Grossenhain in Saxony, Adolf Hitler Platz 1. He was the medical KOB who visited us one evening when we were back at Regiment and whose father has a position as doctor with the Corps hospital. As such, he has the authority to have the wounded transported back to hospitals in Germany. This would be a possibility, should the need arise. Please copy it down and put it somewhere where you can find it. It would be best to put it with my papers. This fellow, who has already been wounded, will do his '*Bajechli*', which is what we call it when someone leaves the regiment or 'polishes the flag', to go back to Germany for further schooling on June 10th. He is the second of us four. Unfortunately, I don't see the battalion's KOBs very often because I am no longer attending the instruction courses. I haven't heard anything about my request to resign as a KOB, but I think something will happen soon.

4 June 1944

This evening I received another letter from you, #8, and I thank you. I had no idea that Lütte was sick. Kidneys again? In any case, I hope she gets better and has some rest afterwards. This evening Ivan was here and really took one on the chin from one of our well-armed and well-supported patrols. That's the way it has to be done. Our own losses—none.

The weather here is probably just like yours—wonderfully warm, sometimes too warm during the day. But then it can also be rather cool and rainy, especially at night. And so goes the time here. I've been here at the front for six weeks, but it's still too early for me to get wounded. We do fewer patrols than before because Ivan is not that far away. Over time, he has moved his line some 600 meters closer, so that now he can gradually start using his snipers. So far, they have hardly used them.

Our duties here are pretty much the same as before. Five to six hours of sleep, four hours of day-time sentry duty, and three hours of work detail. There is little time for writing because we still have to wash, clean our weapons, and keep everything repaired. All that takes longer than you'd think even though our bunker is rather spacious. Otherwise, things are like before. Our food supply is fine. Schnapps, Rum, French and Serbian red wine, occasional *Sekt*, beer, or lemonade, and we get all of this fairly often. There is plenty to smoke; I will probably finish off a pack today.

I just finished it off. A typical 'soldier's package', which we can get ourselves, consists of five packs of tobacco, six cigars, forty French and 106 German cigarettes—long live what is left.

And now Sunday is over—a day on which we usually don't have work detail. I send you my greetings and I will write more soon.

Your Reiner

6 June 1944

Dear Parents,

Today I got your letter with news of Wolf's arrival. That occasion is hardly less important than the news of the invasion.[17] I hope your time together won't be too disturbed by the war. If you are having the same weather as we are, then you can certainly be content. We moved to another position on the day of the invasion, and since then, we've had beautiful, sunny weather. We run around without our shirts, the best camouflage in this sandy region. Almost everyone is more or less sunburned; me, somewhat less.

Last night I did my first patrol here in our new position, which makes fourteen patrols altogether since I've been here. Unfortunately, we had to conclude that it's not as swampy here as claimed. Because of that, we'll be doing more patrols and sending out more assault parties. Tonight one of our patrols ran into a Russian ambush. The third of our four KOBs was probably killed or is in Russian hands. That was bad luck and almost impossible where we are because of the terrain. This KOB was a product of the new regulations and had already been promoted to Sergeant even though he'd been a soldier for barely a year. He had no special qualifications and was quite young and inexperienced. He was always calculating and counted his days until he finished his tour of duty at the front. Well, he miscalculated. He probably would have gone back with the other KOBs for further officer training on June 10th. Now, that is it for him. But we'll all have our turn one day.

7 June 1944

Dear Parents,

I was just with the regimental commander because of my request to resign as a KOB. His name is Behrendt,[18] and I was impressed by him. He reminded me of an Elmering, but perhaps that's only because of his name. He showed more interest in me than my company commander and said that he understood my decision completely. He thinks that I am one of those men who cannot adapt to the standard military concept of appearance and order, but who are no less useful as soldiers—especially at the front. He will discuss the matter with my company commander. But whatever the case, I must resign because without external appearance of an officer, you can't be an officer. But this all sounds like talk to me and won't lead to anything, not even to a promotion as compensation, of which he spoke, for what is the word of a superior when it has to come down through so many levels. But it was honorably intended, and I believe I can be the judge of that.

The situation here has not changed for the worse. There have been changes in position and we are in a new area which is much more quiet. We will probably be doing fewer patrols because of the swampy terrain. Our position itself, though, is dry and as well built as the last one.

Your Reiner son

11 June 1944

Yesterday I finally got a squad. I don't know if it's permanent or not. It wouldn't count as my squad leadership certification even if I went back into the KOB program. You need to know that my resignation from the KOB program came through on the 9th. I don't know what you think about all this, but it all seems strange to me that my situation keeps changing without any goal being reached. How can anyone explain what's happened to me? I don't understand it myself. Am I really a loser? Do others see me that way? Why is it that every time I find a firm foothold and start to climb, I am hit on the head by surprise. I hope the reason is that I do not fit in here no matter how hard I try. In the end, I am satisfied with myself and look upon this, which many people melancholically regard as fate, as only a trifle that will have no importance as soon as I'm a civilian again.

Thanks for your greetings and for Wolf's and Lütte's. They took exactly ten days to get here, like almost all of your letters. But one of them hasn't come. Number seven, that you wrote between May 16th and 23rd. It was the one that must have explained Lütte's illness, so I really don't know yet what is wrong with her.

But I need to close once again because I have so little time to write, and certainly not enough peace and quiet because there is so much to do with this new squad, even though it's Sunday. Please send me another, or several, notebooks or writing pads. And stationery too, but not military paper. I really need envelopes too. Send Wolfgang my greetings in your next letter. I send my greetings.

Your Reiner son and brother

12 June 1944

Once again, we are now getting lunch at noon instead of at midnight. Our mail still goes back with the ration-carriers to the supply depot, so I have the chance to write and tell you that tonight I led my first patrol. We sweated like walruses and had to stand knee-deep in swamp water. But it didn't damage our bodies, and besides, we could go to sleep a whole half-hour earlier.

I send my greetings again, your Reiner

14 June 1944

Dear Parents,

I've been leading a squad for five days now, just like during the best time in my military career (February–March, 1943 Rzhev). The mood of the squad, which was in danger of sinking, has risen noticeably. Even though I have less free time and get less sleep than the men (this is especially true when the squad leader is only a *Gefreiter*), I am still in a good mood, despite other things. I believe you need an assignment to gain confidence in your abilities and to rise to the occasion. I can already describe my first success. I was with the squad that used to be with the KOB who was either killed or captured by the Russians. The men did not like him very much. For the first few days, I had to deal with mistrust amongst my squad, which was particularly difficult because I didn't feel the same way about them. I was challenged to win over the youngest guy in the squad, an eighteen-year-old East Prussian who had already experienced Iron Cross 1st Class conditions twice and who wore a close combat badge and other awards on his chest. Thank God, I was able to earn his trust and now that task is behind me. Of course, it's not all running like clockwork. That isn't possible in this company. But I have the men on my side and I get along without giving orders, which is very different from the other squads. I will write more about this later. For now, I send my greetings.

Your Reiner

16 June 1944

And special greetings to Lütte, who got married two years and three days ago.

18 June 1944

Dear Parents,

We've just finished cleaning our machine gun while singing soldiers' songs and can now sit down with good conscience and write letters. Yesterday I received the correspondence from Wolf, which always has special meaning for me. Partly because things are so different for him in Italy and in another branch of service, and partly because his experience is so similar, particularly the intellectual experience. Especially the question: is the military process of dumbing-down temporary or permanent? This affects not only your intellect but also your overall development as a person. The more that my superiors demand me to order people around, the more I resist this method, which I feel is inadequate. I have finally achieved an understanding in my squad—though not completely voluntarily— that everything we have to do will be done through mutual understanding of the task. Discipline is no worse in my squad than in others. I have the men on my side and a camaraderie that couldn't be better, despite the fact that the men are very different from me. The young guy who has an Iron Cross and who is a candidate for the German Cross in Gold is a decent fellow, though an uneducated rogue who'd like to rest on his laurels. I have to be careful and tactful with this guy or risk being viewed as bad as the leader before me, the KOB who is either dead or captured. The others are harmless guys: one, a strapping young man from the lower Steiermark who speaks Slovenian, an Alsatian stone worker, and a street worker from Thuringia. And there you have it.

Our new bunker is roomy and strong but without windowpanes because Ivan often hits us with mortar rounds, so what's the use getting panes brought up from the supply depot? It doesn't rain much but when the wind blows, sand gets into everything in our bunker. We hardly have anything that isn't covered in sand—from our weapons to our food and drink. It gets into everything— clothes, mail, medical supplies, and even into the bottle of eye drops, which many of the men have to use. But not me. I'm healthy as a fish in water. My cheeks have filled out and have color because of the good food here. We run around barefoot and shirtless when the sun shines, which is hardly surprising. Since we have no windowpanes, we get plenty of fresh air. It's like sleeping out in the open. We lack for almost nothing except free time and sleep. If today hadn't been Sunday, I could have read the copies you sent. Along with your letters—for which I thank you—came a greeting from the aunts, written on the edge of a newspaper article they sent about Richard Strauss's 80th birthday. It was an interesting article, but I felt strange reading it at the front when I'm short on free time and sleep.

Greetings,
Your Reiner

Operation Bagration: The Destruction of *Heeresgruppe Mitte* and the End of the 6th *Rheinisch-Westfälischen Grenadier* Division

The weeks went by, summer approached, and the fields and the roads dried out, but the expected Russian offensive out of the south still had not materialized. The Army, corps, and divisional commanders of *Heeresgruppe Mitte* began to wonder if the Führer's headquarters had gotten it all wrong. The intelligence reports gathered from patrols, prisoner interrogations, and aerial reconnaissance in their own sectors of the front indicated an attack on *Heeresgruppe Mitte* itself—most likely in the north, near Vitebsk, and the south, along the Berezina, just as the Russians had done the previous winter. The German commanders voiced their concerns to headquarters, but to no avail. They were assured by OKW (Army supreme headquarters) and their own Army group commander, *Generalfeldmarschall* Busch, that they need not worry—the Army group would not be attacked, the Russian offensive would come out of Galicia in the south, and the Soviets were only waiting for their western allies to make their landing in France. Such proclamations did little to put the commanders at ease as they watched their overextended lines become thinner and thinner while more of their forces were diverted to the southwest to counter the expected Soviet offensive there or were used to combat the increasing partisan activity to their rear.

Concerned that they could never hold the front line in case of an attack, they requested that a second and even a third line of defense be constructed in the rear, which would give them prepared positions on which to fall back. Hitler denied the request. Instead, he ordered that the cities of Vitebsk, Slutsk, Mogilev, Orsha, Polots, and Babruysk be declared 'fortress cities' and held to the last man. This only served to further deplete the front lines as more divisions were withdrawn to garrison these 'fortresses'.

The field commanders of *Heeresgruppe Mitte* regarded their situation with ever-increasing apprehension; they were woefully short of men, artillery, anti-tank guns, and tanks. They were even short of ammunition for the men. If the Führer turned out to be wrong, they were doomed.

Their apprehension was well-founded. Confronting the 380,000 men of *Heeresgruppe Mitte* was a Soviet force of 2.2 million men, 31,000 pieces of artillery, 5,000 tanks, and self-propelled guns and 6,000 aircraft, which gave the Russians a superiority of six to one in men, twenty to one in tanks, twenty to one in artillery, and 100 to one in aircraft.[19]

The assurances issued by the Führer's headquarters had been correct in one respect—Stalin was waiting to see how the Anglo-American invasion of northern France progressed before he unleashed his avalanche of men and steel against *Heeresgruppe Mitte*.

On 6 June, the Western Allies successfully landed in Normandy. After a few weeks, Stalin was convinced that his allies had established a firm foothold and that the German forces there were fully committed, and he sent word that 'Operation Bagration', the annihilation of *Heeresgruppe Mitte*, was to commence on 22 June, the third anniversary of Germany's invasion of the Russian homeland.

The offensive would be directed at the eastern face of *Heeresgruppe Mitte*. To defend this 700-km front, the Germans had twenty-eight divisions, each of which had to cover an average of 25 km. When one considers that at this point in the war a German division possessed only six battalions of 300–400 men each, this works out to the absurd number of only about 100 men per kilometer of front. It was even more absurd for the artillery, with an average of only one gun per kilometer. As for armored units, there was but one for the entire front—the Hessian 20 Panzer division, with 100 Mark IV tanks. There were just forty aircraft.

Covering the northern flank was the 3rd Panzer Army (with no Panzer divisions) of *Generaloberst* Reinhardt. General von Tippelskirch's 4th Army was in the center. On the southern flank was General Jordan's 9th Army, in which Reiner's 6th Grenadiers were still deployed along the bend of the German line on either side of Zlobin. They had perhaps the longest stretch of front to cover—50 km!

As the Russian assault troops waited in their jump-off positions for the signal to attack, 240,000 partisans operating in the swamps and forests behind the German front line launched the first blow of Operation Bagration.[20] On the night of 19 June, there were 14,000 attacks of sabotage, of which 10,500 were successful. The primary targets were the bridges, railways, and telephone and telegraph lines. When the Soviet offensive began two days later, German transportation and communication within the battle zone had already been seriously compromised.

In order to make it more difficult for the Germans to ascertain the intent and scope of the offensive, the Russians planned a phased opening of the attack, beginning in the north and spreading across the entire front over a period of three days.

On 22 June, Operation Bagration was set in motion as the Soviet First Baltic Front and parts of the Third Belorussian Front launched their attacks in the northern sector against the 3rd Panzer Army on either side of the 'fortress city' of Vitebsk. Although the Russian tactics varied from place to place, generally the attacks along the front began with an hours-long preparatory artillery barrage of unprecedented fury, which would then be lifted to the rearward areas to neutralize the supporting German artillery. Meanwhile, masses of Russian tanks and infantry rolled over the few German soldiers that had survived the hurricane of fire. Incredibly enough, some Germans did survive and manage to hold off Russian assaults, but not for long. Within twenty-four hours, the front was smashed and the 'fortress' of Vitebsk surrounded and bypassed, with its three-division garrison trapped within. The Russians were in no hurry to take it; it would fall in good time. For the present, they were only concerned with rushing their armored columns to the west as quickly as possible.

The next day, 23 June, Phase Two of Operation Bagration began as the Soviet Second Belorussian Front assaulted the center of the German Front in the sector of the 4th Army between Orsha and Mogilev. The story was the same here as in the north. The Russians broke through the thin German line at numerous points. When the German West Prussian '*Feldherrnhalle*' Division—one of the few reserves available to the 4th Army—rushed forward to stop the hole in the front, its commander was asked by General Martinek of the XXXIX Corps, 'Precisely what hole are you supposed to stop? We've got nothing but holes here.'

Despite two days of heavy Russian assaults on the northern and central sectors, the Führer's headquarters maintained that these were diversionary attacks and that the main Soviet offensive would still come out of Galicia. Twenty-four hours later, reality exploded like a bomb at Hitler's headquarters when the third phase of the Russian offensive commenced on the southern sector of the German 9th Army (within a month, a bomb of another sort would explode in the Führer's headquarters).

On 24 June, Soviet Marshal Rokossovsky's First Belorussian Front launched a two-pronged attack against the 9th Army—one prong on the northern flank near Rogatschew, pushing due west to the city of Babruysk, and the other prong on the southern flank west of the Berezina, driving hard north to Babruysk. The city fell to the Russians on 29 June, and the bulk of the German 9th Army was trapped in a pocket between the Dnieper and the Berezina. In effect, the stage was now set for the complete destruction of *Heeresgruppe Mitte*. All that remained was for the tragedy to play itself out.

Within a week, the Russians had smashed the German Front to pieces and had pushed their armored and motorized forces to the west, leaving the German divisions trapped in pockets far behind with no other choice but to surrender or fight their way out. It was Blitzkrieg in the finest German (or rather now Russian) style, only that the Russians had replaced the German rapier with the Russian sledgehammer.

The tragedy played out in similar scenes throughout the entire sector of *Heeresgruppe Mitte*. Small groups of survivors from the original front line desperately tried to find their way back to their units. The trapped garrisons of the 'fortress cities' mounted desperate break-out attempts, most of them failing.

Pounded by ceaseless air attacks, remnants of divisions and columns of *ad hoc* formations of men from scattered units all struggled along the dusty roads, seeking to reach the new German front line that seemed to recede further and further toward the west.

When the Germans came against Russian-blocking positions, they raised a shout of '*Hurra!*' and stormed their way through only to find another Russian fortified line just ahead. Again and again, the exhausted troops shouted and fought their way through—until there was no one left to shout '*Hurra!*'

And what of the 6th Grenadier Division and Reiner's regiment, the 58th? Like the other divisions along the front, the 6th Grenadiers had also had misgivings concerning the Führer's headquarters' directive that *Heeresgruppe Mitte* would not be the target of the Soviet offensive. To them, there was definitely something in the air. Their patrols and their prisoners revealed that the Russian units to their immediate front were being replaced by second-rank troops. Long-experienced in Eastern Front warfare, the 6th Grenadiers understood this to mean that although they would not be the direct target of an attack, an attack was definitely coming. The locations were most probably to the north, near Rogatschew, in the sector of the 296th and 134th Infantry divisions, and in the south, near Mormal, where the 383rd *Volksgrenadier* and 45th Infantry divisions were deployed. If these Russian attacks were successful, the 6th Grenadiers would find themselves trapped. They could not have been more correct in their assessment.

When the rolling Soviet offensive reached the front of the 9th Army on 24 June, the initial attacks occurred where they had been expected: to the north and southwest of the 6th Grenadiers. On the evening of the 24th, Reiner's regiment, the 58th, and the divisional Fusilier Battalion were loaded onto trucks and rushed north to Rogatschew, where they were put at the disposal of the 296th division to help deal with the Russian breakthrough. When they arrived at the 296th headquarters early on the morning of the 25th, they found the divisional staff already destroying documents and preparing for a withdrawal.

The 58th was instructed to take up a position along the Dobriza River, some 5 km to the west, and to prepare to receive the retreating units of the 296th. However, when it reached the designated position, the 58th found that the Russians had arrived before them. The 58th promptly drove them out and established a defensive line but was unable to establish contact with the division on its left (northern) flank, the 134th Infantry. Soon, the 58th regiment soldiers came under heavy attacks by Russian infantry supported by tanks, especially on their exposed left flank. Employing the three *Sturmgeschütze*[21] detailed to them, they fought off these attacks. However, with an open left flank, they soon found themselves outflanked to the north, and at 11.00 p.m. they were ordered to withdraw another 10 km to the west and take up a new position along the Dobyssna near Parchimkowskaya. They reached their new position at daybreak on 26 June, but once again they were unable to link up with their northern neighbor (for good reason, as the right flank regiment of the 134th no longer existed). Throughout the course of the day, they held their line against numerous enemy attacks.

During the night of 25 June, as the 58th Regiment was moving to its new position on the Dobyssna, the rest of the 6th Grenadiers, fearing encirclement, began their westward withdrawal to the Dobyssna some 10 km south of the 58th. On the morning of the 26th, the 37th Regiment found itself involved in heavy combat. Its commander, *Oberst* Boye, was killed; his successor, Major von Ribbeck, fell the next day. The regiment suffered heavy casualties. The division continued its withdrawal in a northwestwardly direction along with the scattered remnants of the other divisions of the 9th Army, all trying to reach the 'fortress' of Babruysk on the Berezina before the enveloping jaws of the Russian offensive snapped shut. Pounded by constant air attacks, they fought their way through the Russian blocking forces—but it was all for nothing. Unknown to them at the time, the Russians had already taken Titowka, sitting astride the Rogatschew-Babruysk highway, and blocked their way to Babruysk. On the 27th, the 6th Grenadiers reached the Ola.

Meanwhile, 10 km to the north, the 58th Regiment on the Dobyssna found itself outflanked again to the north. On the night of the 26th, it was ordered to withdraw another 10 km west to the Ola River, which they reached on the morning of the 27th. Here, however, they were unable to dislodge the Russian forces already dug in there. At this time, the 58th Regiment was operating north of the Rogatschew-Babruysk highway while its sister regiments, the 18th and 37th, were south of the highway. At 3.00 p.m., the retreating German units were informed that the Russian pincers had closed to the west of Babruysk, on the far side of the Berezina, and they were instructed to attempt to break into the city, unite with the 20th Panzer division, and organize a further breakout to the west. Were that not possible, they were directed to break out northwest of the city. All heavy weapons and equipment were to be destroyed; the men would fight their way through armed only with their individual weapons. The time of the attack was 11 p.m.

With the Rogatschew-Babruysk Highway under constant heavy artillery fire, the 58th Regiment chose the route to the northwest. They swam across the stream at Leitischi, all the while suffering heavy losses from the flanking fire. At Dolgoroskoye, they assembled, took up defensive positions, and waited for the hour of attack. All around them was chaos—constant shellfire and air attacks, and scattered soldiers trying to find their units. Contact with the 134th Division and the XXXV Korps was lost, but at 11 p.m., the 58th Regiment advanced; it would be their *Todesritt*, their death ride.

They fought past Chimy, crossed the Mogilew-Babruysk highway near Welitschi, and waded through a broad swamp in the pitch dark. In the morning of the 28th, they overran the Russian positions along the edge of the forest south of Morchowitschi with the goal of reaching Bazewitschi, which was reportedly still in German hands (though the Russians were already there). West of Lyubenitschi,

The artist in his studio—Alf Niemann and his wife, Lotte, in Kassel, 1925. (*Andersson Archives*)

A childhood of happy memories. Kassel, May 1928. (*Andersson Archives*)

The Niemann apartment at Klettenberggürtel 15, Cologne. (*Andersson Archives*)

Reiner at age seventeen, 17 July 1939.
(*Andersson Archives*)

The last Niemann
Christmas together,
Cologne, 1940.
(*Andersson Archives*)

Father and son
surrounded by
books, 1940.
(*Andersson Archives*)

Operation
Barbarossa,
22 June to
December 1941.
(*Denis Havel*)

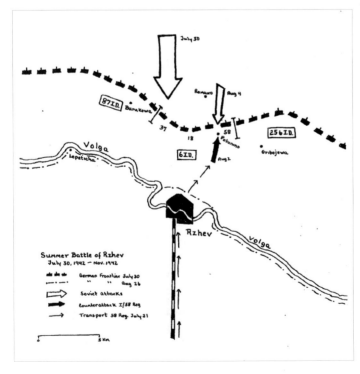

The summer
Battle of Rzhev,
August 1942.
(*Denis Havel*)

Officer candidate Reiner Niemann in snow. (*Andersson Archives*)

A new recruit at Osnabrück, November 1941. (*Andersson Archives*)

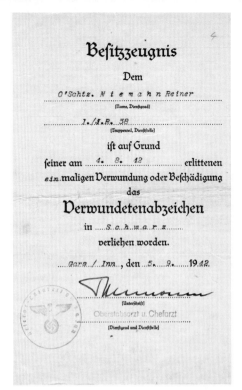

Above left: Reiner's wound certificate. (*Andersson Archives*)

Above right: Commander's directive. (*Andersson Archives*)

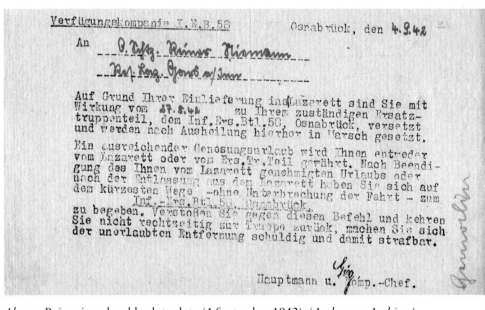

Above: Reiner is ordered back to duty (4 September 1942). (*Andersson Archives*)

Opposite: Oberschütze Reiner Niemann on his first visit back from the front, November 1942. (*Andersson Archives*)

Right: The soldier sons all at home—Alfons, Reiner, Wolfgang, and son-in-law Knud Andersson. (*Andersson Archives*)

Below: Family reunion, Pentecost 1943. (*Andersson Archives*)

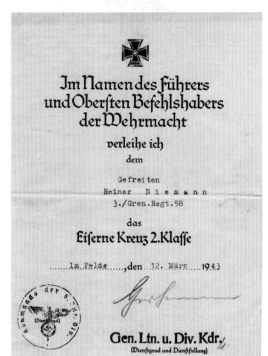

Left: Reiner's Iron Cross 2nd Class.
(*Andersson Archives*)

Below: Operation Büffel, March 1943.
(*Denis Havel*)

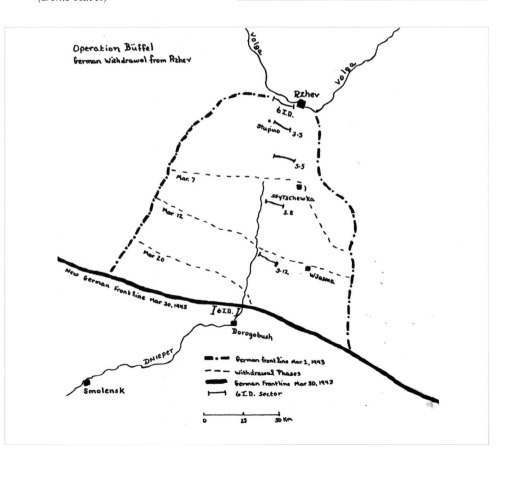

Devoted sisters Lütte and Heidi.
(*Andersson Archives*)

On leave, Breslau, March 1944.
(*Andersson Archives*)

Brothers in arms, Reiner and Wolfgang, Pentecost, June 1943. (*Andersson Archives*)

Last time together.
(*Andersson Archives*)

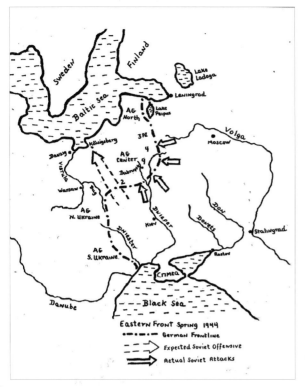

The Eastern Front, spring 1944.
(*Denis Havel*)

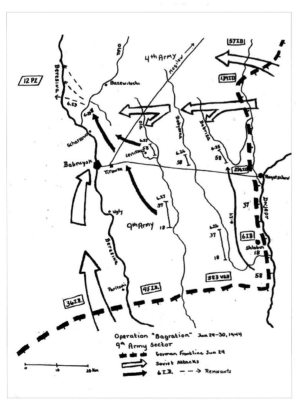

Operation Bagration, June 1944.
(*Denis Havel*)

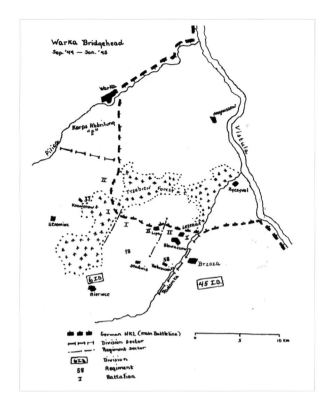

The Warka Bridgehead,
September 1944 to
January 1945.
(*Denis Havel*)

A *Propagandakompanie*
photograph of Reiner in the
Warka, November 1944.
(*Andersson Archives*)

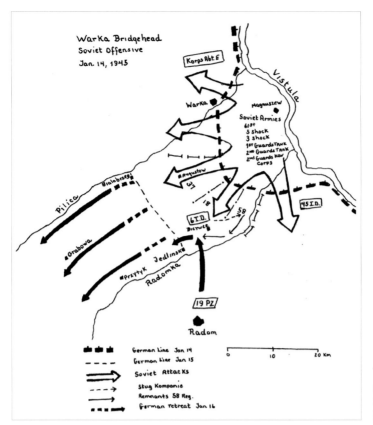

The Russian
offensive,
14 January 1945.
(*Denis Havel*)

Reiner's letter to Heidi, 12 January 1945. (*Andersson Archives*)

An excavated German bunker in the Warka, with Łukasz Gudkiewicz, battlefield detective.
(*Pawel Wyszomirski, photographer; Andersson Archives*)

Looking east, the cemetery at Lezenice and the fields beyond.
(*Pawel Wyszomirski, photographer; Andersson Archives*).

Reiner's source of water, the well at Lezenice.
(*Pawel Wyszomirski, photographer; Andersson Archives*)

Whitney Stewart, finding Reiner.
(*Pawel Wyszomirski, photographer; Andersson Archives*)

they ran into enemy positions, again along the edge of a forest. With a shout of '*Hurra!*', the Grenadiers attacked. Often in hand-to-hand combat, they smashed through one Russian position after another. However, 2 km south of Ssergejewitschi, the Russians had built up a blocking position that was simply too strong to break—but it no longer mattered. By that time, the 58th Regiment of Grenadiers had ceased to exist.

The remaining two regiments of the 6th Grenadiers had a similar 'death ride'. Having destroyed all their heavy equipment and burned important documents, they, like the 58th, chose to break out to the northwest and reach the Berezina at Bazewitschi. They crossed north over the Rogatschew-Babruysk highway and stormed forward, fighting their way through the Russian blocking positions and suffering heavy casualties from the constant artillery and machine-gun fire from the surrounding heights. Their ranks became thinner and thinner. *Oberst* Höke, commander of the 18th Regiment, was badly wounded and later killed when a shell struck the hut into which he had been dragged to safety. The wounded were loaded onto carts, but when they crossed the swamp, their carts sank and the wounded drowned. Division surgeon Dr Lorenz shot himself after being wounded in the jaw. Staff surgeon Dr Schulz did likewise after suffering a stomach wound.

On the evening of 28 June, as they approached Bazewitschi, *Generalleutnant* Heyne organized the remaining troops for a final breakout attempt. However, before the assault could even begin, they were suddenly hit with tank, artillery, and machine-gun fire from all directions. The desperate fighting continued throughout the night, but by dawn of 29 June, the 6th *Rheinisch-Westfällische Grenadier* Division was no more.

Many old, tradition-bearing German divisions met the same fate, collapsing under the relentless onslaught of the Soviet offensive. The commander of the Army Group, *Feldmarschall* Busch, was blamed for the disaster and unceremoniously dismissed. He was replaced by *Feldmarschall* Model, who in the past had so often been rushed in to save a desperate situation; this time, however, even 'the Führer's Fireman' could not avert the disaster that had overtaken the central front. Panzer divisions, which had been wrongly deployed for the expected offensive out of Galicia, were rushed north as *Feldmarschall* Model attempted to establish a new front line between the Dvina and Baranowitschi to halt the Soviet advance, but the tidal wave of men and tanks could not be stopped.

On 3 July, Minsk, the capital of Belorussia fell. Baranowitschi, the southern anchor of the new German line, was taken on 8 July. By 28 July, the Russian forces stood on the borders of the Reich in East Prussia and had reached the Vistula in Central Poland. The last German forces had been driven from Russian soil. In five weeks, the Russians had advanced 700 km and had destroyed an entire German Army Group. It was the worst disaster Germany had yet suffered in the war—far worse than Stalingrad. Stalingrad had cost the Germans but one army, and Germany had briefly recovered afterwards. There would be no such recovery from the destruction of *Heeresgruppe Mitte*. Three armies and twenty-eight of their thirty-eight divisions had been smashed. Of the forty-seven generals of corps and divisions, thirty-one were lost; ten were killed and twenty-one taken prisoner. Three hundred thousand German soldiers had been either killed, wounded, or taken prisoner—but not Reiner.

4, 5, or 6 July 1944

Dear Parents,

I hope this card makes it through since you probably haven't had any mail from me in a while. And you can well imagine why. I have gone through just about everything a person can go through, but I am unwounded and all is well. I'm just a bit starved. I've been out of the mess for several days, and I think I'm in Polish territory. I hope to write more later. I send greetings to all: Brother, sisters, relatives, and friends.

Your old Reiner

6 July 1944

Dear Parents,

Once again, I've managed to get away in one piece. I'm not wounded and I am not far to the rear in northern Poland. I've been lucky again! Since June 25th, I've been in combat. On the 27th, we were cut off, and we managed to get across the Berezina in small groups on the 29th, but then we found ourselves surrounded again. We wandered around for several days, heading to the rear, and on July 1st we made it to the German lines where we loaded onto trains. Nights we froze, days we baked, and we looted Russian villages because we had no food. Each day we covered about 50 km westwards. I'll write more later.

Greetings,
Your Reiner

8 July 1944

Dear Parents,

The storm has passed and now it is the time of the seven fat years. Since yesterday, I've been in a pretty Polish village with a German-like, not Russian, landscape. It's between ... and ... [undisclosed]. Here the division has reassembled, and there are only 120 men, of whom half had been on leave and had not been in the battle. There are no commands and no duties. Not that anyone would do anything. Eating and sleeping on straw is what fills our days, and I feel as if I'm getting my strength back, so I'll outline for you what happened to us.

It all started during the night of 23 June.[22] We were still in our old position.[23] Ivan began shelling the whole area behind us and continued the artillery attack throughout the day, but they didn't attack. The following night we were relieved and were transferred—first on foot and then in vehicles—to the rear area near Rogatschew.

On the way, we were issued two days of rations: chocolate, lemons, candy, cakes, zwieback, wine, rum, brandy, *Sekt*, and tobacco—more than we could pack or enjoy. Our morale was outstanding. I could write an entire letter about it. We all sensed that something big was going to happen. At midday [25 June], our company was deployed along a road. We went into a dug-out position[24] that didn't have a full field of fire and was partially dry, but both our flanks were exposed. In addition, the area was far too large for our small group of men to cover. All day long, we could see Ivan trickling into the area in front of us, but they were too far away for us to do anything to them. Once when they tried to move forward, we fired on them with machine guns and drove them back. They bravely attacked the road with tanks, but our anti-tank guns were outstanding and knocked out their tanks, one after the other. In all, ten tanks in two hours.

As it grew dark, Ivan slipped unnoticed around our open right flank and attacked in battalion strength. We had to get out of the trench and pull back. I was there with my former squad leader at the head of our two squads. (I have nothing good to write about him.) Not knowing that Ivan already occupied the road, we wanted to regroup there. Suddenly, they threw hand grenades at us, and we threw some back. At the end of this song, our sergeant took a direct hit with a hand grenade and was badly wounded; another guy was shot through the stomach, and a third guy was lightly wounded by a fragment to the leg. All the others disappeared into a cornfield, most never to be seen again. The guy who was shot in the stomach went with them. We could hear Ivan groaning, and they didn't come any closer. We gave the Sergeant something to drink and a cigar and dragged him into the cornfield where we had to leave him. We grabbed a machine gun that had been left behind and took off with it through the middle of the cornfield.

The Russians ran after us, so we ran as much as we could. It had rained, so the ground was muddy, and our equipment and clothing got soaked. Later we ran into a remnant of our company—about a third of it—so we kept moving with them through the whole night and the next morning [26 June]. In the afternoon, we rested in the second line of a new defensive position,[25] which Ivan was threatening to break through from the north. In the early morning [27 June], I went on my eighteenth patrol of this campaign. Later in the morning, we launched two long, drawn-out, exasperating, and unsuccessful attacks during which I learned to despise our company commander. Finally, we pulled back and restricted ourselves entirely to defense.

That evening Ivan almost broke into our left flank again, but they were thrown back. When we pulled out, Ivan advanced, so we had to go straight through a swamp and then swim across a river.[26] Non-swimmers, wounded, and the last 100–300 men remained behind in Ivan's hands. I was now the only one from our company, and I continued on. After about 8 km,[27] the column jammed up and that meant we were cut off, and so we were. On this moment alone, I could write an entire second letter, or even a book. Everyone assembled in a large forest clearing, and gradually it grew dark. The ammunition supplies were set alight and exploded like huge fireworks. We plundered all the vehicles, and everyone looked for dry clothing, provisions, etc. Instead of my wet tunic, I pulled on a smock and a padded winter jacket. I filled my canteen with schnapps, my pockets with ammunition, my bread bag with bread and a pound of margarine. In addition, I still had my 'Iron Rations' of zwieback. As it grew dark, the horses were shot and the regiment assembled to march across open country in order to find a way out.[28] I saw eight men from my company but later lost them again. The *Oberleutnant* was there, of course. We marched dull and silent toward the north. When it came to combat, we would all shout '*Hurra!*' so that no one would lose his way. So dull and mindless, we crossed a highway[29] crowded with men. They called to us, even reached out and touched us, but we paid no attention to them. No one dared to shoot at us because we were still 600-men strong.

Then [28 June], we went single file through a swampy forest with water a meter deep. But we lost contact with each other, so by morning there were only sixty of us with a lieutenant colonel whom nobody knew. During the day, we ran into other groups, often shooting at each other first. By noon we had some 200 men from all different units, and we were led northward by a major with red stripes to behind the Russian main line. Nobody knows where the Major went. Now and again, we were fired on from all directions, and then, with forty men, we finally went through the main battle line and waited for evening.

And that is the overall view. The details of what happened are the most important part, but there is too much and it is so indescribable to put down, at least in writing. Well, in any case, that night we attempted to cross the Berezina but had to give it up.[30] The next morning, that is the 29th, we could observe the garrison of Babruysk attacking northwards. That was our opportunity, and we risked it, trying to get across the Berezina in broad daylight. We got over the river unharmed, but we had simply jumped out of the frying pan and into the fire for we found ourselves in another surrounded pocket, which would be totally decimated. We were systematically destroyed during the course of the day as we pushed our way through the Russian forests, but by evening, we had found a way out and took with us several trucks and artillery pieces.

We continued on through the night, and in the morning [June 30] had to fight our way for several kilometers through the partisans in the woods.

Then came the hunger and the exhaustion to the extent that many men could go no further and stayed behind. We would never have gotten out if a German Panzer division[31] had not broken through and held open a ten-mile corridor. Finally, late in the evening on the 30th, we reached our own lines where we collapsed and slept until morning. Then we continued on, half on foot and half on the tanks and armored vehicles. After 25 km, we reached a river with a highway on the other side.[32] I was in the last truck and just after we crossed, the bridge was blown up. We drove another two hours and then were dumped off at the rail station at Rudensk. Then we went quickly through Minsk, which was already burning, Molodecno, Lida, Wolkowvsk, to the area around Byalistok. But even here, we were still not settled but continued in short intervals toward the west. Our rations on the train were as bad as they were on the march. We plundered Russian villages and hauled what we could from destroyed trains, houses, and supply depots onto the train, but it was a drop in the bucket for many of us. We lay closely packed in the rail cars that had no roofs. At night, we froze, and we baked during the day. For the most part, we only had wine to drink. Often I assuaged my tormenting hunger by whatever I could find in the fields. Even now, getting food is hit or miss. Sometimes we live well, but right now, I have diarrhea from eating raw eggs. I'm lucky that I didn't get anything from the swamp water, which was all we had to drink for days.

I must close now because 11 July is almost over and tomorrow we will be traveling back a little closer to you.

I send my greetings to you and to all those who have asked about me.

Your Reiner, who has only found one other member of his company. Once again, I've been lucky. Even the Commander was taken prisoner.[33]

Due to the overall chaos of the situation, and the fragmentary nature of the existing records, Reiner's escape route over the Berezina cannot be determined with certainty. After the dissolution of the 58th Regiment on 28 June, Reiner was most likely with *Kampfgruppe Ohms* and an *ad hoc* formation made up of the remnants of Reiner's own 3rd Battalion and men from various units all led by Reiner's battalion commander, *Hauptmann* Kurt Ohms. As *Kampfgruppe Ohms* approached the Berezina, it split up into several groups, each seeking to make its own way over the river north of Sswisslotsch. *Hauptmann* Ohms did not have Reiner's luck; he was killed on 3 July.

Warsaw
18 July 1944

Dear Parents,

Do you know where I am now? In Warsaw, and in a few days, I will be in Germany, and without even being wounded. So don't worry. I hope to get a leave before we are shipped back to the front, who knows where? While waiting here at the train station to be transported to our quarters, I've had time to read a decent work by W. Raabe, *Wunnigel*, to which I am most receptive after this period of pure, harsh, remorseless reality, which I can say without adornment or embellishment. Also, I've had time for reverie and memories. I am doing all right physically now. Have you received at least one of my letters that I wrote after the battle?

I send my greetings,

Your Reiner

Resurrection

The old 6th *Rheinisch-Westfällische Grenadier* Division, with its three tradition-bearing regiments, had been buried at Babruysk along with many other famous divisions. Over 90 percent of its officers and men were either dead or missing. However, the idea of eliminating such an old division from the Wehrmacht's Order of Battle was unthinkable to the military aristocrats. It would simply have to be resurrected from its grave.

At the beginning of July, the Wehrmacht had finished the initial training of the 29th wave of recruits, out of which it planned to create fifteen to twenty new divisions and eight to ten Panzer brigades. One of these new divisions, the 552nd, was slated to begin its divisional training at Sennelager, near Paderborn, when it was decided to incorporate the 1,100 members of the 6th Grenadiers still on hand into it, thus forming the core of the resurrected 6th Grenadier Division.[34] Its new commander would be the experienced and competent *Generalmajor* Brücker. He would command the 6th Grenadiers to the last day of the war.

The new division was fortunate in that a former commander of its 58th Regiment, *Oberst* von Issendorf, was in charge of the personnel department of the VI AK at the time. He saw to it that they received—as *Generalmajor* Brücker put it—'the best human materiel available at the time'.[35]

With Germany's war crisis mounting on both fronts, *Generalmajor* Brücker realized that he might have only a short time to train his new division before it was thrown into the fighting. Consequently, he drew up a streamlined, no-frills training program. There would be no spit-and-polish parade-ground drilling, marching in step, saluting, or any other such nonsense, only what the men would need to survive and carry out their mission—combat tactics and weapons training.

Perhaps due to his having been a survivor of Babruysk, Reiner was one of the fortunate few to receive a home leave before returning to the front. He spent it with his parents, at his aunts' home in Bad Flinsberg, where he went hiking with his father in the neighboring Isar mountains.

The following May, the 6th Grenadiers would fight their last battle a scant 12 km from the aunts' home.

2 August 1944

Dear Father and Aunts,

I arrived in Paderborn last night at 11.50 p.m. but then had to walk the 8 km to Senne. It was a beautiful night, so it wasn't a march but rather a pleasant stroll through the misty landscape here. And now twenty-four hours later, I've already been assigned to the newly formed division, which had trouble finding room for us. It must certainly be a wild collection of men, mostly older soldiers from all different units. At the moment, the company is out on night maneuvers. Everything is beginning again. I figure we will be marching off again at the end of August.

Greetings,
Reiner

4 August 1944

Dear Parents,

Two years ago I was wounded for the first time but felt secure and sure of the future. But what all I have seen and experienced in the meantime! Now in Germany, you're not safe anymore. A month ago, I just came out of that mess. And now in a month, I'll definitely be back in it. At the end of the month, we are supposed to go to the east—you don't say Russia any more—and that just makes it worse. It's noon now. This morning, starting at 6 a.m., we had target practice, and since I had the best score, I was allowed to leave early, before everyone else, and go back 7 km to the base. Naturally, I caught a car and saved a lot of time. The evening before last, I was assigned to the 1st Company of the newly formed 58th Regiment. The new men (552 Division) have nothing to do with the old 6th Division. Its honor and reputation will have to be preserved by the 300–400 survivors and a similar number of men returning from leave who had originally belonged to it. They had difficulty finding places for us because the division had already been brought up to full strength. In order not to lose any of us 'Tradition Bearers', any new man who could be considered 'conditionally fit for duty' was shoved off into the replacement company to make room for us. Had they not been so intent on this, then I, with my classification as 'conditionally fit for duty' [*KV-Bedingt*], might have been put somewhere else.

The training here seems unsympathetic and strange, especially to those who have just returned from the front. The usual abuse of the recruits is limited, but I think I'll try to get away from here. Our commander is a young *Leutnant* who has the Iron Cross 1st Class and an Assault Badge, which he no doubt earned when he was an enlisted man. He's a decent fellow and conscientious and is good to me and to all the rest. We can also be content with the *Spiess* [Company Sergeant Major]. The company morale is good, despite all the old soldiers and half-cripples in it. One bad part is that we have to travel one and a half to two and a half hours by streetcar or train from our wooden barracks to Paderborn and then still have another 4–7 km to go on foot. And the same when we return. Another bad part is that we have no clothing depot or tailor to make repairs. Consequently, I am running around as ragged as I was when I showed up on leave. The food here is not as good as we were used to at the front, but I'll get by. In addition to the six cigarettes we are issued, every ten days we get a coupon for another thirty cigarettes. That's a lot more than I can smoke. Our duty lasts until 6 p.m., with a three-hour break at midday (which is plenty). After duty we can go to a movie at the camp or have a sauna in the steam room. The movies have certainly been chosen for the soldiers. In the various canteens, you can drink beer that has also been selected for the hard throats of soldiers. I picked up a cheap razor, so you don't have to send me one. We even have an outdoor swimming pool here at camp, but unfortunately, I haven't been able to use it yet.

6 August 1944

What a disappointment. Ever since Himmler[36] became head of the Reserve Army and decided to root out the damn rear-area mentality, we are forbidden from going out on Saturday afternoons and Sundays. According to his wishes, duty will be extended to 6.30 p.m., including Saturdays and Sundays. This will improve the morale of the soldier and make the certain Final Victory [sarcasm] even more certain. Sports, art, education, etc. will all have to give way to the more important necessities of war. I doubt if Father will be teaching school much longer. Perhaps he can do some kind of clerical work in an office—but he's not really a typist!—not to mention his handwriting. Well, that's something the authorities will have to figure out, hopefully to Father's advantage.

7 August 1944

I've been to Paderborn once and it was a let-down in every way. Perhaps I'll write more about it in my next letter, so that I can get this mailed. I send you my greetings, and my greetings to Aunt Annemie and her daughters and their followers.

Your Reiner

8 August 1944

Dear Father,

Just a short letter to let you know what things I still need. I already have a razor, but I need the following: three razor blades, my Iron Cross 2nd Class medal and ribbon, my wound badge with the certificate, toothbrush but no toothpaste, a padlock, my field cap that I left with you, my pipe and tobacco (preferably fine cut), a couple of envelopes (we can buy paper here), something to read (if you have something), a shaving brush, and a small bar of shaving soap. From this list, you can see that all I get here is food and practically nothing else. My equipment has not been replaced, and my clothing hasn't been repaired. I haven't been able to get shaving soap or a shirt. All I've gotten is my back pay—about 150 *Reichsmark*—and finally a new *Soldbuch*.

Wednesday 9 August 1944

Time passes and another day has gone again. Yesterday as I began this letter, I was in Paderborn at the Soldiers' Home having some Army soup after having seen the film *Die Zaubergeige*, indescribably horrible. Earlier in the day, we fired three shots over the grave of a comrade who was killed in an accident and then were given three hours off. Then we were suddenly told we had duty until 6 p.m. I wanted to go to Paderborn and couldn't get the idea out of my head, so after 6 p.m. I went storming toward Paderborn. That was on Saturday. I missed the train by five minutes. Still intent on going, I walked for an hour and a half to catch the streetcar, and I was 200 meters away when it left. So, I waited half an hour for the next one and made it to the city by 8.30 p.m. But I was so tired and out of sorts that even the façade of the old cathedral couldn't raise my spirits. I sat in an unpleasant tavern and read a newspaper. Then later I rode back on a packed streetcar and walked the 6 km back to camp. I was so tired and worn out by the time I got back that I doubt I'll do that again any time soon. Instead, I'll go to the movies here and use the sauna. I'm almost too tired to write.

In closing, I'll expand my wish list. A pocket mirror, but not glass, and a belt or suspenders (long) would be appreciated.

For now, I send my greetings,
Your son Reiner

11 August 1944

Dear Parents,

For the first time in three days, I was finally able to do morning duty. Three days ago, I was forced to go to the doctor to be x-rayed again. I had to report sick for three days to get it done. On the second day, I went to the hospital in Paderborn to be x-rayed and they found another shell fragment, which they wanted to take out. But I had them leave it alone. I'll include the medical report with this letter. Put it with my papers. That's where the other medical report is, I think.

13 August 1944

Today was Sunday. We didn't have any real duties today but we were still not free until 4 p.m. Then I played some *Skat* [German card game] and went to the camp's movie theater. It was a film worth seeing—one hundred and fifty percent! *Herr Sanders lebt gefährlich*. I wish Father could have been there. The ideas and themes in the film impressed me.

On another topic, it seems as if our departure time is not far off. We already have a *Feldpostnummer* and are beginning to cook company meals in the mobile field kitchen. Some men have received short leaves to put matters in order. Yesterday we members of the old 6th division were allowed to buy things from the commissary, so now I have everything I wanted you to send, which is probably already on its way: pipe, soap, mirror, shaving brush, razor blades, a lighter, new eating utensils, pocket knife, deck of cards, shoe polish, toothbrush, toothpicks, shaving cream, notebook, a roll of film 6 × 9, etc. But I still haven't been able to get a shirt or other clothes. You'd be stunned to see how dirty and sweat-stained this civilian shirt is. Sleep is lousy here because every two to three days we have night maneuvers. My digestion still isn't right. Well, I can't go to the front with diarrhea—that would turn everything upside down. Soon I will let you know what else is going on, when I have some peace and quiet to write.

Goodbye for today and greetings,
Your Reiner

19 August 1944

Dear Parents,

You must forgive me for not writing during the week. On writing day—that is Thursday—everything got busy. Since then, we have relentless combat training and target practice during the day. Then after cleaning our weapons, we have a lot of work packing and loading new equipment. This morning we have to pack our gear, but I'm writing this letter in the meantime. First, I must thank Mother for the informative letter that arrived at the same time as Father's on the 15th. I thank you deeply for that and for the package. It went through fast and arrived here on the 17th. Unfortunately, I was able to get many of the contents, so I will be sending them back to you. My wish-list arrived late because I held off sending it while I waited each day to see if those items would show up in the canteen, so Father would not have to send so much. I wanted to send Mother a special letter, but one would need peace and quiet to write such a letter. I still owe her some leave time for she hasn't seen much of me, which as a mother, I'm certain she does not like, and she hasn't been able to look after me as she always has. But then, I'm not like I was before. I've noticed the change but could do no different. It's because so many conflicting impressions and thoughts have been going through my mind—and still are. But enough of this theme. There is no peace and quiet during departure.

Well, my equipment is packed, and our train is supposed to leave early tomorrow morning. To where, nobody knows. We might even be going to the west. We aren't allowed to take more than ten *Reichmark* with us, so I think it might be to the west instead of the opposite. In any case, I sent you 120 *Reichmark* on 10 August, and today I am sending you a package. Only two non-coms and five men have appeared from my old company. One escaped, like me, and one was still in the hospital. Three of them had been transferred back early and so were only in contact with the enemy that first afternoon.

Now I send my greetings. The package is on its way.
Reiner

Sennelager
19 August 1944

Dear Parents,

Now it's time. I have one hour and will see if I can answer both your long letters in peace and quiet. Right now, I'm in the mood to write. I've eaten well, shaved terribly, and am spiritually excited about the imminent changes. True, I don't have a cigar, which I usually have to write a letter comfortably. A cigarette will have to do because cigars are too difficult to pack away for the trip. Therefore, I sent ten of the best cigars I could find in your package. They are for Father. Mother, I'm afraid, is short-changed. Seems she still has trouble with her children. You can send the film roll to Lütte for a late birthday present. The rest goes into the treasury of hard-to-find items for anyone who needs them.

Assembly was just called. The next letter I write will be from Litzmannstadt—East [Lodz, Poland].

21 August 1944

Dear Parents,

Four years ago today was a Tuesday, and I'd just finished my labor service and returned from France for your silver anniversary. And now I've been underway for two days and am going back to the east for a fourth time. This time it seems a trifling matter. One gets so used to it and confident that nothing more can happen to him. Only in the worst case would the train stop suddenly, dump us out without supplies, transportation, or any other support and have us fight our way back to Germany. Must close. We're ready to move again—after a third mishap has interrupted our journey.

Be well and I send my greetings,
Your Reiner

Fourth Time Out:
Letters from the Warka

The German Military Situation, Autumn 1944

The summer of 1944 had been an unmitigated disaster for the Wehrmacht. In June, the Anglo-American invasion force had successfully landed in Normandy and established a secure beachhead. Although the German forces there had maintained a stubborn defense, making the Allies pay heavily for any ground gained, by the middle of July, the German forces in Normandy had been attritted to a level at which a complete collapse of the front was only a matter of time.

That time came in late July and early August, when first the Americans and then the British broke through the German lines on their respective fronts. A German counter-attack, with what remained of their armored forces, failed, and the entire German Front in Normandy came apart. Then began a great *sauve-qui-peut* flight for the Germans across northern France as scattered German groups and individuals, constantly hounded by thousands of Allied fighter bombers, sought to escape the rapidly advancing Allied forces and reach the safety of the Reich. Paris was liberated on 25 August, Brussels on 3 September, and by mid-September the advancing Allied forces had reached the borders of the Reich itself.

Not only had the Germans lost France and Belgium, they also suffered heavy losses in men and materiel—perhaps as many as 300,000 killed, wounded, and missing. After five years of war, these were losses Germany could not afford.

With the enemy troops now on Germany's border, the Nazi propaganda machine could no longer hide the truth of the military situation from the German population. The rumbling of heavy artillery fire was clearly audible to the civilians in the Rhineland. The sudden and unexpected (to the civilian population) collapse of the front in the west created a panic both among the civilians and the political leaders. There was talk of evacuating cities in the Rhineland. The *Volkssturm* (People's Militia) was created on 25 September, with all men (and boys) between the ages of sixteen and sixty not already in the armed forces being required to register for duty. Reiner's father was taken from his teaching duties and sent, along with old men and boys, to dig trenches for the defense of Cologne. Propaganda Minister Joseph Goebbels once again called on the German people to wage 'Total War'. One could certainly forgive the average German civilian a moment of perplexed head-scratching at Minister Goebbels's rants. With many of their cities in smoldering ruins and 2 million of their sons already dead, they wondered just what kind of war Mr Goebbels thought they had been fighting the past five years.

The Allies, however, were now having problems of their own. The rapid advance from Normandy to the German border had seriously over-extended their lines of supply. Shortages of fuel and materiel slowed the Allied advance, and the German Army, again displaying its remarkable ability to recover from disaster, was able to stabilize the front. The immediate crisis had passed, and for now, in the west, the Germans could breathe a sigh of relief.

In the east, the summer of 1944 had been an even greater catastrophe for the Wehrmacht. As previously described, the entire central front had collapsed. *Heeresgruppe Mitte* had been annihilated, twenty-eight divisions had been smashed, and some 300,000 men had been removed from the German Order of Battle—and this had only been the opening act of the Soviet summer offensive.

Having amassed and obtained the resources to maintain an army of over 6 million men, 90,000 guns, 14,000 tanks, and 14,000[1] aircraft, and with the war industry fully mobilized, the Russians owned the Eastern Front at this stage of the war. Since the abortive German offensive at Kursk the previous summer, the initiative had passed completely to the Russians. They no longer needed to fear a serious German offensive anywhere along the front. They could choose the sector of the front they wished to destroy, amass an overwhelming force of men, tanks, guns, and aircraft, and crush the German forces whenever they wanted. They could then pursue their gains as far as possible, halt and amass another overwhelming force on another part of the front, and smash through a sector weakened after the Germans withdrew to defend the first sector. The Russians were confident the Germans could not protect all of the sectors at once.

By employing these alternating attacks, the Russians drove the last German troops from Russian soil during the summer of 1944. On the central front, the Russians reached Minsk, the capital of Belorussia, on 3 July, and the Polish border on 18 July. On 25 July, they reached the Vistula River and stood at the doorstep of Warsaw. There they halted; not so much because of German blocking forces that had been rushed there to stop the Soviet advance, but because they had shifted the impetus of their offensive to the Baltic states in the north and to the Balkans in the south. Though estimates of the German losses vary, in addition to the 300,000 lost in the collapse of *Heeresgruppe Mitte*, they could well have lost another 300,000–400,000 men during this phase of the war in the east.

Not only had Germany lost field armies and hundreds of thousands of irreplaceable soldiers, it had lost allies as well. Italy had abandoned Germany the year before, and with German prospects quickly fading, other allies were desperately seeking a way out of the war. In late August and early September, as the Soviet armies approached their borders, Romania and Bulgaria arranged an armistice with Russia and promptly switched sides. On 19 September, Finland was forced to sign an armistice with the Soviet Union and dropped out of the war.[2] Even Hungary engaged in negotiations with the Soviets, but the country was pressured by Germany to remain in the war.

Even with the relative stabilization of both fronts, the immediate threat that Germany would be overrun from both east and west had lessened. Still, the German situation in the autumn of 1944 was one of desperation. Stalin, Churchill, and Roosevelt had made it abundantly clear from the outset that there would be no negotiated war settlement; the war would end with unconditional surrender. Germany would be destroyed as a nation state, and as for the German people—*Vae victis*.

In the fall of 1944, Germany entered the sixth year of the war. The Nazi leaders were aware of what their personal fate would likely be in defeat, and they could only cling to their self-fabricated illusion that somehow there would occur a break between the western powers and their Soviet ally that could be exploited to save their necks (literally). The German generals, knowing the war was militarily lost, put on the blinders of their professionalism and lost themselves in the daily tasks of their particular sector of the front. The German civilian just waited for the horror to end, and the German soldier soldiered on; he went where he was sent, and he did what he was told. Some of the men still believed in the Führer, that he might yet have a last trick up his sleeve that would pull it all out in the end—perhaps another wonder weapon of such unimaginable force that it would sweep Germany's enemies from the field. Others knew that Germany would lose the war, and that tens of thousands would have to die. They could only do their duty and trust their soldier luck that it would be others—not them—who died.

The Warka Bridgehead

Not only had the Russians reached the Vistula River with their summer offensive on the central front, but they had also established three bridgeheads on its western bank. The southernmost was the Baranow (150 km south of Warsaw). Next was the bridgehead at Pulawy (110 km south of Warsaw), and the northernmost was at Magneuszczew (40 km south of Warsaw), which the Germans called the *Warka Brückenkopf*. These three bridgeheads would serve as the crucial jumping-off points for the forthcoming Soviet winter offensive.

Although the Russian advance had halted at the Vistula as their efforts were being shifted to the Baltic and the Balkans, the front was not quiet. German and

Russian units clashed in bitter struggles as each sought to gain a local advantage. Warsaw erupted in revolt. In the meantime, the Soviets sought to expand the bridgeheads. Early in August, the Russian forces in the Warka emerged from the forest of Trzebien, pushed beyond the Glowaczow-Warka road, and even took the town of Glowaczow itself. In bitter combat, the newly arrived 'Hermann Goering' Panzer division brought the Russian advance to a halt, retook Glowaczow, and threw the Russians back across the road, establishing a line that would become the German HKL (*Hauptkampflinie*, main battle line) and remain so with a few alterations until the Soviet winter offensive.

In mid-August, the 6th Grenadier Division, rebuilt but not re-equipped, loaded onto trains at its training base at Sennelager and returned once more to the front—less than two months after its destruction at Babruysk. The front was no longer in Russia; it was in Central Poland.

Generalmajor Brücker describes the return of the 6th Grenadier Division to the front:

> The transport of our division from Sennelager took place during the period of 15–20 August. The Ia of the division Major J. G. Heitzmann with some of the divisional staff was sent on ahead as VP [advance team]. The first regiment to depart was I.R.37[3] with II/AR6 and it was followed in accordance to capacity of the train stations at Paderborn and Paderborn-Neuhaus in intervals of one to one-and-a-half days by I.R.18 with I/AR6 and I.R.58 with III/AR6 and the remaining units of the division.
>
> The transport proceeded rather quickly by rail via Berlin-Frankfurt an der Oder-Litzmannstadt to Radom where it turned north to the unloading station at Bierwce, which had been the depot of a former German training base. The available ramps there enabled a quick de-training. In this unloading area there was considerable activity by Russian fighters and we suffered our first losses from bombing and strafing attacks.[4]

Reiner described his experience of the new front in a letter to his parents:

22 August 1944

Dear Parents,

Today at noon, the train dropped us off within hearing distance of the front. Now we are lying scattered about on the ground in the shade of the fruit trees and have some time for ourselves. Now you hardly need two days to get to the front whereas before it took at least ten to fourteen days. On the trip here we had three unplanned stops. The first one was when an ammunition car began burning for some unknown reason. It and the cars before and after it had to be unhitched from the train. After that, one of the axels on our car overheated and broke and then another. I can't say why. Aside from these mishaps, the trip went smoothly. Those were the only long stops except to switch locomotives a couple of times and to take on water. So, in three days, that is, exactly two months since the beginning of that previous mess, we are back in position at the front. From what I can hear from the front lines, it seems that things have come to a standstill, but our being here until winter is highly unlikely. Anyway, if we should have to make an orderly withdrawal from here, at least we will have something to eat. Potatoes, cabbage, and all kinds of garden vegetables and fruit are abundant. Even the meat ration is not that bad. We do have blackberries, but they are no more abundant than in Flinsberg. I'll close for now and send you my greetings.

Your Reiner
(*Punktiert*: east of Radom)

Deployment in the Warka

The three threatening Soviet bridgeheads on the west bank of the Vistula lay along the front of *Generaloberst* Josef Harpe's *Heeresgruppe A*, whereas that of the Warka was in the sector of *General der Panzertruppe* von Lüttwitz's 9th Army. Assigned to its defense were the three infantry divisions (the 6th, 45th, and *Korpsabteilung* E[5]) of the VIII *Armee Korps* and the two Panzer divisions (the 19th and 25th) of the XXXX *Panzer Korps*. The bridgehead formed a westward-projecting bulge 40 km south of Warsaw and 25 km northeast of Radom. Its base ran some 25 km along the Vistula and was 20 km at its deepest. The VIII *Korps* deployed its three infantry divisions in the HKL (*Hauptkampflinie*—main battle line) along the perimeter of the bulge, with *Korpsabteilung* E in the north, Reiner's 6th Division in the center, and the 45th Division in the south. Here, they relieved the Hermann Goering Panzer Division and took over its positions. The 6th *Infanterie* Division sector of the front was essentially that part of the HKL between the two tributaries of the Vistula—the Pilica in the north and the Radomka in the south, which flow almost parallel to one another in a northeasterly direction.

Generalmajor Brücker deployed his division with the 37th Regiment on the left flank, the 18th Regiment in the center, and Reiner's 58th Regiment on the right flank adjoining the neighboring 45th *Infanterie* Division. The commander of the 58th Regiment, *Oberstleutnant* Müller, arranged his two battalions on their 6-km front with Reiner's battalion, the 1st, on the right between the Radomka and the village of Lezenice, and the 2nd *Bataillon* between Lezenice and the village of Lipa. To support the three infantry divisions in the HKL, the XXXX *Panzer*

Korps placed the 19th Panzer division just northeast of Radom and the 25th Panzer division further north at Bialobrzegi.

The terrain between the Pilica and the Radomka is essentially flat, or gently rolling without any commanding heights. Its main feature is the Trzebien forest. Consisting mostly of conifers, it stretched before the German HKL and made the observation of Russian troop movements difficult in the rearward areas of the bridgehead—even in winter.

When Reiner was deployed on the front line, he was part of 1/I/58 (1st *Kompanie*/I *Bataillon*/58th Regiment). Here, he and his comrades found only the hastily dug defenses of the Hermann Goering Panzer Division, little more than shallow trenches and individual holes. It took months of hard work to build a viable defense system, and during this time, Reiner was rotated back and forth from the front line to the rear areas for 'rest' and building defenses.

Unfortunately, no existing maps or documents describe the deployment of the individual companies (1–4) of the *I* Battalion, but in all his letters Reiner never once mentions a stream or a river, so it can reasonably be assumed that his company (1st) was not on the extreme right of the battalion, near the Radomka, but rather more to the left, near the villages of Lezenice and Glowaczow.

Generalmajor Brücker wrote:

In the first days after relieving the *Hermann Goering* Division there was lively combat, especially in the area of Glowaczow-Lipa. Numerous attacks mounted by the Russians were beaten back with heavy loss to them. Likewise, the Russian attacks on the left flank of the 37th Regiment where our Fusilier Battalion was also deployed. However, from the beginning of September, the fighting eased along the entire front and there ensued a period of relative quiet that one could only describe as the calm before the storm—that was our sense of it.

Reiner's letters continue:

23 August 1944

Dear Parents,

I am writing to you from our front-line position. Exactly four months ago, I had just come back to the front... '*DONNERLITTCHEN*!' A heavy artillery shell just hit 300 meters away and sent the breadcrumbs flying. The Sergeant here with me is still sleeping, but it was noticeable. It sounds worse than it is because usually here at the front line we infantry don't have to worry too much about heavy artillery. For us it's merely a show that helps the time pass faster when we're on duty. I can't complain: you get what you pay for. But if you stick your nose out too far, you'll certainly hear a few rifle rounds go whistling by. But they're fired from way off, and you can easily avoid them, unless they're fired directly at you.

So, when we took up positions here this evening, we did so with the utmost precautions according to a plan someone had thought up. The front was not expected to be here long, so we have to put up with poorly constructed positions that run for about 100 meters in front of a sparse forest. It's not possible to leave them during the day. Eating, washing, etc.—all have to be done at night.

Today got off to a good start. We were completely covered with dust from all the sandy roads and paths, and we wished for something to drink, but we were out. I have little more than what I was able to bring out of Russia, at least as far as clothing and equipment are concerned: my old tunic, my half-dead boots, my very ragged socks, no gasmask (which is actually a plus), and an Italian shirt. And, I still need to get myself a new field cap. My belt is too large, my suspenders too worn out. They would constantly be hanging around my knees if I didn't use every trick I know to keep them in place.

Despite everything, things can only get better. We certainly don't want to lose spirit just before a 'speedy victory' [sarcasm]. You see I am in a good mood. Whether it is simply gallows humor or the joy from the greater freedom one has at the front over that at the barracks. In any case, I trust my luck and don't think we'll be here long. I need to close now for St Peter has finally shown us thirsty souls some mercy, and after long negotiations with the sun, has sent us some rain. Hopefully not too much, though, because I don't have a shelter-half either. A hole in the ground like this doesn't have a roof like a bunker does.

I send you my greetings. Yesterday I sent you a letter with a ration coupon for white bread. It was the first one we had received since our departure, and it was stamped #2.

27 August 1944

Dear Parents,

For five days, we've been here in the front-line position and have gradually learned what to expect here. I am just back from a bombed out farmstead, and from its large garden I brought back tomatoes, cucumbers, carrots, and onions. There are plenty of these to be had in the fields here. You don't have to look for long before you have filled your containers, but you have to be careful when you go looking because both sides have brought in more heavy artillery. When they start pounding, the skies turn dark and the sun disappears behind clouds of smoke. We of the infantry aren't all that obvious. We just lie here in our primitive holes, fortified with straw, and accompanied by other tenants, mostly frogs. They are a pretty, grass-green color but with a loud, deep croak so you have to toss them out of your hole if you want to get any sleep in the morning.

Worse is that during the day we have no water for washing and you can't leave your position. I have managed to shave but not to wash up. So here we are, sweaty and filthy like pigs. We do eat but have so little to drink, except at night. Our only warm meal is two or three sandwiches a day. At least these are thick ones. As for fruit, there is none. There are so many flies and gnats that it's almost impossible to sleep during the day.

That is how we live—sometimes good, sometimes bad—and we always watch out for when the artillery lets loose. That's when you don't want to stick your nose up too high. Originally, they had me as number two machine gunner[6], but soon enough they advanced me to platoon-runner.[7] It's a rather more eventful job and you don't have to do much digging or stand watch as often when something is happening, which are two things that determine how much sleep a person can get.

The day before yesterday when I received your package of sweets, for which I thank you deeply, a heavy barrage had just started. And it did me good to be reminded of home. Thinking of home, I find it best to imagine what you are all doing at that moment. Are you sitting in a streetcar or standing in line at one of the shops, or are you at a concert listening to beautiful music, though there probably isn't much of that anymore? Anyway, I have to take a message off. Be good and I send you my warm greetings from your Reiner.

The last day of the fifth year of war

Dear Parents,

On the evening of the 27th, I sent off my third letter to you and the following night I received Father's second letter, a letter from Mother with the field cap and one from Lütte with the series of nice pictures, and I thank you all for them. I had to laugh when I held the field cap in my hand because I was wondering if Mother's cake also found its way in there. Not that I am in any great need of it for we are all well fed for now. We have so much meat that I forgo the bread and just eat cheese and sausage with tomatoes, so that it won't spoil and Ivan won't get it. But we don't have cake here. If we did, we'd be fully satisfied. However, it is almost a crime to receive calories from those who hardly have enough of their own. It's a double crime considering this is almost the sixth year of the war. And it's a triple crime that in order to make room for something from home, you either let some of the food here spoil or stretch your stomach.

Anyway, I'm already having my old stomach trouble, which can only be cured by fasting or not drinking. As you can see, I've reverted to my old front-line principles. I've been in the east too long. The scant eight weeks I was away provided no sharp separation, no neutral period as did the time between my entering the hospital and my leaving the barracks and the home-front army, completely fed up. In the eight weeks that I was away from the front, I have not changed or grown accustomed to the comforts of home any more than if I had spent two days in the rear area with the supply train. I have had little trouble adapting to conditions here and accepting our life in the open without the shelter of bunkers. Some of the men have put wooden boards over the top of their foxholes to provide themselves some shelter. The day before yesterday, as it started to rain, I merely covered my hole with a thatch of straw that will be fine as long as it doesn't rain too much more. But when the sun comes out, the flies do too and become a burden when I try to write. Actually, my solution for shelter is simpler and more practical for I can sit up in my hole. Our holes are rather shallow because you hit ground water around eighty centimeters deep. The trenches are also shallow and because of that, our company commander was hit three times by a burst of machine-gun fire. The wounds were not that serious, but he will be leaving us. He reminded me a great deal of Wolfgang, who, I imagine, as an officer is open, honorable, direct, and somewhat indifferent to formalities. Our commander, with his calmness, his presence of mind, his single-mindedness when necessary—not rigid like his superiors—had impressed us all. He was a good man and not a traditional officer type in his demeanor. He didn't demand respect; it was freely given by the decent men here with whom there was mutual trust and respect. I would have liked to have known him better, as a person if not as a friend. But that's not possible between officer and men. That is one of the reasons why I didn't apply to be a squad leader. I didn't want to have any official dealings with an officer I didn't know that well. But that isn't the main reason. My view is that since I have managed to survive three years of war as a common soldier, ambition could hardly serve any purpose now that the war only has a few months to go, unless it concerns staying alive. But I see things darkly, for even after the war, ambition will be of little use, even a hindrance.

Anyway, what I would like to know is what happened to my Iron Cross ribbon and Wound Badge along with the certificate that I wanted sent to me? I hope the package Father sent hasn't been lost, or if you haven't sent it yet, please do, but not the certificate for there is no copy of it. Maybe it will get here before the front moves again. I thank you for the post and send you my heartfelt greetings.

Your Reiner

2 September 1944

Dear Lütte,

I've just finished gathering tomatoes from a large field. We roughly estimated the yield to be from 100–200 tons. The field lies behind our front and belongs to a nicely situated and charmingly landscaped, almost castle-like property. It's a pity to see it now. Every time I pick a couple of helmets full of tomatoes from the surplus—unharvested because of the artillery fire—I go into the manor house, which sadly is now fully destroyed. I've tried to draw it from memory and although I can still see it in my mind, I just can't do it. It is similar to Eichenberg [an estate near Kassel of family friends] in its overall arrangement. There are round rose beds with individual tree and flower gardens. The manor house is long, one storied with a flat roof. The entryway has a few steps and slender columns. The work yard with sheds and tractors is some distance off, so that the noise and traffic would not disturb the life of the owner of the manor house as it sits, surrounded by the well-tended grounds and gardens.

But now I have to break off and eat the chicken that I have been holding in my left hand as I was writing....

[Later] The chicken also came from the manor. It fell into my hands one night when I was there looking around for some timber for our shelter. I only had to lift it off its roost as it slept. I left the plucking and cooking to others in our bunker.

And now I want to thank you for your letter with the outstanding pictures. I greatly enjoyed looking at them and will continue to enjoy them in the future. Again, I thank you. I am doing better here than you probably think and will be fine as long as the good weather holds, but it's been threatening to change for a while now. I hope I've protected myself adequately by putting a light thatch roof over my foxhole. If only the ground water doesn't rise. For now, it's low tide.

I am closing now and wishing that your good fortune continues through the remaining course of the war as it did during the last attack on Trier [which Lütte survived]. I send you my greetings and wish you the best.

Your brother Reiner
Give my best to Knud who must be waiting for things to break loose down there.[8]

5 September 1944

Dear Parents,

Actually, I am writing this letter two days late, but then here not everything goes according to plan. Things have become quiet even though at first it did not look like we could hold out here for three days. Except for occasional artillery attacks or a few mortar rounds, we don't have to put up with much, not even anti-tank guns.[9] The nights are usually moonlit, and Ivan is more scared than we are. The reason I've had to re-write my letter was that the rain brought me to the realization that my hole is not quite rainproof. Consequently, I was stuck in my hole wet and shivering. The next day was spent bailing out my hole. Now though, the sun is shining and I hope the next rain does not interfere with my writing.

In the meantime, I received all that you sent for which I thank you. Last night the package with the cake arrived and this morning I ate it with my spoon, and it was delicious. It was proof that despite the war shortages and wartime ingredients, Mother's skill is still at the same high level of baking. The aunts sent me a newspaper article about Sibelius, which I must study sometime when I have some peace. Also, your package arrived with the Italian cigars and many of the things I needed when I was in Senne, and with an alteration of its contents will soon be on its way back to you. The cigars and the fantasy of sitting in a *Ratskeller* in Bremen will help sustain me here in my foxhole on rainy days. They bring up memories and thoughts on days when it's raining outside, and also inside me. I have to make sure they don't get wet. They, like the cake, are a reminder that only their production has suffered from the war, but not the masterly skill that creates them and that we are defending something that is worth the sacrifice, if you think of them symbolically. Yes, the good cigar, and the outstanding cake.

Anyway, I am extremely thankful for them and the reading material. For me the most interesting thing about Wilhelm Schäfer and Kleist is their style and composition, and I always enjoy reading Hermann Hesse even though I have read him countless times. Today I received from Heidi some magazines from Munich and a nice notebook, which I am reluctant to use here for I have a far less nice one that I can ruin. I thank you for the letter with the returned letters from Russia in it. It looks like Father had the house cleaned at the right time. Everything must have been covered with plaster dust. And you will probably be hearing the Western Front rolling toward you soon. Looks as if Lütte is next in line.[10] Everyone here is thinking about these sudden war developments. Nothing but special bulletins and constant attacks. Seems I am on the most stable sector of the front. But that can always change. I hope I don't have to spend the winter here. In my estimation, something has to happen here by 1 November. And then where will my family all meet up again? The best thing might be to just get a caravan wagon with two horses, a radio, and a gypsy fortune teller who can direct us to the safest spot in Europe. That would be something. I will see if I can bring the necessary equipment from here for such an odd vehicle.

Enough for now. I send my greetings to you and your interesting guests.

Your Reiner

7 September 1944

Dear Father,

Today is not a warm sunny day, as most of them have been, where one could almost believe that time was standing still. Instead, an autumn wind has kicked up and blows through the trees and whirls about, picking up sounds here and taking them with it. It seemingly speeds up the time; that is, the present, and like the sounds, also takes it far away. It creates a mood where one finds himself thinking about earlier times. In the present war situation, a similar wind has risen. We have fallen from the pinnacle on which we have stood for so long and now the long expected tipping of the scales has come and we will come crashing down. The war cannot last much longer.

A year ago, I wished you on your birthday that your next birthday would be celebrated during peacetime. I no longer need to wish you that. I only wish now that in the coming year you will be spared too much sorrow and that the family will once more be together. We can help each other, take one another by the arm, and steer each other safe and sound into a more normal life. I find it sad that the parent of four children must spend his birthday alone, marked only by a few letters arriving from all different places, one today, one tomorrow, and so on. I would be happy if I could arrange a short leave so I could be home for Mother's birthday this year. Can you understand how worried the common soldier is about his home and family and how homesick he is after all the recent frightening events? I feel the same as the others. I'm just not as frightened. I just wish we were all together again—it doesn't matter where. Then we could find our way again. We would be complete. We could be a country in and of itself. But now, I have to go and clean some weapons. I hope I am in a birthday greeting mood when I finish!

The weapons cleaning was followed by the sun coming out again, which is hardly an exciting event that would lend itself to any interesting letter writing. But despite that, I did light up a cigar and will now continue with my scribbling. Lately I haven't experienced anything noteworthy. One day is rather much like the next. Now that the sun is no longer bearing down on us so hotly, our appetites have returned and mealtime is the high point of the day, although suddenly it seems somewhat more meager than before. But it only seems that way for the food has remained good and because of casualties, there is actually more. As before, there is plenty of meat and as a welcome addition there are as many tomatoes and cucumbers as we can get from a field not more than 1 km from our positions. As for drinking, my stomach can't handle it; what they have to drink around here is not tolerable. There is coffee, but not much water for washing, shaving, or rinsing our mess kits. The only water we have is when the rain trickles through the covers we've put over our foxholes. Our only other sources of water, the pond and the well in the village[11], are within the view of the enemy and are too often brought under fire. I only get there once a week at the most to wash off some of the dust and sand.

Well, it's getting dark now in my hole. It seems the wind is bringing in a storm. I need to close now so that I can send this letter back with the rations carriers. Dear Father, once again I send you my heartfelt congratulations and best wishes on your birthday. I hope that your life will be much easier after the war. Have Mother bake you a cake, one as good as the one she sent me. To say '*Guten Appetit*' is superfluous.

Take care and give Mother my warm greetings and special greetings to you from your Reiner son.

p.s. Do you still remember when we used to 'climb the mountain' up to your studio where you would try to teach me and usually had to answer your own questions because little Reiner couldn't? And do you remember when I turned six and you couldn't believe it and asked me, 'Are you really that old?' And I was so proud that I could keep up with you when we walked. In any case, a month and a half ago, when we hiked together in the mountains, I was just as proud, but more so of you than of me. Take care and we will be together soon.

10 September 1944

Dear Parents,

We had a heavy rain here but the 'roof' of my fox-hole kept the rain out so that when I awakened in the morning, shivering under my waterlogged roof, I was able to go back to sleep. However, when I woke up at noon, I was lying in a couple inches of water. That's how much the ground water had risen. Thank God, the sun is shining again so that I can dry out. The nights here are gradually turning colder so that it is difficult to stay warm surrounded by the damp, cold walls of my hole. It's a good thing that the aerial observers are pulling out of their bunker so that we can move in. They are so low though that one can only sit, but at least they are warm and dry and provided with bunks to lie on. You can't really stretch out, but there is enough room for three men. This we can deal with, especially when it gets colder.

The package with the things I was sending back from Sennelager was returned to me because it was too heavy, so I had to put them into two packages. One, I sent off two days ago and I'm sending off the other one today. The two certificates are in it [Iron Cross 2nd Class and Wound Badge certificates] for they have already been entered into my *Soldbuch*.

There isn't much new to report from here except that I have been promoted to *Obergefreiter* [Corporal] effective 1 September 1944. The pay is the same except that I will receive seventy-five *Reichsmark* per month for front-line duty instead of sixty-two for homeland duty. It will probably be a while before that goes into effect, and if the war ends before that, I can always collect my back pay.

I see here now another *Gefreiter* [private] who has also been promoted to *Obergefreiter* and who now seems to have dedicated himself to taking part in every undertaking as though he feels he has to earn his stripes. Perhaps what has already happened to me will happen to him: that is, when the decisive moment comes, those for whom you have stood up and supported are nowhere to be found. That's not a nice thing to say, nor should it be a basic life view for me. As for now, I am satisfied to know that I have been able to do things that I wasn't necessarily endowed by nature to do; things which I had no great ambition to achieve. Today I feel as though I am capable of a great many things. I feel I would even have the self-assurance to lead a platoon or even a company. I sought to acquire the character necessary to hold a position more than I sought the position itself. When things occurred to impede my progress, I would say to myself that too many young officers have too quickly achieved their position and have been given tasks they cannot perform. I feel that I have the self-confidence that such would not happen to me. Anything good takes time. That is certainly a maxim of the middle-class, which should not be used to excuse laziness or indifference. However, in my case it is definitely applicable. I see that clearly, particularly now in these times. To survive as a common soldier for six months and then suddenly at five minutes before midnight, strive with all your might to achieve something—that has no point. And no, these are not the words of the fox when he saw the grapes were too high to reach. For me it is best to accept the present situation, a life for now with no greater responsibilities. If my withdrawal from an officer candidacy seems to have been too hasty, it does not seem so now. My promotion to *Obergefreiter* was a result of it. I would have been an *Obergefreiter* long ago if I had not been an officer candidate. I think this a correct justification of my decision, particularly with respect to my brother who did manage to succeed. I don't want to claim that it was any easier in his branch of service, but that branch was more suitable to those of a particular background and technical education. But when one has been in the infantry for three years and has been constantly pulled away from his background and education, and has had his abilities diminished, then my actions were no mistake.

Your second letter that you sent me in Russia has arrived with your letter #5, and I thank you for them. In the letter sent to me in Russia was the information I needed for my last leave. Had I had it, I would not have ended up in Cologne, standing in front of a locked door. In order to avoid that in the future—that is, after the war—we will need a well-thought-out plan because our family is now so widely scattered. Perhaps some central location that would have all the addresses of the family members or changes of addresses, as well as where one will be able to find a place to stay or get help. In the coming confusion, who knows where everyone will end up? Many things have to be thought out and prepared—like finances and everyday needs. But there is still some time for this.

With that, I will close.

My most heartfelt greetings, from your Reiner.

14 September 1944

Dear Parents,

Things are quiet here for now, and we have dug ourselves new positions. We've provided our holes with new roofs, and so far, the ground water hasn't seeped in. We should be dry for a while.

Yesterday your letter #5 of 1 September arrived. It seems it took some time to get here. I am glad to hear that the package I sent by way of Sennelager arrived. I don't know if I packed it as well as Heidi does. I had opened and closed the package a half dozen times because I kept finding something else to send or something new showed up at the commissary that I thought you needed. Finally though, I wrapped it up and mailed it off even though I missed a company instruction course to do so. Anyway, it all worked out.

In the meantime, many here are worried about their families. Lütte and you are not far from the advancing allies, but I trust Father's prudence and Lütte's efficiency. True, you can't save everything, not by a long shot. I hope the war will not be pushed deeper into our country, but if the front does not stabilize or if there isn't an armistice in two weeks, it certainly will be. And where will you go if it does? You must send me your plans soon so that our connections will not be broken off. Now the sun, which was a red glow among the pines and the white birch trees, has gone down and the first stars are coming out. Now one can go to sleep without much worry. We won't have to do any more work here and we have almost a normal life. We don't have to be on edge all the time or duck every time a shell comes whistling over. If you can all remain in an upbeat mood, as I am, I will be happy.

Be well and I send you all my warm greetings from your Reiner son.

16 September 1944

Dear Father,

It is a sunny but windy autumn day; the wind rushes through the pines here and brings with it the smell of smoke and cooking. For two days, we've been living a wonderful soldier's life. One could almost say it's like an excursion without the war. I'm sitting on the steps into my hole and letting the sun shine down on my back. I have been reading newspapers that the aunts sent, and I want to thank them. It occurred to me as I was writing that today is Father's birthday. Are you busy packing today, as I am sure you have been for the past several days? Today we had a couple of hours of informal instruction and this afternoon it was announced that there would be a lecture by an officer from the National Socialist Relief Agency.[12] We're excited about it as if it were a championship-boxing match.

He doesn't dare take questions or he will get an earful because the soldiers no longer hold their tongues. Many think it impossible to carry on the war within Germany, and if there is any truth to the rumors of the new weapons, and these weapons are not used to defend the borders of Germany, the rumors are nothing more than bluff, which many already think our entire military strategy is.

Where will you go if Cologne is evacuated? If I lose touch with you, I will send my letters to the aunts.

I will be thinking of you again tonight, Father, at your coffee time in the evening. I hope that Lütte is already with you and that perhaps she will remain with you in the coming days. There is a great deal of talk around here about the evacuation of Trier. I wonder if Heidi is there, helping you celebrate your birthday. And are you having perhaps a plum cake? It could be. But then again, you might be standing in line at some shop or already preparing to leave Cologne. It almost seems childish that I worry about this and maybe in the beginning you will feel childish as you prepare to leave, as childish as your sons were when they first went into action. But we Niemanns always remain cool, thoughtful, and practical. I am completely calm in the knowledge that you, Father, will always know what to do next.

I must close now. This evening I'm making potato pancakes if there is enough butter. Yesterday I made roast potatoes with meat, nicely browned and delicious the way Heidi makes it. I send you my warm greetings, and to you especially from your Reiner.

20 September 1944

Dear Parents,

This will be the last letter I send to Cologne. I assume that Cologne will be evacuated and you will be somewhere else. Until I hear where you are, I will send my letters to Flinsberg, and I hope the aunts will know where to forward them to you. I hope this is an unnecessary precaution, which will prove to be superfluous. Above all, I hope whatever you have to do that everything goes well with you as things have with me so far. Then nothing else matters, not that wreck of an apartment or the large or little things that you couldn't take with you. Things are pretty much the same. We are still living a life of luxury. Often we cook better food here than the field kitchens. I've been doing a great deal of baking and feel I'm completely capable of cooking anything here. I hope things are going as well with you.

Warm greetings from your Reiner

Reiner's family wrote to him often during his fourth Russian Front assignment. Their letters reveal the challenges they faced and the plans they made:

10 September 1944

My dear Reiner,

This Sunday the local 'High Command' decided that for a slight change the day would be work free. I wanted to slip off to Cologne and so yesterday I stood for two and a half hours in the evening in the train station of this little Lower Rhine village and since the train hadn't yet arrived and that there was little chance of catching the last connection in Düren, I gave up the idea and left the other men to their fate. They were fortunate though and somehow made it to Cologne.

There are about 130 men here digging a tank trap in which all the British tanks will get stuck. This is the first step towards victory. That's what you need to be doing in the east! [Sarcasm]

In any case, other measures are being taken. Today the Russians are leaving town and heading east just like the Poles had done a few days ago. Leaving on wagons piled with refugee goods. There is no small number of them—just as the military traffic eastwards is greater than that going west. Lotte and I were packing up ourselves, and now Lotte has to finish it all alone. And that is a great deal for only one head and two hands that also have to maintain the household and finances. I believe I have already written it, but I will repeat it again: in case things unravel here in Cologne, Paul Elmering, Aken an der Elbe, Elbstraße 5b will be the meeting place and communication center for the family. But until further notice, continue writing to the Cologne address.

We work from seven to noon and two to seven. Not everyone has been provided with shovels and so there are many breaks. Most of us are of the older age group,[13] but there are a number of the younger age group and even kids. All professions are represented. An artist and I are living in the neighborhood. We are building human relations here. The food is good, the mood uniform, which even the arrival of ten SA men didn't change. They came out of Saxony and weren't too happy. The air-raid alarms cause us to have many breaks. Yesterday, an attack with hundreds of planes flew over us. Today in the gray morning came a second, followed by strafing attacks by individual aircraft on the rail station where two lines intersect.

The work is to be for about three weeks. After that, it's not clear—like with all the rest. In three weeks! What all can happen in that time!

I'm enclosing four photos so that you will have several with you. I found them while we were clearing out the apartment and brought them with me for you. Goodbye for now. I'm sitting here on the edge of my bed because there is no table in the room. Heartfelt greetings, dear Reiner; be well.

Sincerely,
Your father Alf

Reiner responded a few days later:

20 September 1944

Dear Parents,

I had just sent you a letter this afternoon, telling you that from now on I would address my letters to Flinsberg because you would probably be evacuating Cologne. Then the ration carrier came with the mail. In addition to a letter from Heidi mailed from Aken, and one from the aunts, I also got one from you saying that if you left Cologne, I should write to Aken. This then is the first letter I will send to Aken and should you still be in Cologne, then Heidi can forward it to you. The last letter I sent to Cologne was the letter of 16 September and this morning's letter. For Father's letter from Baal, I thank you, and also for the four pictures, which besides showing the entire family, also showed the apartment in a more peace-time condition. I don't think you will be able to move much more out of the apartment, but it is good that you have been able to get the important things out. What will happen to all those who are digging entrenchments around the city if Cologne is evacuated? Will they be let go or will the core of our family, that is, the parents, be separated? I live in a much clearer and thereby a better situation than you. It is still quiet here. We only change positions and build new bunkers. The weather hasn't changed, and it would be enjoyable if I didn't have to constantly think of you. How is Lütte? I've noticed the mail is running much slower now. Each letter is no longer relevant and it is difficult to get caught up on events. I need to close now. The sun is going down and I am going to cook a hearty bean soup and use the meat I saved over noon to flavor it. Maybe I'll write more tomorrow. For today, I send warm greetings from your Reiner son.

The soup was great but I wouldn't compare it to Mother's vegetable soup.

Bye. R.

Building Defenses

Because the Russians had shifted the emphasis of their attacks to the Baltic, the Carpathians, and the Balkans, and a relative calm had descended on the central Polish Front, the German commanders there realized they had time to build a defensive system. Just how much time, they did not know, so they wasted none.

First, the hastily constructed positions left by the Hermann Goering Panzer division would have to be improved. The shallow trenches and individual holes would have to become a genuine *Hauptkampflinie* with bunkers and deeper, reinforced, connecting trenches. The troops needed livable conditions for the approaching winter. In addition to the HKL, a 'defense in depth' would have to be constructed extending all the way back to the supporting artillery positions (6 km), which would consist of strong points with flanking machine-gun posts. Further to the rear, more bunkers and accommodations for the troops would be constructed, including a theater for the men. What this meant for Reiner and his comrades was much work and little rest.

Although *Generalmajor* Brücker had remarked that a relative quiet had descended along the front, it was the peculiar 'quiet' of the Western Front of the First World War. The routine daily death, or 'wastage', would continue to be dealt out by the young men on both sides of the line through a sudden burst of machine-gun fire, the sniper's bullet, a mortar round dropping out of a clear blue sky, patrols colliding in the night, and, of course, the murderous trench raids.

23 September 1944

Dear Mother,

Yesterday evening as I returned from work I found your nice long letter and one from Lütte with two enlarged photos from Wolfgang's leave showing you with a smile on your face and your large summer hat in your hand. When I had finished reading your letter, it was already dark. Maybe tomorrow I'll be able to answer your letter.

For the past couple of days, I've been going to the village and helping there to convert a barn, the best we can, into a cinema and theater. We get up at 6.30 in the morning, and one hour later, we march off and then come back at 6 p.m., tired, worn-out, but in good spirits because we are really building something. But now, you will be reading the cloddish pages that I'm able to write while I'm at work.

25 September 1944

I still remember that while in the RAD [Labor Service], I had to write on paper like this. That was back when I lost one of your letters and then found it by chance stuck to the bottom of a cow's muddy hoof. Then, we were hauling old material out of a French factory and had no time to write except for what little time we could steal from work. Here, for the moment, it's rather like that, since we're gone the entire day trying to get the theater built.

The situation here hasn't changed, still quiet. We haven't been sent back to the front-line positions, so we can continue our regimented lives here in the rear area. It is so regimented that those who aren't working are constantly training like they would back home. I like what I'm doing much better. Every day a certain officer comes from the regiment, benevolently watches the progress of our work, and brings us schnapps and cigarettes. He was here an hour ago and now the whole work party, enlivened by schnapps, is discussing the bullshit about medals and honors, about V-1 through V-67,[14] about what will happen to their savings accounts after the war. I just sit around and use the time to write, but it's not that peaceful. Things can get pretty loud when soldiers argue. Now they're talking about who's been through the most air raids and I now realize that I'm dealing with a bunch of 'Home-Fronters' rather than 'Eastern-Fronters'. Other than that, the desire for importance and recognition goes on unchanged. People are such caricatures!

The drawn-out discussion ends with each complaining about the bad luck he had at the masked ball at Carnival, how they danced with their masked partners so enthusiastically, and how disappointed they were when the masks were removed. You need to be around when soldiers really get talking. I enjoy listening to them. Some of my finest hours in the Army have been spent listening to soldiers talk.

For now I need to close, and I send you both warm greetings and hope that from tomorrow you are together again and can sleep through these times.

Reiner
Punktiert: 30 km northeast of Radom

28 September 1944

Wolf is constantly moving, one change of position after another, but always backwards. In his last letter from 17 September, he writes that he is living in a covered foxhole where a mouse is constantly digging and kicking dirt out onto his head and he hasn't lived like this in a long time.

Your Mother

27 September 1944

Dear Parents,

I have now been here in position at the front for five weeks and I had always thought that in four weeks we would be withdrawing back to Germany. For four days now it has been quiet. It is a beautiful, if somewhat cool autumn evening. We've just finished our cooking, having been busy at it all day because today with our rations we receive two loins of veal and for the first time here our weekly ration of sugar. I don't know what we will make with it. Mostly we roast here and fix potato pancakes and fried eggs. Imagine what we could make if we still had flour, but there is a limit to everything. There's the problem with people—the more you have, the more you want. If people would admit that, we wouldn't have wars. But you have to learn that yourself from experience, and then you are seventy years old and no longer have the strength to make mistakes.

14 September 1944

My dear Reiner,

The pen is empty so now I have to write with this miserable pencil, which makes it even worse for the reader. Right now, there is an alarm again. From here, we can hear the sirens from four different villages and since they don't go off at the same time, we often don't know what is meant. Also, the mooing cows in the distance make a similar sound!

The front seems to have stabilized here somewhat, at least as far as I can observe. The traffic from the west has thinned a bit. Yesterday a fellow returning from Cologne saw a poster in Jülich, which basically said, 'Soldiers, you are entering a region hardened by the constant bombing. Your loose talk won't diminish the courage of the inhabitants.' The misery of the refugees is bad enough. Old women sitting on the caissons of the retreating artillery, men and women, often on crutches walking alongside, their possessions piled on a cart being towed by a military vehicle. They can take very little with them. At the drug store in Türnich where we buy razor blades a young girl said: 'We have to win!' And when we said that that would be great with us but that we were doubtful, she repeated, 'but we must win!' A passing soldier with a retreating artillery column called over to us with a broad grin: 'Hey! The Rhine's still open.' Yesterday, the entire village passed by our window loudly repeating the Lord's Prayer and '*Gegrüßet seist du, Maria*' as they went to bury a young boy from the village who was killed along with several others by a strafing attack while they were digging. Our trench is proceeding slowly. We've started a second section and are digging machine-gun positions behind it. The rainy weather makes the soil difficult to dig out and shortens our shifts—and we would all rather get back to Cologne as soon as possible. Bread is in short supply and that dampens our mood, and butter is often replaced by margarine. But despite that, one must praise the food supply.

Gradually we get to know one another. Some stand out because of their intelligence and behavior—and this impression never deceives—but the circumstances prevent anything more than a fleeting acquaintance. Some have been sent home. Lotte keeps her head up and manages her daily work, but certainly, she feels herself to be deserted and alone. A whole batch of packages has been sent off to Aken, Hartenstein, and Dresden—hopefully the boxes will still be able to be shipped—they are only partly packed. There should be only a few of them. Naturally, this is difficult for Lotte to do alone. I live here completely without newspapers—I never even hear the Army bulletins—and so

I hardly know what is going on in the world. I hope things are going relatively well with you. The most important thing you need is the shelter-half. It doesn't seem that you are very far away from Ivan. Be well dear boy! With many thoughts and even more wishes,

Your father Alf

28 September 1944

Dear Parents,

We are in reserve now behind the front. The movie house here is finished, and today I saw my second film. For duty, we had weapons and field training. We spent the morning gathering surplus beans, berries, and other fruits. There are plenty of pears here but mostly wild and sour, and cooking doesn't seem to help them much. Rye, millet, and potatoes lie un-harvested in the fields. Occasionally we harvest a single louse from our own bodies and a not-so-singular flea. But they are not so bad because they don't multiply like lice.

Today Father's letter of 14 September arrived, and I thank you for it. I'm getting more letters from you now probably because you think I have less time to write than you. I hope Father was able to return home from his duty today, as expected. We were also busy today digging trenches, and when I thought of Father doing the same, some of the ridiculous slogans one sees today came to mind such as: 'The German People Dig at Home!' or 'You have Two Duties: Family and Country', and other such nonsense. I also think of them in relation to the present tragic situation. I know Father will make the best of it, if not in the length of it, then certainly in the width and depth of it. Please keep me informed, and I send you my warm greetings.

Your Reiner

7 October 1944

Dear Parents,

After several days of rain, we are having another beautiful day. There is hardly any wind and in the bright sunlight, I can see glittering threads drifting about in the air. I once read in a nature book that these are the webs of a certain type of spider that spins out a long thread—as much as 200 meters—over its area and then climbs to the top of bushes or blades of grass. In the morning when the warming rays of sun cause thermal winds to rise from the ground, the spider leaps from the bush or blade of grass and allows itself to be carried along by the drifting web. It's a trip into the wild blue, and this way the spider travels across continents and oceans. I wrote this only as an introduction. The aunts regularly send me articles from magazines about important people and times and events as well as poetry and critiques of performances. There are often scientific articles as well.

Rurich[15]
16 September 1944

My dear Reiner,

There you sit in your shallow, water-filled hole and wave towards the west and I take my shovel into the tank ditch and salute towards the east. And far on our horizons, our images appear and it is as if we have taken one another's hand. You are the last one to receive greetings on my birthday. Perhaps Lütte is drinking a birthday coffee with Lotte and afterwards will follow her belongings and go south. Whether all will work out is still unclear at the moment, because everything now has become so uncertain. Here we now have Georgian[16] and Walloon soldiers[17] digging next to us. They came up over the past two days. After a couple days of good progress, our trench has slowed down. Tommy will probably pinpoint us before we finish it. Lucky that we have good weather. Thinking of you without a shelter-half makes my teeth clatter. Not having one in the summer is not good; but how will you get on without one now? Lotte writes that your digestion is not good—take care that nothing serious happens to you! A shame you lost your nice *Leutnant*. Take care old boy, stay healthy and safe. My thoughts are with you.

Your father Alf

Cologne
26 September 1944

Dear Reiner boy,

Today your card arrived which should be the last one to Cologne, and I thank you for it. Today I am writing to all our dear ones because yesterday there was another heavy attack. Klettenberg was spared. We only lack gas, and water we must fetch from the cellar. I can cook well enough though at other people's apartments. The alarm came suddenly at 10.30 a.m. and the bombs began falling immediately so that many people were still in the streets. Carpet [bombing] over Lindenthal, Sülz, Hohenstaufenring, Neumarkt, Heumarkt, Richl, Mülheim. All the streetcar lines are kaput.

Now it's 10.30 p.m., and I want to go to sleep, but like letter-writing, that takes place in the kitchen. I always remain dressed and lie on the chaise, and only get up in the morning to wash. It calms me down when I have finished. The evenings when Father was gone were mostly quiet—that is, no alarms. I have only had to go to the cellar once or twice. But when transports constantly fly over Cologne or when the wind is right and one can hear the cannon fire from the front, I get disturbed. Every morning shortly before seven, I am standing at the post office with one to two packages. One time, Schnuk, last year's stoker, brought three crates to the *Eifeltor* [train station] for me, and then I had thirteen boxes for the express freight. Since early yesterday, there has been snow—even at the *Westwall*. How glad I am that so many of the heavy things have already been sent off!

But goodbye for now, my dear boy. May God protect you as well as he does me! I'm usually in good spirits when I work, but I feel it necessary that your father return.

I truly hope that Father returns this week for the trenches must be finished. Up until now, the schools were still in session but the way is too far and dangerous because strafing attacks by fast fighters occur so often and so quickly that one doesn't know if they should continue their journey.

When will we ever meet again? Now Heidi is the ground floor for the family. For today, goodbye. I've given you all my news and now it's evening. Greetings my dear boy and God protect you!

Your Mother

[Undated]

My dear Reiner boy,

You write me so often and I get so much mail from you children and of course from Father that I hardly notice my loneliness. I notice it mostly when I am packing and have a question that I wish I could ask Father; or when there is shooting[18] or when I listen to the fearful talk of the neighbors, which raises my fear a bit of what is to come. Mostly though I live here with you children and feel myself surrounded by your love and concern such that I feel happy and thankful to you all. Today your letter of 16 September arrived (it had no number) and the package with the two certificates. What strong bands you wrapped it with, you could have used them for suspenders. Yesterday your letter #7 of 14 September arrived; #6 from 10 September with the 'report' from the *Obergefreiter*[19] and the birthday letter to Father of 7 September haven't yet been acknowledged or thanked for. I just can't keep up with the writing. I hope that Father returns this week. Tomorrow, his three weeks are up and the trench they were to dig should be finished in the next few days. Admittedly, it's uncertain if he'll return to his regular schedule of writing. Perhaps we will never return to our usual every day.

Sudden attacks happen more often now. They shoot up the railroads and all the people have to throw themselves on the grass or in the bushes. It took Lütte sixteen hours to reach Trier, but there were no attacks. I learned this over the phone from *Frau* Andersson.

Lütte has sent several boxes of things to her friend Gertrud Hildebrand in Biberach. The safety there has recently become questionable. Her new sleeping room is in the cellar and she can sleep there even when they are shooting. She wants to remain in Trier as long as it is feasible in order to save her things. The Borscheids are always there if she needs anything. They aren't leaving either. Trier isn't occupied yet. When Lütte was here, we got a friendly greeting from Wolf—that is, a man from his battery, who had a special leave because his wife was dangerously ill, visited us. They are still retreating. The battery is now on the Adriatic but still has the Po plain between them and the Alps. The seventeen bridges over the Po River have been destroyed by fighter-bombers. Now a pontoon bridge is put up every evening and taken down every morning. The salvage work proceeds very slowly. Wolf hopes for spring and the new weapons. Two letters came from him today, dated 10 and 17 September. In the latter, he writes for the first time of a covered foxhole in which a mouse is annoying him.

I take joy in your military advancement if it is the peak, and I am content if that means the war won't last long enough for any further advancement, I believe you think the same way.

Your Mother

8 October 1944

Dear Parents,

Today Father's letter #11 and Mother's of 28 September arrived, and I thank you for both of them. We, too, are digging trenches night after night. Each trench is ten meters long and one and a half meters deep, one hundred centimeters wide at the top and sixty centimeters wide at the bottom. The digging is causing the shell fragments still inside me to act up. I've been to the doctor twice for nothing. All he did was to give me the same pills he gave me for bronchitis. Around nine in the evening, we go out to dig and come back between one and four in the morning. Then we sleep until 11.00 a.m. From 2.30 p.m. until 5.00 p.m. we have duty in the form of peeling and preparing potatoes.

As for my digestion, it changes from time to time. Since we've been digging, it is good except that I have no appetite. My overall condition is adequate. Today the weather is mild again, warm with no wind, but I am rather slow and lazy and not feeling like doing much. It's even difficult to write letters. The front is no longer as quiet as it was. If I felt like reading, I could probably borrow a book from the company library. I have borrowed a few: *Das Befreite Herz* by Hans Löscher, but I didn't read much of it. Also *Brigitta* by Stifter, but again, I haven't read much of it. To be able to read, I would need a change around here, and things may change, just not the way one thinks.

I hope that things are going relatively well with you and that Father is back from digging entrenchments. You should really leave the western region as soon as possible, for when the official evacuation comes, it may be too late. Do like the spiders with their long webs. Hang all of your belongings on it. Just don't forget to grab on yourself. Then up and away. And when you find where you want to land, you need only to reel in the thread like a wash line or a spool of wire.

I need to close now, and I will write again soon. For now, I send my greetings.

Your Reiner son

10 October 1944

Dear Parents,

From 3.00 a.m. to 8.00 a.m. this morning, we were busy digging trenches. When I got back, there were four letters waiting for me: one from Flinsberg, one from Aken, one from Cologne, and one from Rurich. In Heidi's letter was also a letter forwarded from Trier. So, I have now received news from all the sectors of the Western Front as well as the home front, informing me of how things are going. I have to say that I am deeply impressed and filled with pride that every member of our family, scattered though we may be throughout Europe, has managed to be brave, high-spirited, and clear-headed enough to see what needed to be done and has done it. This is a result of the unique Niemann-Elmering mixture for which I need no words of praise. Though we are all facing different situations, we know that not one of us will despair, break down, or act in some foolish way. From you, Mother, we have inherited your always positive outlook, which seems to grow stronger the more dire the circumstances and has allowed us to regain our balance in the face of fear and worry and do that of which we did not think ourselves capable. I could send a hymn of praise to you, but from Father we inherited the basic rule: let deeds speak for themselves. That is Father— always clear-thinking, considering all factors but not allowing himself to be diverted from his path—always doing what is necessary in the interest of us all. I could speak boundlessly in your praise, but words have now become hollow and empty. But one must remember their meaning and the spirit in which they are used—the love and the humanity. As I am far away from you, words are all I have to use. If all of us can manage to come through this mess, then we can all be proud of each other. Let us hope that our good fortune continues.

11 October 1944

Dear Parents,

Yesterday I received Father's twelfth letter. I thank you for it. And Mother doesn't think you write. Yet, you so diligently write me long letters despite all the work you have. Yesterday your letter of the 26th arrived, obviously overtaken by your letter of the 28th. I thank you for both of them.

12 October 1944

I have just finished reading *Das Befreite Herz* by Hans Löscher. It was quiet in our bunker. Another guy was reading as I was, and a third was sleeping. And the ever-inconsiderate guy from Kappo was not there. The book had a peculiar composition and wasn't abundantly expressive, but it was not that bad. It dealt with the life of an all too quiet and seemingly weak character who remains insignificant and misunderstood by men who in their tightly supervised circles unthinkingly exclude he who is different.

But now to your letters that arrived with the small package of chocolates and bonbons. I enjoyed them greatly and I am glad to hear that you haven't been bothered again. With regard to Mother's lecture on *Mär* versus *Märr*— Mother has often written *dass* instead of *dasz* and also because it reminded me of the mother instructing her youngest child in Keller's *Frau Regel Amrein*. I also remembered how Mother would seek to instruct us children.

As concerns Knud, I don't think you have to worry too much. In many places, including rear areas, there are restrictions on mail or other disruptions. To hear from and about Lütte, who is near the front, was good. I can't really judge, but in general, it is not wise for civilians to remain in the war zone, especially if it's for the sake of personal property that can always be replaced. I understand it and perhaps it is courageous to remain but what I have had to witness as a soldier, to imagine my sister going about barefoot, poor, exhausted, and neglected is not something I want to think about. Perhaps I would do the same when one considers the impression it would make on those about one; I'm thinking here about the local city council. In any case, I hope that things go well. The rations carriers have arrived and so I need to close this letter so I can give it to them to mail. I send my greetings to you and especially to Heidi who is probably reading this letter aloud to you in Aken.

Your Reiner

14 October 1944

Dear Parents,

I am sitting here in the late afternoon sun in our strip of woods, writing this letter. This sun has just disappeared behind a huge, solitary oak tree that crowns a small rise. It seems to be winking at me through the branches as though it wants to call out 'Cuckoo' before it finally disappears from a cloudless sky beneath the horizon. The sun now is warm for only a couple of hours a day when it shines. We usually return from digging trenches around dawn and then we finish off the rest of our rations and sleep until noon when they bring us up some food. Then there is time for reading (I recently borrowed Kolbenheyer's *Meister Joachim Pausewang* from the company library) writing letters, washing, cleaning our weapons, and putting things in order. Then the day is over. We eat, discuss politics, or tell stories and then around 6.00 p.m. we go to bed, interrupted of course by two-hour watch duty. Then between 11.00 p.m. and 3.00 a.m., we are awakened to go dig trenches. But it's time to close now. Supper has arrived.

15 October 1944

Sometimes I think it's hard to believe that we're still lying around in peace, a kilometer behind the front where shells rarely land. We're having good weather and better days, only the mail is late in coming, but then I've been somewhat spoiled. Otherwise, nothing here seems to change and each day repeats itself every twenty-four hours. Things are as regular here as in the barracks. Even my mood, which is good, remains the same. My digestion has improved and doesn't seem to bother me anymore. The beans and the fruit in the fields that were not harvested are beginning to sprout and blossom again. Otherwise, we have bright fall colors. The half-shot-up trees though are sending out green shoots as if it were spring. The war is to blame for the confusion of seasons. But when the front comes, the seasons will get back in order and the war, which has come to a standstill (indeed almost going backwards) will continue its course.

I often wonder if Wolfgang has already retreated north of the Po River, and if Lütte is still in Trier, or if you haven't already left Cologne before the railroads are kaput, which would make travel difficult with more than just a minimum of your possessions. All too often Cologne is mentioned in military reports that we get to read fairly often, and so it is obvious to us how things stand in the west. But in the Balkans, things are moving so fast that one needs a map to have a clear idea of the situation. East Prussia appears to be safe again, and our sector is the most quiet of all the fronts on which Germany must fight at the same time and almost alone. In the newspapers one reads about the capitulation of Warsaw[20] and the arrogance of the Polish national character and how modest the average German is, how reasonable and obliging. And they still crank out this insanity from us.

4 October 1944

My dear Reiner,

Today it has been four weeks since we began our work here in the west. Because of assurances by a number of people, we thought we would be sent home after our trench was finished—but we've been misled. Our trench and some other work were finished, but Sunday they marched us off in a heavy rain to Lövenich. Many of the young women were clever enough not to leave until Monday. Here, we who had previously been quartered in private homes have no place to stay. We sleep, or more often don't sleep, on a bed of straw strewn on the field. Tuesday morning, yesterday that is, several of the men, me included, put in a request to see a doctor. The Captain said that such things were allowed here, but that it wasn't necessary to make a request. Anyone over fifty-five could just go and see a doctor. So, we sat around the whole day because one can only travel at night because of the fighter-bombers. Everything was arranged but we are still sitting around today because it seems our transport was sent to another place—you know how that goes! But I won't dig anymore; I am somewhat overtired, my digestion is bothering me. I lack both appetite and sleep. It seems though that our sojourn here is coming to an end. We are accustomed to thinking in terms of weeks. The front has become quite lively and pushes ever closer. We are in a new place somewhat further back. The fighter planes are making themselves unpopular: the Americans because of their zeal; the Germans because of their complete absence. And Cologne is supposed to have been attacked again.

That you are being 'promoted' to *Obergefreiter* is a real crock of crap. You certainly got your receipt for refusing to be a KOB quick enough. Couldn't you refuse it and just remain a *Gefreiter*? But, everything will pass, even the war and this dissatisfaction with the military. When we have gotten over this, then we will look to getting over all the other dissatisfactions. Lotte is very busy at home. How happy she would be if I suddenly showed up this evening—but that is a joy that we will have to wait for!

And what are you doing now? Are you still so close to the enemy that you can't leave your hole during the day? Do you still not have a shelter-half? That too is a crock! Dear Reiner boy, be well and I send my greetings.

Sincerely,
Your father Alf

Cologne
4 October 1944

My dear Reiner son,

Today your package with the tobacco, writing paper, notebook, and socks arrived. And I thank you for them! It's a sign of life from you and I'm happy to have the tobacco because I use so much for trade. Unfortunately, Father is not home yet to enjoy it. Tomorrow it will be four weeks since he left. The trenches at Rurich are finished now, but instead of sending them home as promised, they've sent them to another position near Lövenich, near Baal. Father had hoped to be home next Sunday, but because of this new employment that has become doubtful. The weather is often bad, the heavens pour; but one is happy about that because it gives us a break from the air raids. After the enemy ran into such strong opposition in Holland, he now bombs the hinterland all the more, particularly the rail lines. Münster has been hit hard several times, and here and in the vicinity there is damage almost every day. After the last heavy attack on 27 September, nothing has been cleared away. There is still no gas, and I cook my food on someone else's fireplace, which takes up a lot of time, as do the conversations, which are pleasant and friendly nonetheless. Most of this morning, from 9.30 a.m. on, was spent in the cellar. My packing was brought to a standstill. All kinds of things have been sent off and much of it has arrived safely.

Sunday I had a nice surprise. Knud called me from Bonn. I had been concerned about him. Up until 6 September, he had been writing from his isolated corner in Albania. They were lucky and were able to get out. Now it seems he will have leave for three weeks. At the moment, he is on military business and yesterday wanted to go to Trier and surprise Lütte. The trip will be difficult because everywhere the rail lines are kaput.

Recently a letter arrived from Meinhard [unknown]. He has finally escaped from headquarters and was writing from Wiesbaden. He will be posted to Trier and would like to visit Lütte. That was good to hear. Now an officer's protection will be provided. Gundula [Alfons' niece] had a baby on Father's birthday. Brigitte's husband [Lotte's niece Brigitte] has been missing since June.

So, be well for today and thank you for the card. You wrote on it that you would now write to Flinsberg. Write to Aken, which is our new Family Central—they'll know how long they can forward mail to me here. God protect you my dear boy and may He grant us a joyful reunion soon. My deepest love to you.

Your Mother

Aken
[Undated]

My dear Reiner brother,

Now I need to get caught up on all that I have missed: my congratulations on your promotion to *Obergefreiter*. Then I must thank you for the two letters which actually only passed through here and then one came today that was for me—I thank you for it. It's not actually necessary to write separately a letter for me— only if you have spare time on your hands. I always read the letters to the parents and thereby have the advantage of having regular news—that's the main thing.

That you don't mind the fleas shows how badly you are living there. I find them a most unpleasant plague. I have them constantly here in this outstanding, clean, and well-kept household because Uncle Paul [Lotte's brother] has so many foreign workers to treat [in his medical practice]. They get them from the cattle. Aunt Käthe [Paul's wife] also gets fleas but they don't bite her. Me, they bite all over, and many times I don't find them for days. I once put one in a medicine bottle to see how long it could live without nourishment. After a week, the bottle tipped over, opened up, and the flea hopped out as if nothing had ever happened.

Excuse me for this short letter. My nose and eyes are running from a bad cold so not much would come of letter writing. You can always mention in your letters to the parents when you get mail from me—then I will know that you received them. And from the greetings you send to the parents, I take my share of them. I hope things remain quiet where you are and that the food remains good.

I send greetings from me and the Elmering family.

Heidi

16 October 1944

This morning Father's letter (4 October), Mother's letter (4 October) and Heidi's letter (10 October) arrived and I thank you for them.

Reiner

16 October 1944

Dear Parents,

Because I wanted to send the previous letter back with the supply truck, I could only thank you for your letters. Now I will try to answer them before the sun goes down. Now and again in your letters I get the idea that you think I have no shelter-half. That problem was solved some time back. When we first took up positions here, especially over the first three days, we had a number of casualties caused by a drumfire that Ivan was laying down on us with his *flug-flupp*, which we call his mortars, and anti-tank guns. It wasn't difficult to find an extra shelter-half. I even got a gasmask and a bayonet though I didn't really want them. On the other hand, I was able to exchange my old, worn-out boots for a brand new pair, which I then tastefully laced up with bright red telephone wire.

And no, I am no longer lying in a foxhole, as Father asks. For thirty-two days now, I've been behind the front and beginning today, we will be training for a week instead of digging trenches. As for Father's letter, I hope it is the last one you write from Cologne. Digging trenches makes for slow time.

19 October 1944

In the meantime, I received a letter from Heidi that contained two older letters. I thank you for them and especially for the pictures. Again, the letters are piling up here and I need to get rid of them or Ivan will just get them. The older letters probably sat around in Warsaw so long because for a long time our division was not reachable.[21]

Right now, I am returning from training again. For the most part, it consists of our having to crawl on the ground back and forth across an 800-meter stretch twice each morning and then to cut our way through barbed-wire entanglements. It takes one to one and a half hours to complete this course. Our *Leutnant*, though, is considerate and often turns his back to us so we can save our energy by crossing long stretches standing upright. He certainly knows what we are doing or he would have caught us long ago. But everyone must carry out orders as they see fit. The regiment strictly ordered that we must crawl around on the ground. Somehow, we are to overcome the superiority of the Russians through patience, agility, and crawling around. Utter nonsense! We can endure it though because the breaks we take are extensive. The afternoons are mostly for weapons cleaning. Only once did we get to see a movie instead of cleaning our weapons: a well-staged though kitschy film *Der Weisse Traum*, which though exaggerated was a really interesting film for all that. I need to close now. I don't have much time left before the supply truck comes. I thank you for all your letters. I send my greetings to you all in Cologne and in Aken.

Your Reiner

22 October 1944

L.E.! [*Liebe Eltern*, 'Dear Parents']

We have just finished our Sunday noon meal and dessert (cherries dipped in milk) and we were exceptionally satisfied, even me, though they did serve red turnips. This morning we have special duty. Two sergeants and two men, of whom I was one, were driven back an hour from the front in order to conduct an instruction course for some of the older men in uniform in the use of our new automatic weapons: MG-42, MP-43, the semi-automatic rifle G-43, and the panzerfaust[22], about which we don't know much ourselves. It was too much. It was terrible. Bent-over old men, some of them construction engineers, they were anxious and their hands were shaking when we put all this dangerous iron into them. Otherwise, they were decent fellows, but just putting on a uniform doesn't have much effect on a personality that has developed over a lifetime. It wasn't like being around old front-line troops.

The drive back was the best part. I rode in a one-horse cart with a *Leutnant* and the weapons. The weather was mild and the sandy roads were full of ruts and large puddles of water. The clouds hung low over the fields and the varied landscape. At times, we traveled at a trot through the splashing puddles and had to duck down in the swaying wagon. I felt like a Baron out surveying his lands— the only thing missing were the workers along the road greeting me and trying to avoid the splashing water. I was totally content and thought deeply of peace.

23 October 1944

Three days ago, I was able to write a letter to Böhm. I visited him on 20 October 1942 in Jettingen when I was traveling from the hospital in Gars to the replacement battalion in Münster. I had been released from the hospital at noon on the 19th, spent the night in Munich, and arrived in Jettingen in the morning. But since I had already sent you a telegram in Cologne, I could only stay and visit with my architecture-master teacher until lunch. On the 21st, I was with you in Cologne, and then at 9.10 p.m. I continued my trip to Münster by train.

Many times I think that after the war when we have all found a place to live, which is questionable, that maybe I could continue my studies, to go to Böhm and by working with him and studying in my spare time make progress in the profession. But whether Böhm could use me or not is another question. That is one of those wishful dreams I have here at times. However, the most important thing is that during the poor times, which are coming, a family is provided for. Whether one can advance a career is secondary. If I could earn more as an errand boy, that would be better. One hopes to have good relations with decent people, but I fear that all will be swept away in the struggle to prolong one's own life and to get bread, shelter, and clothing. And many an old soldier who was glad to be able to shed his uniform will perhaps look back with longing on his carefree life as a soldier when he had food, clothing, shelter, and everyday necessities.

24 October 1944

Today we started building a new bunker for our squad because in the approaching winter one won't be able to move about in the open. Our old bunker was only one meter high and perhaps 2.20–2.90 meters wide for six men. It had hardly any support and the walls were hastily covered with straw. We now have a new company commander. The former was a big man among small people. The new one acts decisively in all matters, which sometimes we like and sometimes we don't. The first thing he did was to have our cheap summer housing properly supported with boarding. He may be a regular fellow, but he may be a fanatic; it doesn't matter. I haven't written in five days now[23], and the letters need to go out today. Tomorrow I will have been here eight weeks, which is about my average for being at the front.

Now enough. I send my greetings to you in Aken, and to the parents in Cologne from your Reiner.

28 October 1944

Dear Parents,

It's been a relatively long time since I've received news from you. The last letters were from October 4th. I hope it is due to the state of the transportation system. Connections with Trier have been broken for some time. What concerns me is that Cologne is so often mentioned in the military bulletins. What I want to know is, has Father been allowed to return home or has the *Volkssturm* called him up? I guess I'll just have to wait for news. You need to know that I can still get a *Bombenurlaub* in case something should happen. Whatever the case, I need to hear from you.

A few days ago, the weather suddenly turned cold here and there is a sharp east wind that causes us to work faster just to keep warm. We are busy building a new bunker, which is definitely needed right now. By tomorrow, we should be able to move into it. Often I think it a good thing that I am busy building bunkers. When I am reunited with my Father and brother, at least I will know how to build one.

Now I have duty until seven in the morning, and I am using this time to write letters by firelight. During the day, there is little time to write. My duty is almost over and so I need to close. In case Heidi isn't getting mail from Cologne either, then she should write me soon so that I know what's happening.

With warm greetings from your Reiner, who is still in Russia.[24]

29 October 1944

Dear Heidi,

I'm sending this letter to you because I haven't received any mail from the parents for a while and I assume that the postal connection with Cologne has been broken. If not, then could you forward this letter to Cologne? Since yesterday, I am again at the front line. To be blunt, I doubt if I'll be able to write two letters a week. We've just received our postage stamps for Christmas packages, which I'll be sending to you. There are two brown stamps that are good for packages up to 100 grams, and the green stamps are for packages up to 500 grams or you can use two of them for up to 1000 grams. The green ones have to be used before 30 November. You know that I can send back heavy packages from here, so be reasonable, as we all are, and don't feel as if you have to send me heavy packages stuffed with *Flinsberger* chocolates and heavy cakes. We have here good quality and more food to eat than you have at home, and at Christmas we will certainly get plenty of sweets, alcohol, and tobacco to gorge ourselves on, more than you get for an entire month.

I have a comrade here from West Prussia, and in exchange for some tobacco, he will arrange for a package (probably peas and white flour) to be sent from his home to you in Aken. He is a dependable type and comes from simple, but honest and decent people.

Other Deployments

As the warring powers were deploying their forces for the final battles of the war, the Niemann family made its own final deployments. In two years of Allied bombings, the family home in Cologne had only the minor damage of shattered windowpanes, but in the middle of October 1944, that run of good luck came to an abrupt end. The apartment on the Klettenberggürtel suffered extensive damage during a bombing raid, rendering it uninhabitable. Obviously, it was time to go.

Soon after the first bombing raids, the ever-practical Alfons wisely decided to disperse both family and belongings so that a single bomb would not destroy them. The war had already dispersed his sons. The youngest daughter, Heidi, moved in with relatives in Breslau, while the eldest daughter, Lütte, worked as a librarian with the central library in Trier. Alfons and Lotte Niemann packed up and shipped their most important belongings for safekeeping with friends and relatives throughout Germany.

Now, however, with the approaching storm, it was time for Alfons to concentrate his forces. Aken an der Elbe, a town in north-central Germany, was selected to be the family's base of operations at the home of Lotte's brother, Dr Paul Elmering. When disaster struck, this would be the family's rallying point. Heidi was sent on ahead to Aken to establish the 'central office'. She received the family's letters and forwarded the painstakingly typed copies. Lütte joined her when she was released from her duties at the Trier library. Alfons, finally released from digging entrenchments, still had to attend to family matters. He and Lotte traveled to Bad Flinsberg, where he could recover his health and see his sisters one last time before the storm broke. When he was well, he and Lotte would join their daughters in Aken. There, they would wait out the end of the war; there, they would await the return of their sons.

31 October 1944

Yesterday I finally heard from Cologne. A green postcard dated 15 October with a poem on it brought me proof of life from the parents. I also received your letter #5 (15 October) and a postcard from Lütte and Knud with greetings from Meinhard. I am glad that I received them, and I want to thank you, each and all. I am especially thankful for the copies and the poems by Mörike. I don't have much time for reading around here, but since it is a small book, I can always carry it with me and in quiet moments inhale his poetry.

That I am at the front line again is not so bad. It's almost an improvement. Here one can focus better on the war situation and its outcome and be content in the knowledge that all who are wearing a uniform—indeed our entire people—are suffering the same from the war. I'm here in a cellar with five men and a KOB sergeant. We have no light, but it is roomy and warm. There are more rats than mice. During the night, which is now about thirteen hours long, we all have to stand duty outside and can only come in one at a time to warm up. During the day, we don't see much because that is when we sleep. In order to see at night, we open the oven door because we have hardly any candles left. But it is bearable. The position is well fortified with barbed wire and land mines, and directly in front of us is another strong point. Our meals arrive in the evening and are better than they were, although they weren't that bad before. Gloves, winter coats, and rubber boots are available, and I've managed to acquire a pullover and a new shirt.

For the past few weeks, my digestion has been fine. All in all things are good, especially now that I know good fortune has decided to linger a while longer with our family. To be honest, I no longer try to calculate how things are going to turn out in this war. No one is going to escape unscathed. One must not be miserly with the little life one has. Those who are anxious and fearful will be struck first. But one must not gamble with one's life either for one will get what one has earned. That is the lesson of this war.

Write to the parents and Lütte that I think it is time, especially for non-swimmers, to get across the Rhine, and though the Rhine has no sharks swimming in it doesn't mean one should risk swimming.

I will close now and send you all my greetings.

From your old Reiner son, brother, brother-in-law, nephew, cousin, and even uncle.

3 November 1944

Dear Parents,

I thank you for sending me your *Lebenszeichen*.[25] I must limit my signs of life to this form and no letters from me because I am at the front again and don't have much time or opportunity to write. I have been here for six days and I can assure you that I have never been in a quieter sector. The weather is still mild, and the rain doesn't cause us problems because it is quickly soaked up by the sandy soil here. Anyway, we have rubber boots and have pulled a shelter-half over our trench in case it does rain. We have been well equipped, even for winter, with a stove in our bunker, scarves, gloves, and of course winter coats. I have even managed to acquire a second pullover and shirt. Regular winter clothing will be sent up soon. We can probably wait out the time here more peacefully than you can at home.

I am constantly thinking and having dreams of you at home and of earlier times. Of course, I have plenty of time for this during our thirteen hours of night watch and the remaining time in which we sleep. Today we had a bottle of Rhine wine, and although I didn't have the preferred company, surroundings, or festive atmosphere, I did manage to drink to your health and well-being. I hope that it helps. I hope that Father hasn't been put in a uniform and stuck in one of the trenches he dug as a civilian. I also hope that you will get out of desecrated Cologne soon.

Warmly,
Your Reiner

11 and 19 October 1944

My dear Reiner,

I wanted to write you sooner and now I no longer remember all the things I wanted to tell you. I wanted to read your letters again and now it's been an entire week since I have written. Again, there have been fires in all parts of the city—in some of them, quite bad. The anti-aircraft defense is still limited here and so Tommy can do what he wants. They used the situation well and came flying in constant waves for over an hour and dropped their bombs. No railroad, no streetcars, no water, and no electricity. We haven't had gas for a long time. The Mülheimer Bridge is *kaput.* Our days now are rather short. It is dark at six and then we eat by the light of a candle stump. Then we go to our night quarters without undressing because many times the bombs fall without the warning sirens going off. Then we must rush down the dark staircase—I'm always too slow for Lotte. Sometimes the sirens don't go off at all. Mostly they are irregular and unreliable. The explosions of the flak have now melted away to a few individual shots. We no longer hear ambulances or fire trucks; apparently there aren't any left. As such, the evacuation is in chaos. The evenings we have written off and the days are spent in the cellar. We have to stand in line for at least an hour at the few available water pumps (the nearest one to us is on Luxemburgerstraße near Leybergstraße). Because it takes longer to cook on a strange hearth, it's difficult to do the daily chores. Where then does one find time to write? So far, we have come through it. An incendiary bomb outside the kitchen door did little damage. The next high explosive bomb landed on one side of the street, and another on the other corner of Siebengebirgealle on Ölbergstraße. The damage to the windows was less this time, only the dirt—one can't imagine how it is all blown about. My exhaustion is a bit less now. I prefer to doze the entire day in a recliner. A doctor has determined that physically there is nothing wrong; my symptoms can be attributed to over exertion. I hope now to get a leave. Today it is pouring so badly that I don't want to go the long way on foot.

In the meantime, Heidi has sent the first two letters you sent to Aken—I thank you! Mail is rarely delivered and considering the situation with traffic, it will be that way for a while. Here, one is somewhat stranded! When this letter will get off, I have no idea. Don't think anything bad if our communication with you is rather slim in the near future—but I send my greetings dear one.

Always, your father Alf

12 October 1944

My dear *Reinerkerl*,

Actually, it is a prerogative of your mother to call you that, but she has made an exception and has allowed me to. You have certainly noticed in the salutation that a change in the scenery has arrived, and this change has given rise to a certain high spiritedness. But as you can imagine this cheerfulness is of a modest quality because it is certainly no time to be as happy and unconcerned as a child dancing about in a field of flowers. But finally, on Monday night I arrived home. In our second war theater, Lövenich, I did considerably more—partly out of protest of the promise that was not kept, and also because I had had enough. Under other circumstances I would have just kept working at half-power, but because of my sometimes better, sometimes worse intestinal trouble and the nightly colic, and because we were told the older men would not be sent home; I went to the doctor again—a student in his last semester who gave me some pills and classified me as capable to work. I told him that I wouldn't work anymore. Then the High Command got involved, came to me, and said they knew that I had always worked hard at the digging and that it had become too much for me, but that I should go back to my work detail. They said they would talk to a doctor. I refused; I wasn't going to be treated like a malingerer. They wanted to send me home but couldn't without the doctor's cooperation. They arranged it that a private doctor in the town would examine me. He immediately classified me as unfit for work.

The next day, Monday evening, I traveled with a flak unit that was bringing four vehicles to Cologne. From seven until after midnight we were on the road, delayed by flat tires and alarms. Then I slogged my way, carrying my rather heavy pack through the dark city to the Klettenberg where I found Lotte still reading at two in the morning. Now I am catching up on all the sleep I lost by trying to sleep on the straw they had provided us. I am alert and in better spirits. I've done little else but read through the letters that had piled up here. In addition, I've consumed a couple of cutlets and cognac, some French wine from the lower Rhine, all helped along by a box of your cigarettes and which I—God be praised—brought home with me. To all this, the farm wife added a good pound of thick bacon, which despite its powerful appearance after the slaughter, melted in your mouth. Yesterday we had noodle soup with *Geschnorre*, and today half the beast was roasted and we drank the red wine that Möwe had brought to my birthday celebration. The other half was preserved. Because we have no gas, *Frau* Meier [neighbor] cooked everything in her fireplace. Now it will soon be time to turn our backs on Cologne.

From your letters—and I have had to do without all children's letters—I now have a slightly clearer picture of your situation, and I must say that compared to your situation, I lived like a prince on my straw bed. At least I didn't have to clear out the frogs before I occupied my bed. Even though the front was many kilometers away from our work site, I found out a lot about the war from soldiers coming from the front, either because they had been pulled out, or were fetching supplies and other necessities from the rear, or were being newly deployed—and also from refugees, whose numbers have increased in the last days. The picture is clear: it's all been brought to a rather compromised formula. That is, the common soldier will have to defend himself with hand-grenades and small arms against an overwhelming mass of tanks and aircraft while the newly deployed anti-aircraft is too weak. This dogged defense, which currently is being performed by soldiers of the older age-groups, will certainly continue for a while longer along this stationary front, but no soldier doubts that one day the opponent will be able to mass his forces for an offensive for he can supply himself with weapons and materiel in a way that we cannot and so in the future will do what we can't. I've spoken to men who fought in Normandy without any relief, to men who fourteen days ago were in the Navy or the Air Force and are now being used as infantry. The idea of employing the new weapons is regarded by the soldiers with laughing skepticism.

The reliability of our soldiers is beyond question, but so too, the war weariness. If the latter overcomes the former, then a point will be reached where some of the troops will break—even if against their will. When I speak of the refugees—and there's been quite a few—it's not a matter of despair— what would be the point?—but rather a mood of resignation, indifference. Notable is when one group of refugees calls to the other, 'Fahrt ins Blaue,'[26] and the other calls back, 'You bet—KDF!'[27] Basically, the mood of the people, even those who are still in their home territory, is embittered that it has all come to this. Though outwardly calm, the people are indignant, and many have decided to take matters into their own hands. It's not quiet everywhere. If there should be breakthrough, however, then chaos would ensue, the breadth and depth of which would be difficult to estimate.

Yesterday here in Cologne, we heard heavy cannon fire from the front all day and night as well as frequent air-raid alarms. My plans are not firm yet. In any event, I will consult with the doctor.

Just now mail has arrived from Aken, and as I can see some of your letters are there—I must first read them—I thank you for your two letters and now I will write some more. Today, things are not going well—with the mail there came more bad news: Konrad, Suse Wolf's fiancé, was killed on 27 August. Käthe writes, 'Truly, we have lost a second son.' If one seeks solace, one must only look about oneself, and then fall quiet and bow his head.

Dearest Reiner, I send my greetings. Stay safe and sound and do your best to remain so. I think of you often. One cannot number the thoughts I send to you and Wolf every day.

Always your faithful father Alf

Cologne
12 October 1944

My dear Reiner,

You will be happy to know that I now have Father back home again. It's not much of a life for the two of us. The worst is that at the moment, I cannot cook—but I won't complain. The little things wear me down—but when I think of Käthe Wolf, then things don't seem so bad. I send my greetings my dear boy, and thank you for your letters.

With love,
Your Mother.

19 October 1944

A third letter of yours sent to Aken has arrived. Many thanks. It's so good to have Father here. It does me good under these conditions although I'd rather be on our way east. But how? That's a bag full of questions. One cannot go over any of the bridges either on foot or as a passenger in a vehicle—when there's no streetcar—without being stopped and checked as to who you are and why you are traveling. Even so, we'll keep our spirits up and hope for a reunion of the family. God protect you, and stay well. I send my greetings.

Your Mother

5 November 1944

Dear Parents,

I thank you for your letter of 19 October that arrived here today. What happened to me with your mail is now happening to you with mine. It doesn't really matter what's in a letter. All that counts is that there is a letter, a sign of life. Now you are living a life like the one we live at the front, no less uncomfortable, no less difficult. I hope you are able to finish things there and get yourselves moved to a more civilized life in Aken. With Tommy bombing so often and so heavily, one of these times, things are going to go badly for you.

I lead a true dream existence here. From five in the evening until six in the morning, we are on watch duty here and from about seven-thirty to whenever in the afternoon, we get to sleep, with interruptions of course. And I use the time to the fullest to sleep and dream. It is the only good side to our dark and comfortless existence here. I always have the same dream, but always it is new. I dream about the old days with their various, distinct, and different emotions. Things that cannot be put into words, described or translated. Everything is always more beautiful in the blossom of memory. When you spoke of your childhood and youth, it made me feel warm in the heart, and yearn. I regretted that I could not have been there in that time with those wonderful people and their friends and their simple, untroubled existence. And I, too, regret that this time is gone and will not return. Those days only appear to be better and that is because they have been conveyed through the memories of positive people. That is what caused their transformation. Even those times of the greatest discontent, which usually make the strongest impression, can likewise be transformed. And so, when I light up a cigar to help me write a letter, I do it instinctively. As I enjoy the aroma and give into the drifting and ever-changing rings of smoke, I feel myself supported as I sink down inside myself into the world of dreams and feelings. Man is the creature whose most pronounced characteristic is his inclination towards that which cannot be fulfilled, the unworldly, the irrational, the boundless. In this respect, even the war has its purpose; its productive side. War, which arises from baseness, imperfection, and a hatred of mankind, has its most important impact on the positive nature of man in that it is a self-chastisement and a self-purification of mankind. I am surprised that even I have arrived at this conclusion, but it satisfies me in that in this way I can take away more good than bad from the war. This should be proof to you that things are going well with me and that I have much time to reflect upon things. All too often, however, it degenerates into contradictions where one battles with himself and his surroundings. But this too is peculiar to man—strength and weakness at the same time. Whenever things are going badly with me, the negative dominates and should this prevail upon all the participants of this war, then comes the last and worst part of the war, the great chaos, which we all fear but which is unavoidable at the end of war. We can only hope that we will be spared and somehow come through it. We are standing before the last act of this war, and we have no choice but to be here. Today is Sunday, but only inside us. As with you there, there is little outward sign that it is Sunday. In three weeks comes the beginning of Advent. Often I think that perhaps somehow the Christmas season will bring reason to the world and a willingness to negotiate. But I am too naïve and I wish to remain so. I wish you well at Advent time and will continue to think of you and all the Christmas arrangements under Father's direction and the aroma of Mother's cooking.

I leave you with warm greetings,
Your Reiner

11 November 1944

Dear Parents,

It's exactly eleven minutes past 11 a.m., and so the carnival can begin. For us it arrived yesterday with the first snow that then melted and turned our bunker into a rain bucket. Everywhere it was dripping through—on your cigar, if you were smoking; on your face, if you were sleeping; down your collar and sleeves; and on your paper if you were writing. Even the trench is full of mud and water and the sandy clay walls have partially caved in. But we have rubber boots and the whole night to dig it out and repair it, better than standing on watch and freezing. I sleep the same way I stand watch, under a shelter-half, which is our main piece of clothing now. It is being seen to that we don't get too dry around here. Since the 9th, we have been given beer, a half bottle of Rhine wine, and a quarter liter of schnapps. The wine was drunk this morning, and I am drinking the schnapps now, to your health, of course, for I think you need it.

Your letter of the 19th remains the last one I've received. The mother and sister of one of the guys here are still beneath the rubble in Essen. I keep thinking of you and your life there, and I wish you could get out of that staging area of the Western Front. If something does happen, send me a telegram certified by the police and then I can get a leave. But I would rather see you healthy and safe and would gladly give up a thousand such leaves for a year. Here things are still quiet. This morning we could hear artillery rumbling somewhere in the distance. It happens often. I guess you have to do something on 11.11.[28] I would just like to be happy again. Now I am only happy when my night watch is over. I wish it were only days or weeks before this witch's sabbath were over and we could all be sitting around the table again. Here it will be quiet for a while. What we heard this morning was just someone releasing tension, and it didn't last long. I try to imagine how we will manage our not-too-pleasant life in the future. I would gladly share the meager portions and the daily unpleasantness of a hopeless time if we were all together. Working together will lighten the load of each of us, and mutual love will overcome all eventualities and show us the path to a more bearable life. I often wish it were already time for this, but Father admonishes me against this easily spoken phrase. But we have lived too long among brutish men, and despite all protestations, not even our family will escape wickedness. But the main thing is we speak honestly to one another and have good will. Not like here where the soldier—the longer he lies in the filth, the longer he is a soldier, the more bitter, the more uncooperative, the more secretive and envious he becomes.

I must close for now. I need to get a letter off to Wolf for his birthday.

Warm greetings,
Your Reiner

Unbeknownst to Reiner and his family, Wolfgang Niemann was killed in a sudden British artillery attack near the Futa Pass on 10 October. His parents did not learn of his death until 27 November 1944.

14 November 1944

Dear Wolfgang,

You probably already know that I have been on the front line since 28 October, that is, if you are receiving any mail, considering the prevailing conditions where you are. Now we are having a quiet time and things are really heating up in your sector, and it really doesn't look like things around here are going to be any different. I'm sitting in our bunker, which is the cellar of what used to be a house. The door is open so that we can get some fresh air. Right now, I'm sitting on a wooden box with a half-moon shaped board across my knees. It's called a *halb Brett*, formerly a *Rückboden*, fashioned from the base of a wooden barrel, which we use to eat on, write on, and whatnot, because there isn't enough light where the table stands. I'm smoking a cigar without a paper band, fat and big, and in the characteristic style of some rich industrialist. It's thick at the front and tapers toward the end. Unfortunately, it's somewhat damp in our bunker because for the past several days it has become a dripping cave. That's because after the first snow fell on 11 November, it has been melting every day since. We are all hoping for a hard frost to arrive soon and put an end to this condition. And now, to the introduction of this letter: the main reason I am writing you is for your upcoming birthday, which unfortunately won't be the last war-time birthday if we are going to try to win this war, but willpower doesn't always make a difference. I hope we can celebrate your next birthday, or better yet, my next birthday [19 May 1945] in peacetime. So, for this year, let me shake your hand and wish you the best and continued good fortune during the coming difficult times. You can't believe how often I dream about you and think of you, whether while sleeping or on sentry duty. And though in my dreams we often argue, I must smile when I awaken, because after all, we have grown into such reasonable young men. And I imagine how it would be if we could later study together, but I don't know if we will be able to. The main thing is that we and the family get through this. Somehow we will, if we have inherited just a part of our parents' character. I wish it were already time for us to show and confirm it. I wish you the best and hope that we will soon be together again. I don't have much to tell about me here. I live more in a world of dreams than in reality, though the reality here is not that bad. The situation is as good as it can be with regard to food and our everyday life here. It's the dreams, hopes, and memories that keep my spirits up.

Nothing much happens here. I've had to do a patrol, which is a rare thing around here, and that only because our squad leader is a KOB. But he'll soon be going back to Germany. It bothers me some because it is something I could do because there is nothing in my papers that says anything about my cancellation as a KOB, and I haven't cared that much to mention it either. I hope the situation doesn't continue—to see someone take over the squad that I could lead better. I haven't received much mail from home and when I do, it's the high point in my monotonous life here. Since the postcard of 15 October, in which they informed me that they were alive and well, I have gotten one letter, that of 19 October. That's not very many and I worry. One of the men from Essen received notice that his mother and sister were killed in a bombing raid. I am afraid that one of these days, things will go badly for us if the war continues as it is without any discernible goal. Unfortunately that is something we must reckon on. But for now, I will close this letter and send you warm greetings. All the best, dear Wolfgang, and be well.

Your brother,
Reiner

20 November 1944

Dear Parents,

And now it's your turn to have a letter written to you. Around here, it seems everything has its turn: eating, cleaning our weapons, washing, repairing, and putting things in order. One always is losing some sleep time in order to take care of something that concerns the squad. There is some time each day for sleeping but never a full day when one can catch up on sleep. And when you have to go back to the supply depot or the regimental HQ, then you are on your feet for forty hours. How do you make up for that? However, for right now the sleeping is all right, but in a month comes the longest night. We'll just have to manage. Last night something special was going on that made the night go faster. Loudspeakers were blaring out propaganda from our positions. Before, only Ivan did that. First, they played a couple of jazz records, and then came the speeches, and that was followed by folk music. And all the while the ukulele twanged, the saxophone crooned, and the drums thumped. We could hear the droning of Ivan's sleds and trucks. This all didn't last long before Ivan opened up with his anti-tank guns and mortars and other infantry weapons and began blasting away at the loudspeakers. But we must not blame ourselves for the music or shut up shop just because the artillery interfered; otherwise it would be the same old boastful propaganda speeches. They finished the broadcast, which is the most important thing. Anyway, as the music played, we stood, two to a foxhole, and looked at one another and let the beat of our beloved jazz take us back to happier times. And then I thought what rubbish this war is; what a cheap and unjust matter when compared to a war between two Germanic tribes. We enlivened our thoughts and memories with swigs from our flasks that each of us had stowed away. It wasn't that cold, but we drank it anyway so that we could turn in the empty flask at noon the next day. The day before yesterday we received a 'gift to the Infantry from the Führer': a package of cookies and chocolates, one-sixth liter bottle of synthetic brandy, and one half bottle of white Bordeaux. The schnapps should have been saved for colder weather, but we have never been permitted to save it up.[29] Last night it thawed after a couple of days of frost. We thought the snow might stay, but once again, it melted and disappeared, and dripped through our bunker as before. The trenches are full of slush and mud and at times, it rains. We would rather have the frost. I have been preoccupying my mind during my night watches with the construction of a clock based on the stars. After three nights of thinking about this, I came up with a plan that could work for two thirds of the men in our trench. We just need one watch in order to make it work, but we don't have a single watch in the entire platoon and so we are always having arguments because everyone thinks they are being shorted on their time to come inside the bunker to get warm. In my head this star-clock is already finished. It could be made out of an oven ring with 12 spokes of wire stretched from the center to the outside ring. The center wire would be the polar star and the hours would be marked off by the other wires as the stars rotated around the polar star throughout the night. It's a pity we don't have clearer night skies, but when we do, the system will work. And I hope that things are working for you.

Sending warm greetings from your Reiner

22 November 1944

Dear Parents,

Another strange date, right? But I would have written anyway. First, because it's your turn for a letter. And second, because I received your letter of the 14th—the first from Flinsberg. I feel loaded up like a fresh battery of guns brought out to the field, ready to fire away. But now, to my letter.

I'm writing on this paper because we get so much of it, and with all of us here in this damp cave, it accumulates. And with your contribution, I have a nice store of it. I thank you for yesterday's letter, and the two old letters from June, which have gained, not lost, significance with age.

How nice it would be if Wolf suddenly showed up! You certainly deserve it after all that you have been through in the Western sector. I would like to have seen the humorous drawing that Father wrote about. I believe that I, too, have learned something about drawing, although in the past few years it had hardly led to any picture with a good composition. There are many elements of drawing that seem to be unconnected. Apart from a concept of the eternal, there also needs to be a mature objectivity and a basic standard of life. In the three years I have spent in the Army, I have experienced a great deal such that I feel like an old man. Often when I am visually impressed by something, I think about drawing it, but then I become uncertain. And to draw, one must be certain from the beginning. I often cut pictures from newspapers that impress me with their visual effect and composition and impatiently wait to see if by drawing them I confirm my artistic impression and impulses. But soon we won't have time for such unprofitable work as this.

How long has it really been since you last heard from Wolf? Certainly, nobody has messed up the mail. Your letter was carried to me by a guy who returned from bomb leave. We had been in a squad together before my most recent trench duty. The first thing he said to me was, 'Hey Reiner, you're getting fat.' And I believe him, because physically I'm really feeling great, and I'm in good spirits too, just as I was in Münster when I was certain I was finally going back to the front. Looking back, Münster was a dark spot in my life where I never had any peace. Here, I have peace and people leave you alone. The mood in the squad is so irritable that we all stay out of each other's way to avoid an argument. We rarely address each other face to face, except when I bring up my favorite subjects: home and family. Then everyone is sociable and talkative. I would like to write down and send you all that my sentry-duty partner has heard about my home, my parents, my brother and sisters, my childhood Christmases, and my hobbies. I've mentioned that Mother is a regular '*Frau* Regula Amrein',[30] and that Father was and is a passionate soccer player and still hikes so much in the mountains that his long-legged son who is accustomed to long marches has trouble keeping up with him. But to balance that characterization of him— as if that's necessary—I also mention that he is a professor. I talk about old music, playing the organ, of music chambers, early architectural endeavors, Baroque churches and castles, modern churches, photography, and decorating the Christmas tree. And when my partner has a chance, he talks of his work as a gardener in the Henkelgardens in Düsseldorf, which I often passed during my time with the *Landeschützen* in Hallenbad. Now whether the other listens or not is unimportant. What's important is that we share our visions and memories of the human warmth of family, to which we all want to return. We don't talk about war experiences or anything connected to the war unless it's to say how the war could go favorably. He only sees two possibilities, whereas I am just glad that it's not too late for a decisive solution. We don't lack topics of conversation when we are in the mood, and sometimes we're in good spirits. You can tell that Christmas is coming. The NSV has distributed their packages of fabulous cookies and chocolates, as well as wine and good schnapps. The only thing missing is the atmosphere, and the warmth and closeness of family.

Your Reiner
And greetings also to the aunts and Uncle Fietche [Fritz Niemann] and Breslau as well.

26 November 1944

Dear Parents,

They are burning up an old wooden washtub in the stove, and it smokes and smells so bad of rancid soap that even on the 'third floor' (i.e., upper bunk), it's impossible for me to sleep. So, I prefer to use the time well instead of being angry about not being able to sleep. Besides, today is Sunday after all and it is your turn for a letter. It's a rather dreary Sunday, and the pale light coming through the 30 × 30 cm opening in the door into our stone cellar is barely enough for letter writing. My bed lies far in the back, in the darkest corner. Yesterday, the whole damn structure collapsed with me in it, just as I suspected it would after all the climbing and twisting it takes for me to get in it. This happens to all of us because we didn't have enough nails for our bunks. The nails we did have were taken from charred timbers and were damaged by fire and so were only 'conditionally fit for active duty'. But in Total War, everyone must do his part, from the *Volkssturm*[31] down to the last rusty nail. Right now, I need to get rid of my beard because it's the first Sunday of Advent if you don't count Christmas Eve. But I don't know whether to or not—oh, too late. Two old soldiers just got up to shave, and one needs as much peace and quiet and more room for shaving than one does for letter-writing. I'll have to wait now. Perhaps I'll have my chance later. Otherwise, I'll shave in three days when I am outside on alarm duty.

And now to my letter. After a period of little mail, the good times have come again. I received your letter #22 from Flinsberg (17 November) the day before yesterday, and yesterday I received an overdue one from Heidi (3 November) both with copies of letters for which I thank you. The old letters have become almost historical but no less interesting than the new ones. The times are changing so quickly, but even so, could you send me some military press releases from time to time? Just put them in with the newspapers that the aunts send me, which I always appreciate. Around here, they are saying that the Yanks have already reached the Rhine at Strasbourg and Mulhausen, and that Tommy is already advancing near Eschweiler. We haven't received any Army press reports for over a week, and I spend long nights trying to calculate how things are going to turn out.

27 November 1944

I finally have to give it up. My comrades have so increased their proclivity to inform everyone of everything that I have to give up trying to inform you. I've just received a letter from Cologne dated 13 October, which I will answer later. I must go to bed now. It's quite late. I send you thanks and greetings.

Your Reiner

29 November 1944

Dear Parents,

Once again, I enjoy a period graced by your letters, and that is good. Yesterday I received two letters from Flinsberg: letter #23 postmarked 21 November, and a letter from the aunts postmarked 23 November, so it only took five days to reach me. I thank you and the aunts for them.

As before, things are going well with me. The weather here is probably similar to yours. For the time being, we have light frost, even during the day, but no snow, which is just the way we want it. Yesterday we received our thickly quilted winter clothing, which is reversible. The inside is completely white, and the outside is gray and both are waterproof. The jacket has a hood to protect the head and neck in snow and wind. If it gets much colder, however, we will need felt boots and a second pair of heavy mittens. Then we'll be ready for anything. Yesterday we received fresh, un-carbonated apple juice in our provisions. It was almost as good as Oberwinterer's. I'm always glad to receive things that you wouldn't expect during 'Total War'. In four weeks comes the shortest day of the year and then Christmas. But time will pass as it will, despite all impatience. Yesterday the second guy to go on *Bombenurlaub* left for Düsseldorf, and another guy just came back to replace him. He talked about the conditions in the west and about the V-1 and V-2 missiles and so on. If I get a regular leave— the members of the old 6th ID are supposed to be next in line after those guys who get bomb or marriage leaves—I'll be happy if I don't have to spend it in some cellar in the west. But let's not get too hopeful, especially since the present three percent [quota of leaves] isn't even enough for those seeking bomb leaves. Hope is premature. But thoughts are free and I certainly enjoy my thoughts.

What do you know about this year's harvest? And how are the aunts and the Breslauers [Alfons' family in Breslau] doing with the potatoes. The outcome of the war can depend even on such things.

30 November 1944

I've just gotten out of my bed because something is making me uneasy, and I can't get to sleep. I'm bothered by something and I need to shake it off. I tried eating and reading but nothing helped. What I really need here is a piano. It would conduct my troubles and feelings of pointlessness away from me like a lightning rod. Or I need some task that involves me mentally and emotionally. Or perhaps someone here I could talk to, not about the war or reality, but about the good things of life. But that is best found when one is alone.

So with this hope I sit down with the letter I started yesterday, and gaze at the photos of you, light my cigar, and begin writing, not knowing how the letter will end up. I would much rather be touring in the mountains, hiking in the fresh air of the Isar mountains. But there's nothing left for me to do but whistle some Hayden melodies, loudly enough that the mice in our cellar quit scratching and hold their ears. Otherwise, I feel completely empty inside and need some external stimulation. Since this is the last day of the month, I'll put the October letters in order and get them ready to send back to Heidi for safe-keeping. I need to close now because it's already getting dark. Since yesterday, we've only had to spend half the night outside on duty, so it's still night when we come back in to sleep. Even if it's only a short time, it does us well, and the mood of the men has visibly improved. However, that just gives the men more chances to argue over whose turn it is to be relieved. But that's people. When they have it good, they get dissatisfied and bitch endlessly or argue over everything, large or small. There is nothing more peaceful than when I am dreaming, which is an antidote for all the bleakness of the present reality.

Be well, and I send my greetings,
Your Reiner son and nephew

On Wolfgang's birthday [3 December 1944]
Between 2.00 a.m. and 4.00 a.m.

Dear Father and Mother,

Yesterday evening, the night before Wolfgang's birthday, I received your sad news. I have seen it coming for a long time and one guy in our group had just asked the date, and I said it was my brother's birthday and hopefully he is still alive. After I read both letters, which consoled me with your love, I got ready quickly and went out alone on watch while the others went to get food. So, I was able to be alone to face the first wave of pain. The choking in my throat was only relieved by sobs. Never have I wept so hard. I felt like a stranger to myself. But finally, I overcame it. My thoughts and feelings were scrambled as I tried to grasp the scope of what had happened. I realized I couldn't change it, and I was finally able to control myself and calm down. This process of introspection happened under a clear, star-filled sky, and one bright star in the distant southwest was blinking at me and seemed to be whispering words of comfort. Earlier it had moved restlessly across the sky, but now it seemed to have found peace, as if Wolf was taking pains to calm me and return me to reason. Take your time. I will wait and then we'll be together again. So now, I'm calm and can write to tell you that I don't feel so alone and you needn't worry that I'll be overwhelmed by this blow. It hasn't thrown me off course. I only hope that this war, which has become senseless and still hasn't reached its climax, will not bring on our people more heavy blows to bear. I want to do my part. You've had the heavier burden with Wolf's departure, and many German families have lost their sons and other loved ones. We've been on this course for a long time. I didn't trust that we'd be spared and I feared that our good fortune wouldn't last.

Midday

You know my relationship with Wolf. Often just to have some human connection while on sentry duty, I'd talk to my comrades about our family. I often found sympathy and understanding, and they all agreed that our family has a special and close relationship. And it's true that this makes the loss twice as hard, but the sadness is lighter. One could and should, but I won't use more words. Things will get better over time, but right now, this feverish hangover robs me of clarity. Basically, all our thoughts and wishes should be on Wolfgang's last hours and on our duty to him and to our family.

Evening

Right now I'm writing between two periods of sentry duty to tell you what I did this afternoon about getting a leave—though there is little chance of it. I presented the matter like this: that Father must leave Cologne because he became sick while on duty digging trenches, and he hasn't been able to pack up all of our belongings. The company commander said that without a telegram certified by the Nazi Party Office[32], it would be pointless to try to get a leave because all leaves must be granted by the regiment. Getting a leave is highly uncertain even with a telegram. As an example, he pointed out that a captain who lost his child in the complete destruction of his home was refused a leave with a statement that said an officer's wife would have to handle the situation alone, without her husband getting a leave. Another guy in the company lost both his parents, his only living relations in the city, in a bombing raid. He's been waiting for over a month for a telegram, probably because there is nobody left to send it. So, that's how things stand here. For me to have a chance at getting a leave, you will have to get a certification of Wolfgang's death and Father's illness from the Nazi Party Office (difficult because the official news is not there yet) and have everything verified, including the fact that there are still necessary items to pack in the apartment. Maybe we should give up the idea and not make more heartache for ourselves by dragging out this hopeless affair. I've considered things from all angles, and considering how things are right now with the mail, a certified telegram would probably come too late. The main sticking point is the certification from the Party Office. Becoming hardened during wartime is unavoidable, but we must become so, and carry this out successfully with our belief and our willpower. I pray that you do not become embittered. We have nothing more to expect from these times. Maybe something will come from my part in the retreat last summer.

The whole matter is still being processed throughout the whole time I've been here with this bunch. Everyone says it's about getting medals and a leave. On 5 October, I submitted my personal report,[33] and I've been hoping to be able to surprise you some day. But the process is ongoing (the last inquiry was 28 November). Hopefully it won't run itself to death.

4 December 1944

And so, that's how things went on Wolfgang's birthday. I had to deal with it alone and without you, but your dear letters greatly softened the blow, and I had a lot of time and quiet. So perhaps it was not as bad with me as you thought it might be. Though alone, I was thankful that I could concentrate on remembering Wolfgang and not tormenting myself with dark images. Now I will have to travel my path alone in life and not how I had dreamt it would be—working and learning together in the same profession with mutual encouragement and inspiration. Though there is still much to say, I will do so in later letters while I have the chance and more importantly when we are all together again and have more control of our fate. Wolf's industry and energy will always be an example and encouragement for me. I will do all I can to lighten the blow of his loss. I thank you for your letters—Lütte also, whom I hope yet to write. Let us always think of him in the light of the southwest evening star. For now, I send my greetings to you, to Lütte and the aunts also, from your Reiner son and brother.

5 December 1944

Dear Parents,

Yesterday I received your Advent package with the red candles from the aunts. I thank them, and you as well. Now we are doing fine with candles, and I too have plenty of soap. We wash only every few days. But then, thoroughly. Today is another Wolfgang's birthday; that is, Wolfgang Amadeus Mozart. He was also a cheerful fellow despite all the hardships of life that he had to endure. If one can judge from his music and letters, he seems never to have become bitter. And so it is without a doubt that our Wolfgang's will is that we never lose our high spirits in life. In contrast, his last thought certainly would have been of his parents and siblings and that they should not grieve too much. And perhaps he asked them to understand that he had to change his life, and that he did not carelessly risk his life but did what he had to do so he could face himself and that they would forgive him if his death added to their pain and sorrow. Certainly it was easier for him to die in the trust and knowledge that he had parents like you who do not deceive themselves and therefore will continue living upright and steadfast, and had they been in his place would have done no different, as simple and stale as that may sound in these times. But we must be proud of our Wolf. Sometimes I become depressed because he wrote me once and said that he wouldn't have made it out during the retreat of the 6th Division because he couldn't swim. But I swam across. On both sides, there was an ever widening and deepening swamp, and I had to leave behind a comrade who couldn't swim, partly because he couldn't find the courage to try and partly because I would have held up the entire group. But if an officer like Wolfgang had been there, he would have taken up a position on the other bank with a direct line of fire, and he would have laid down covering fire, keeping the Russians down so that even our last wounded man could have been brought across. In our case, more than one hundred, even two or three hundred men were lost. Even our company commander must have tried to get out this way. He held the Iron Cross 1st class and the close combat badge, but instead of being promoted to Captain, he later gave himself up with a small group of our men. Well, I wasn't there; I had swum across. There must have been other officers who broke under these conditions. This probably wasn't the only case; otherwise, we would not have had to experience this shameful retreat, this defenseless, chaotic flight, which strictly speaking, no officer should have allowed himself to survive. Perhaps Wolf was in a similar situation and took the burden upon himself, and thereby spared many other German families the pain that we must now accept and let influence our lives in a positive manner. Now with me, I still feel a painful wound whenever I think of Wolf, but I also gladly remember him for he is always a bright star in my dreams, filling me with his gentle light.

Earlier I received a letter from Heidi and your letter #26 from 29 November, and I thank you. Dear Father, you write that Wolf should have better protected himself by transferring to a heavy battery or staff headquarters. But for someone who believed in victory, who did not feel himself pressured, who was young and did not believe himself to be fully tested, how could he have—without disappointing himself—not actively put himself where the greatest danger was? For him, that was the basis of self-confidence and strength, and always had been. But it is pointless to wonder about this and that and to try and analyze it. Each man does what he must, and from my point of view, Wolfgang was already a complete person who impressed me even though I had been allowed to see the weaker side of him. But we need to let it all rest.

7 December 1944

Dear Parents,

I still haven't mailed off my Christmas post, but I must thank you for your package from Flinsberg. In all seriousness, with the way things are here, one can hardly wait to open packages. The front is completely quiet, although we have had to anticipate a heavy attack by the Russians for the past month and a half. Now they say that Ivan is waiting for a hard freeze so that he can use his tanks unhindered. I have already opened your Christmas package and with all spiritual respect, sampled some of the sweets. The small book of Angelus Silesius really did it. What is not in it? So much wisdom. A single page filled my entire soul, which was so often desolate and empty since Wolf's death, but no longer. Since then, I have hungered for such food, that which will console me, support me, and strengthen me. Is it that way with you now? It is far better to read than to quietly brood and give oneself over to dark thoughts. True, the old proverb: The wise seek after only one thing and that is the highest good. The fool seeks for the man and the small. I thank you so much. Please know how much value there is for me in this 20-page book. Angelus Silesius will certainly help me express how I believe when it comes to God and the last things, and in this, Mother and I are so similar. But dear Mother, I could never so quickly dismiss matters as you could with your articulate manner and understanding. I never had that ability nor the wide choice of maxims at my command, as you have. That is mostly because I always had a certain reluctance and hesitancy when it comes to Christianity or the Church, which is still not completely clear to me. But that, I will leave to itself. Even so, in all that I do, I place a great value on the Christian perspective and always try to bring my world perspective and that of Christianity into harmony. Dear Mother, don't be angry and do not worry that I haven't really answered you, and perhaps will never be able to. I know from experience that for all the matters that you have alluded to, I will find a resolution. It may be unconscious, but if so, then it will be all the more certain.

Friedrich Deml, I have already read. A true pleasure and even in the sketch, already attractive and charming. But can one get the necessary funds for the basic elements? I thank you deeply for Father's postcard. Unfortunately, I haven't had the chance to look at it more closely because of the lack of light here. You sent me an impressive package of cookies, so it must be Christmas. And I won't say anything about who needs them the most and who gets them the least. I will simply thank you for them and thanks also to the dear benefactors—the aunts, in particular. Now I need to go fetch our rations and take this letter with me. I send you my greetings.

Your Reiner

8 December 1944

Dear Parents,

This evening I was once again pulled back from the front-line trenches and am now back at the company, which lies to the rear in reserve. And I will use this first night that I don't have to stand out in the cold to get my rather meager Christmas package sent off. I could have had more to send but in the present situation where we had to constantly reckon on an offensive, I didn't store up much, although we were given more to smoke than we needed. What I didn't smoke, I shared at the front, and then the rest I divided with the company today, with favors exchanged for a few cigars. I can now give you the happy message that Father's letter to the company commander seems to have been fruitful so that now I can at least turn in a request for a leave. They say it's almost certain that one can leave. It's a question of when. If there is no fighting going on, then it could be the beginning of January. And that's enough for today. I can only quickly wish you a Christmas blessed by beautiful and happy memories (of which I need not mention) and that the love of so many good and true people will help you over all the difficult paths and make this Christmas a fest of peace in which you find comfort in one another and find peace in your soul again. I have yet to write my actual Christmas letter. So, in this spirit, I send you and the dear aunts my greetings and hope that we will see each other soon after Christmas.

Your Reiner

9 December 1944

Dear Parents,

Briefly, two bits of good news:

1. Father's letter to the company commander has succeeded. Today I can hand in a request for a leave and that is half the battle. Unfortunately, I won't be able to leave until after Christmas.

2. I am off the front-line trenches again and back with the company where it is always quiet. Only one squad is sent up to the front. I was only temporarily assigned to the squad because I couldn't dig ditches because of the shell fragments in me. So now it's back to instructing. I would just as soon have remained up front, but I know you would rather I were not. Anyway, a change is always good. Back at the company, the bunkers are first rate, and it's good to be able to stand in the open and enjoy the fall weather and have the landscape in front of you instead of the trench wall, and to be listening to the rustling of the trees instead of to detonations. I thank you heartily for your many letters and send my greetings.

Your Reiner

10 December 1944

Dear Parents,

Today I received mail from you with the date of Wolfgang's birthday, and I thank you for it. You write almost every day. I would write every day too if only I had peace and quiet around here. In the trenches up front, I can usually sit alone and write while the others sleep. Back here in the rear area, either everyone is sleeping or up moving around, which takes away any quiet time that we have left. That's a great drawback compared to life up in the front trenches. I no longer have the peace and quiet to think about Wolfgang. We are up at 6.30 a.m., then we have twenty minutes of exercise. From 8.00 a.m.–11.00 a.m. we have field exercises just like in the barracks. Then we clean our weapons until 1.00 p.m., and then more instruction. Then from 2.30 p.m. on there is always something to do until twilight. But then we have the long nights, and each man only has two hours of sentry duty. We certainly have more comfortable quarters here, and more opportunity to keep ourselves clean. But those are just formalities that one would gladly forgo.

Gradually I am starting to work on a prospective leave. I have the feeling I might be able to clinch it before Christmas. The man in line for a leave before me has been transferred, and so our company won't be issuing his leave. I submitted my request on the 9th. If it is approved, I still have to wait until the man who went to Düsseldorf on bomb leave returns. He's the gardener I spent so much time with on sentry duty and told him so much about home. Perhaps then I'll be able to celebrate Christmas with you, and maybe Heidi and Lütte will come to Flinsberg. Then after Flinsberg, I could immediately continue on to Cologne. But whether it would be easy to get there is highly questionable.

I've been thinking about putting together a photo album from Wolf's Italian pictures, if you have the materials for it or could get them somewhere. Böhm put together a type of illustrated biography of his sons that showed all the important episodes of their childhood and youth with existing examples of what they had written between the photos. If you have time in Flinsberg, it could be a welcomed and comforting endeavor to put something like this together, which we children could then expand and complete from our viewpoint. Certainly, the various diaries that Wolf so diligently kept still exist. With all that, and perhaps with some clarification from us, as well as the collection of photos of Wolf's life, the photo album would be a testimony to his life and industriousness. With something like this, a person would not believe that he simply comes to an end, or that he suddenly no longer exists. It would give our children an understanding, a sense of respect, and perhaps with love a certain longing that these people were still here. Wolfgang certainly wouldn't have anything against it. Perhaps just an indulging smile at those of us still clinging to this earthly life and admonishing us, saying that it would be more fruitful to concern ourselves with our own future. And we will. But it is from just such a book of memories that new inspirations will arise.

Anyway, the situation here is supposed to remain quiet, so I don't think we need to fear that anything here will interfere with our reunion. But let's not get our hopes up too high so that we are disappointed later. And with that, I will finish for today. I send my greetings to you and the aunts.

From your Reiner son. (The quota for military leaves is supposed to be set at four and a half percent.)

15 December 1944

Dear Parents,

This will be my Christmas letter, which unfortunately will have to begin with the sad news that my request for a leave has been denied, and you will have to celebrate Christmas without me. I really wish that I could have had different news for you in this Christmas letter. Now we must try to accept things as they are. There is nothing else I can do except wish you in writing what I wanted to wish you in person, that you will find peace with the world and will be open to its better side so that joy can find a place in your lives. It is easy for me to say, for I am still young and healthy. But that doesn't necessarily lead to anything good if your physical well-being does not go hand-in-hand with spiritual well-being. So be reasonable and make an attempt, for despite all our setbacks, we must be fresh and strong when the war ends or we will not be able to manage the struggle for our continued existence. When I think about last Christmas, and how I wasn't feeling that great—I had no reason for that back then. But when I opened your packages Christmas Eve, with the various Christmas letters, they warmed my heart and I saw things differently and hurried back to the barracks under a clear night sky. But there, once again that heavy mantel of musty atmosphere descended upon me both spiritually and physically, for at the time I was still suffering from the shell fragments inside me. I often had to turn trifling matters into major things in order just to get myself to do them. In many respects, I find myself in a better situation this Christmas because physically I am doing well. In addition, we have a small but nice bunker of six men. Yesterday we got the first prize in the bunker competition. Our bunker is completely decorated with evergreen branches and juniper. Above the table hangs an Advent wreath, and on the table stands a candleholder with the red candle that Heidi sent me and by whose light I can write during my two hours on duty. In front of me lies Father's card with the quote '*Auf Erden die eines guten Willens sind*' ['On earth are those of good will'], which is unfamiliar to me but beautiful and clear, and just as beautiful and clear and simple in its printing and design. To me, good will is where love is, and peace. And for the honor of God, one can also say the reverse. And war is not for honoring God, especially in today's form.

Our first prize in the bunker competition consisted of a bottle of wartime *Steinhäger*. In addition, yesterday we received a bottle and a half of *Kirschwasser*, which unfortunately we drank up in turns. That is what's called comradery, and one must take part. That's why I couldn't write to you yesterday as I had intended, and today it wasn't my turn. We have so little space at our table that only two men at the most can sit there and write. Also it's not as quiet here as up at the front in the trenches when those who are off duty are sleeping. It's nice that I have two candles from you so that at night I can write undisturbed without using up the squad's lamp, which if I did, we would have to fill up with frostbite salve, shoe polish, or gun oil. Two days ago, it finally turned cold and windy here. Soon everything will be white with snow as it probably has been for a while where you are. We have already been taken off duty. Instead, we are building a couple of bunkers for the battalion. That is not so bad.

Now I will close so that I can get some sleep in the tiny bed that I have to give up every few days because it's too short for me. This Christmas let us remember our beloved Wolf, quietly and without pain. Every evening I look for the star that so comforted me with its light on the day I received the bad news. Have a reflective Christmas Eve with the aunts and hopefully also with Heidi and Lütte. I hope you all can have time together. I send them all my greetings, and also my greetings to you.

From your Reiner son.

18 December 1944

Dear Parents,

Today I received a letter with newspapers, a small package, and a telegram from you. The day before yesterday, I got your letter #31 and the card from Koblenz of 3 November. I am most grateful for the blessing of mail. I have also recently received some things from Heidi: copies of Wolfgang's last letters and two small books among which were *Vom Grossen Abendmahl* and other war poetry by Walter Flex,[34] actually intended for Wolfgang. Now I receive so many things that could have gone to Wolfgang that sometimes the feeling creeps up on me that I am better provided for because he is gone. As crazy as it may sound, it is as if he had lived his life for me even though, and I always admitted it, he was the more important one, the greater personality, more disciplined, goal-oriented, conscientious than I. That was never a problem for me. But now the words of Walter Flex, Rudolf Binding, and others qualified to speak have a great effect on me. In my own words: without any over-glorification it can be said that those who have fallen are the best of the German people. But they do not fall for a victorious outcome of the war. They fall for the purging and purification of mankind. Through their death and our pain the true worth of a people will be raised up so that it will not be that the best have fallen but rather that they have multiplied. The masses will once again be aware of their natural origin, and there will arise a new, more respectful, more honest, uncorrupted sense of purpose that is sound and powerful enough to fill the gaps of the fallen, to take over their task and bring it all to a good end.

But enough of this.

As I wrote that, the hours passed away. Something like that you cannot write quickly and without reflection. You need time and to be alone. Often while writing, my mind wanders. I really need to use the precious quiet time I have more productively.

Your telegram came directly to me and shortly thereafter, I took it to our commander. Since nothing has factually changed, I doubt if 'The Telegram'[35] will be enough. Nevertheless, I will try everything I can.

And now to your letter, Father. '*Raube das Licht aus dem Rachen der Schlange*'.[36] This saying is at first applicable to the theme. It sounds somewhat pretentious. I would almost say it's rather like one of Mother's mottos the likes of which Heidi and I have inherited from her. But the passage is also so encompassing and abstract that it can hardly be comprehended directly. Easier it is just to think of Mother's natural ability to find the best in any situation.

Otherwise, things are still going well for me here. I only suffer from a lack of peace and quiet, for time to reflect on things and think. I had been somewhat spoiled in this respect. Otherwise, it would have been more difficult to accept Wolfgang's death. I had the soft glow of memories to help. Now I have bad dreams, and against all reason, crazy, grotesque thoughts of death. I have no more time to think and reflect in peace. Therefore, I am almost happy that tomorrow we will be relieving another company at the front. The training is finished. For the past few days, we've been digging ditches, but only during the day and with two hours rest at noon.

Now it's time for bed. Therefore, I leave you with my warm greetings from your Reiner son.

Send my thanks to the aunts and my greetings to Heidi and Lütte, who, I hope, are with you now. Also to Uncle Fritz and the Breslauer Schneider family.[37]

Final Preparations

By any objective analysis, the German military situation was beyond hopeless; it had reached the level of absurd. Although both fronts had stabilized and entered a period of relative calm, it was only a pause before the inevitable final offensive on both fronts, which would crush Germany. Caught between two massive forces, Germany could either sit on the defensive, where it was, and wait to be destroyed at a time of its opponents' choosing, or it could seek to shape its own fate and attempt some dramatic action that might change its fortunes. The Allied demands of unconditional surrender meant that surrender was no option at all. No military, as long as it possesses any means of resistance (no matter how meager), can deliver the people it is sworn to protect unconditionally into the hands of its enemies.

Because of the stabilization of both fronts during the autumn, Hitler, always predisposed to attack, decided to go on the offensive as soon as possible. The relative lull gave the Germans the chance to build up a force to achieve that end. The Panzer divisions destroyed in Normandy were rebuilt and refitted; new divisions were created from the last scrapings of the manpower barrel until a force of some twenty-five divisions, with 240,000 men, 2,000 guns, and 700 tanks, was ready to strike the enemy. But where? Thrown against the east, even such an impressive force as that could have achieved little more than a local success, gaining ground that could not be held. Numbers such as these would make little impression on the vastness of the Eastern Front. So the decision was made to strike in the west, to break through the Allied lines in the Ardennes, race northwest, seize the strategic port of Antwerp, and drive a wedge between British and the Canadian armies in the north and the Americans in the south. Who knew, perhaps they could force another Dunkirk on the British—or so Hitler fantasized. More sober military minds were thinking in a less grandiose fashion, believing that at most they might inflict heavy casualties on the Anglo-American forces and thereby disrupt and delay their final drive into Germany. Then, hopefully, these forces could be sent in time to the east to counter the expected Russian offensive. This hope was based on the assumption that the Russian attack would not begin before mid-January, when the ground had sufficiently frozen to support heavy traffic (which was always a consideration in the east). Unfortunately, this strategy meant that the German forces in the east would be starved of the badly needed reinforcements and equipment and would simply have to somehow get by on their own until then.

After the war, serious discussions would arise concerning German military decisions during this campaign, but the truth is that considering the great imbalance of the opposing forces, any decision the Führer, OKW, or even the generals made in the field would inevitably prove to be the wrong one. The disparity of numbers in the east dwarfed that of the west. For their offensives, the Soviets had amassed a force totaling 6,298,000 men; 15,100 tanks and self-propelled guns; 91,400 pieces of artillery; and 14,500 aircraft. Opposing them were only 700,000 German soldiers. The German Command was correct in its assessment that the Russians possessed a superiority of eleven to one in infantry, seven to one in armored vehicles, and twenty to one in artillery. Hitler angrily rejected this assessment, dismissing such numbers as the greatest bluff since Genghis Khan. Chief of Staff Heinz Guderian's remark was by far the more accurate—the Eastern Front would collapse like a house of cards.[38]

The situation in the Warka Bridgehead was reflective of the overall conditions on the Eastern Front. For their breakthrough offensive there, the Russians had amassed 400,000 men; 8,700 guns and mortars (250 per kilometer); and 1,700 tanks and self-propelled guns into the 240-square-kilometer area. It was no bluff. The 9th German Army was aware of the massive force arrayed against them in the Warka; in some respects, they had actually underestimated the Soviet strength, giving them only 800 tanks and 3,000 artillery pieces. To oppose this force, the Germans still had only the three infantry and two Panzer divisions with which it had first deployed in the Warka. In the early years of the war, three infantry and two Panzer divisions would have represented a powerful and effective force of some 80,000 men and 300–400 tanks, but in this fifth year of the war, German divisions were mere shadows of their former selves. In 1939, the regulation strength of a German infantry division had been 16,977 officers and men. After the first winter in Russia, it became impossible to maintain the divisions anywhere near their required strength; replacements simply could not keep up with casualties. In addition, Hitler preferred to raise entirely new divisions, thus diverting the ever-dwindling supply of manpower away from the older divisions, which were left to wither away.

By necessity, many regiments were forced by casualties to dissolve one of their three battalions just to be able to maintain the other two at an effective level (the 58th Regiment had done so in July 1942). Finally, bowing to reality, the Wehrmacht introduced the Type 44 Infantry Division with a required strength of only 12,000 officers and men, but even this lowered number was illusory as few divisions could reach or maintain it. The three infantry divisions deployed in the Warka numbered only about 7,000 men each. Rifle companies averaged eighty men (instead of 150–200), and battalions numbered some 350 men (instead of 800). Reiner's regiment, the 58th, the proud tradition bearer of the old imperial regiments—*Prinz Friedrich der Niederlande*, *Graf Barfuss*, and the 7th Battalion of Westphalian *Jägers*—which had marched into Russia, 3,000 strong, on 22 June 1941, now deployed a mere 750 officers and men in the Warka Bridgehead.

Even the Panzer divisions, those elite strike forces of the Wehrmacht, had fared little better than their brothers in the infantry. Their regulation strength had likewise been reduced in 1944 from 14,000 to 12,000 men and 150 tanks. However, this was the end of 1944, and the two Panzer divisions allotted to the defense of the Warka possessed a mere fifty tanks apiece.

Not only were the German divisions short on manpower, but they were also lacking in essential weapons—artillery, anti-tank, anti-aircraft, and communication equipment. The 6th *Infanterie* Division had been sent off to the

Warka without a *Panzerjäger-Abteilung* (anti-tank battalion) with its anti-tank guns. Instead, it was given forty-eight *Panzerschrecks* (shoulder-fired, anti-tank rocket launchers)—an effective weapon, to be sure, but hardly an adequate substitute for the deadly 75-mm and 88-mm anti-tank guns.

Constant requests (or rather pleas) for more of *anything* eventually produced some results, but it was a rather hodgepodge collection of whatever could be scraped up:

A *Nebelwerfer* regiment of some sixteen rocket launchers (160 mm and 320 mm)
Two heavy mortar batteries (210 mm) with four guns
A platoon of heavy anti-tank guns
A platoon of 20-mm anti-aircraft guns
A battery of heavy *Feldkanone* (170 mm)
And several light *Feldhaubitze* (105 mm).

The most important reinforcement was the arrival of a *Sturmgeschütz* brigade of three companies (fifty *Stugs*[39]) under the command of Major Kapp. They would play a critical role during the Russian offensive.

However, even with these efforts to strengthen the defense of the Warka, a comparison of the opposing forces still presented a rather grim picture.

	German	Soviet
Men	35,000	400,000
Tanks	100	1,700
Artillery	200	8,700

With these inadequate forces, the German soldier was expected to resist the Russian onslaught. Although *Generalmajor* Brücker expressed himself as confident that his division could fulfill the mission assigned it, the idea that these forces could have been anything more than a 'speed-bump' to the Russian steamroller on its way to Berlin is essentially a case of professional optimism on steroids.

Reiner and his comrades could do little but continue their front-line existence, bailing out their trenches, maintaining the night watches, writing letters home, enjoying the Christmas packages from family and Führer, and waiting for the inevitable Russian offensive.

21 December 1944

Dear Parents,

Instead of being home with you at Christmas, I am once again crawling through trenches, so different from two weeks ago. We are also in a different sector. At first, the conditions here appeared rather hopeless. But one has to get used to them. The bunkers are only 1.30–1.50 meters deep[40] at the most and can only be heated at night. Smoke from fires during the day would give away our positions. The beds are short and only shoulder-wide and stacked over one another. Turning over in bed is impossible. The fireplaces in the walls are half collapsed and smoky. Mice are everywhere. Connecting trenches are hip deep and across the way—snipers. There are landmines behind us, but none in front. Neighboring positions to the right and left are hardly visible. Mood: gallows humor. Weather: frost, even during the day, sometimes windy, but no snow. The ground is frozen too hard for any digging. Consequently, my future letters will be short, hopefully not too seldom. I have no idea how we'll manage to sleep here. There is one advantage here: at the front, one actually feels a bit freer. Once again you have the opportunity to think and to imagine yourself in more pleasant surroundings. Then, nothing else matters.

For your last post, the newspaper, the aunts' traditional chocolate.[41] I thank you most heartily. I am enclosing two package stamps. If you can, please send me some salt. Send it in a practical, substantial box or other container. We could also use some sweetener, but sugar is not practical. It gets too dirty during storage. Please excuse my cold practicality, but at the moment, I'm not capable of anything else. I wish you, the aunts, and the entire family a less difficult and perhaps a peace-bringing 1945. Sorry my greetings are so short and concise, but you surely understand. So, greetings from your Reiner.

We had a demanding night last night.

23 December 1944

Dear Parents,

First, I have to make myself some room in order to write. The CO wants to visit all the bunkers and have a little Christmas celebration in each one. Therefore, we've put up our small Christmas tree on our small corner table and hung some decorations. Father's '*Ehre Sei Gott*' ['Honor be to God'] is displayed next to the unavoidable motto of the Infantry, '*Die Treue ist das Mark der Ehre*' ['Loyalty is the essence of honor']. Anyway, these two mottos stand next to each other, agreeing less in their execution than in their level of validity. They are so different in their nature, almost contrary, that choosing or even preferring one or the other demands that one make a sharp distinction. Considering all circumstances, it seems to me that one should just drop the soldier's motto, for it is so unsound and false. Why it should be used as a Christmas'decoration, I don't understand as well as I understand the decorations on the Christmas table. There are things: three impressive bottles of Steinhäger, partly filled with 'peace-time' [pre-war quality] Steinhäger and partly with 'war-time' Ei-liquor. Also, a bar of chocolate of modest—certainly not *Flinsberger*—quality, and a Christmas *Stollen* baked by the company cook, which earlier had been wrapped in cellophane just as it would have been in any bakery. Everything was in it, eggs, butter, sugar. Each of us also received a 'close-combat' package of forty-eight German cigarettes, a half-pound sausage, and a couple of handfuls of spice cookies. These were intentionally sent up so we could begin celebrating Christmas.

Today your letter #32 arrived, for which I am most thankful. Because of your telegram, the company commander let me submit a request for leave. However, he told me that was probably pointless as two other similar requests for similar reasons (bomb damage at the parents' home of one of the unmarried men in our group) had been rejected by the regiment. Consequently, I withdrew the request.

Be thankful and send my greetings to the aunts and sisters from their Reiner who right now has to clean the machine gun. Hopefully more soon.

25 December 1944

Dear Parents,

Such is Christmas Eve on the front. Both sides are nervous and suspect that the other might use the holiday to gain a cheap advantage with a sudden trench raid. Here you must always be on your guard. If you let your thoughts wander, you can find yourself quickly destroyed by a sudden artillery attack. Those who suffer the most are the infantry in the trenches who swear that the firing of our artillery only causes the Russians to fire on them. That's how it was yesterday evening at least. Tonight at midnight, it's much quieter because the bright moonlight makes the whole battle area clearly visible. But in a half-hour, the moon will be gone and then maybe all hell will break loose again.

Now it's the first day of Christmas. Your letter #33 of last Sunday arrived today wit' our meal. Thanks for writing. I hope that things have worked out well with Heidi and Lütte and that the four of you and the aunts can sit around the Christmas tree that you have surely obtained by now. Here we have three Christmas trees: two made from packages and paper from home and one real tree some 40 cm tall. This one will only be placed on the table when the officers come by like yesterday when the company commander came by and joined us in an unskilled singing of '*Stille Nacht*' and '*O, Tannenbaum*', or tonight when the regimental commander[42] visited our position. As he came through our trench, he was wearing a white fur hat that I honestly thought was part of a Santa Claus outfit, and I couldn't help but laugh when he asked me who from the company would be playing Santa Claus. He laughed as well, and clapped me fatherly on the shoulder and told me the *Unteroffiziere* would be bringing up a chocolate bar for each of us. His adjutant was rather less amused and later explained that the commander always wore a fur hat in winter. I wasn't too concerned. Later while on sentry duty, I had a discussion about Christmas songs with a comrade, a fellow from the Black Forest. I said that in our family that our favorite was '*Grünet Felder, Grünet Wiesen*'. As we sang '*Gelobet seiest du, Jesus Christ*', I remembered how we sang it at matins in the Brüderkirche in Kassel with the organ playing and the entire congregation singing, and how it echoed in the high vaulted ceiling of the church. And afterward, there were still three hours before the streetcar ran and we strolled along the streets all decorated for Christmas and passed all the shop windows of the stores. That's how it once was, but that was fifteen years ago.

29 December 1944

Now begins the third day of Christmas. Ivan has remained quiet. Only our commander was anxious and ordered patrols to be active all night. Consequently, we got no sleep. But as before, it came to nothing. Washing, shaving, and celebrating Christmas in platoons and squads seem to have come before writing letters even though with me I felt it urgent to send you and my sisters and everyone my Christmas wishes and thoughts and to thank you for yours. Yesterday I received another letter from Heidi with two beautiful Christmas cards and the oft-discussed reading notebook. The day before yesterday, I received a nice letter from Lütte. I've really been well provided and lack for little. As for sweets, cookies, and beverages, we were surprisingly well looked after. In addition to the Christmas *Stollen*, there was also streusel cake, a 20 cm by 30 cm square per man, twenty apple strudels, one and a half liters of schnapps, which around here we call *Ratschbum*.[43] The leadership, it would seem, tried to give us all that we would normally have for Christmas. What they couldn't give us is a peaceful Christmas at home with our loved ones. Pardon me for writing so officially, but I'm writing this letter between two night-sentry duties. To the left and right of our sector is constant fighting.[44] I would like to go in and warm myself up. I need to close this letter or it won't make the evening mail.

The weather is not too cold here, nor is there any snow. Even our feet are no longer cold. In the past few days, we've been issued felt boots. Gradually we are getting used to eating bread again instead of cakes, cookies, and sweets. My issue of sausage for the past five days is still outside in the cold so that it won't spoil. I would like to have wished you all such an abundant Christmas as we had even if during these times the stillness of Christmas can grow heavy. To write such things takes time and concentration, neither of which I have at the moment.

I send you again my greetings and thanks.

Your Reiner

30 December 1944

Dear Parents,

Yesterday the birthday letter that I sent Wolfgang was returned with a note announcing his hero's death. I am sending the letter along with this one in case you would want to keep it.

31 December 1944

In celebration of the last day of the year, I washed, shaved, and even combed my hair, all without my unbreakable mirror, using only the sense of touch. Around here we often say, 'Why wear a helmet if you get shot in the stomach?' In the same manner, why have a mirror if you have no light. I have a little time before I go on sentry duty. I want to thank you for the simple letter of Christmas Eve. No matter how much suffering the Angel of War brings, he is bound like brother and sister with the Angel of Annunciation, and in the end, both give more than they take for they bring us all closer to God, the saved and those seeking salvation. War is a law of nature and only an apparent contradiction of it. The harmony will not be destroyed, the eternal cycle will not be pulled apart but rather it will be confirmed, made stronger, and pulled closer around the Highest, as with all the unfathomable laws of nature. They say that Christmas is a fest of love, and to give that impression that is what people speak of. In war, one does not need that external impression. The war reveals to us here what the Angel of Annunciation reveals to other people, what will be in this world as well as in the eternal kingdom of God. At Christmas, one can think about eternal and worldly things, about God, nature, man and his work, and about the individual self. In each of us is the other preserved.

Father I thank you for all your woodcuts and the writing of good words and wishes. And we must thank Wolfgang and always think of him and all that he did for us.

I must close now and send you all heartfelt greetings from your cheerful Reiner.

Final Decisions

At this late stage in the war, much of the German military planning at both the strategic and operational level was characterized by compromise and hope. With ever-shrinking resources, the Germans had to make compromising choices between one alternative and the other and then hope that the God of War would favor them with good luck in battle. Nowhere is this more evident than in the German plans to defend the Warka Bridgehead.

The first decision that had to be made was the actual deployment of the three infantry divisions. From bitter experience, the Germans had learned to appreciate the Russians' ability to amass incredible amounts of artillery for an offensive and the destructive fire it could bring down on defensive positions—often to the extent of the elimination of a quarter to a third of the soldiers deployed there. To counter this, the Germans had often resorted to the tactic of evacuating the front lines just before the expected attack and then occupying a new, previously constructed front line outside the range of the preliminary Russian barrage (some 10 km), sparing their troops from its destructive effects. The hurricane of fire would all be wasted on deserted trenches, and the Russian assault troops would find themselves punching an empty sack. It would then take the Russians another one to two weeks to bring their artillery forward to within range of the new German front line and to re-emplace and re-register the guns.

However, it was decided that in the Warka, the German infantry would not be pulled back to safety. They would remain in position and ride out the storm of steel the best they could. With good luck, perhaps enough of them might survive to mount a viable defense. This decision not to evacuate the troops was made on the basis that any such withdrawal would do nothing more than put off the inevitable Russian attack for a week or two. Additionally, the front-line officers and men expressed both a confidence in the protective qualities of their fortifications and a preference to conduct the battle on ground with which they were intimately familiar rather than some new position somewhere else. They would fight in the Warka.

As previously mentioned, the defense structure was one of 'Defense in Depth', with defensive emplacements extending from the HKL all the way back to the supporting artillery. Rather than a series of trenches, there were strong points utilizing all arms (mortars, anti-tank, and machine guns) scattered throughout the entire battle zone with well-concealed flanking machine-gun posts. When the Russian assault troops entered the battle zone, they would find themselves in a 'kill box', with fire coming at them from all points of the compass. The intent of such a defensive arrangement was not to prevent a breakthrough *per se*, but to ensure that the Russian advance was scattered and uneven. Russian troops who had somehow managed to fight through the battle zone and emerge on the other side would most likely be isolated groups of men from various units, lacking any coordinated command and control and thereby highly vulnerable to the counter-attacking German Panzers and *Sturmgeschütze*.

The next decision demanding attention concerned the tactical deployment of the two Panzer divisions at their disposal, with their limited number of tanks. There were two options, either of which would have serious consequences if it turned out to be wrong for the developing battlefield conditions. One option involved keeping the Panzer divisions well back from the battle zone, thus giving them time and space to best assess the direction and threat of a Russian breakthrough and how best to counter it with their meager forces. The danger involved with this option was that the Russians would also have time and space to strengthen and consolidate their breakthrough, gain momentum, and thereby become unstoppable. This tactic of holding the Panzer well back from the front had been employed in Normandy with disastrous results for the Germans.

The other option was to deploy the Panzer divisions close to the battle zone so as to be immediately available to smash any breakthrough, drive into the battle zone itself, and seek to re-establish the German line by linking up with whatever infantry units had survived and were still holding their position. Likewise, this option had its dangers. The armored forces could well end up caught in the fighting in the battle zone, lose their ability to maneuver effectively, and be unavailable to counter a more threatening Soviet thrust elsewhere. They could be caught up in a flood of retreating troops, unable to reach the battle zone.

The second option was adopted; the Panzer forces were kept close to the front. With their limited number of tanks, they probably could not deal a serious blow to a Russian advance once it had gained strength and momentum.

The final decision involved how best to employ the artillery. Here, again, the German command was dealing with limited resources. Not only was there an inadequate number of guns *vis-a-vis* what the Soviets could bring to bear, but there was also a critical shortage of ammunition. The normal daily allotment of ammunition for an artillery piece was termed an *Ausstattung* (225 rounds for a light howitzer, 150 for a heavy howitzer). Considering the Russian force facing them, the Germans would like to have had at least two to three *Ausstattungen*. Despite all their efforts over the past months, they had not been able to stockpile even one *Ausstattung*. A debate naturally arose about how this limited supply could be used most effectively. Some argued that the bulk of the supply should be used for a heavy, pre-dawn, preemptive bombardment of the densely packed jumping-off positions of the Russian assault forces, causing massive casualties and disrupting the attack. Others (particularly the artillery) argued that the limited supply of ammunition should be reserved for direct observable fire during the attack itself. The decision was made to compromise, with one third of the available ammunition to be used in the pre-dawn bombardment and the remaining two thirds for direct fire during the Russian assault. This proved to be the wrong decision, and it would have disastrous results.

1 January 1945

Dear Parents,

The New Year has just begun, and it has immediately greeted us with an exchange of fire. At the blast of our CO's whistle, the game took off. Every machine gun and heavy weapon had received its full allotment of ammo. The machine gun fired without jamming, as always. Only after 150 rounds did we have to change barrels, but I burned my hand so badly that I can barely write. Shortly thereafter Ivan sent us his greetings, and we now had to run for our foxholes. Now everything is quiet as before. Again, we received Steinhäger and wine for New Year's. Also, the mail came. From you and the aunts came the newspaper from December 24th, and from Heidi came a small package of cakes, a candle and tin candleholder, and two pieces of Flinsberger chocolate. I'm certain that was her share of the Christmas chocolate. That's the way she is.

Today I even have the chance to write during the day. The Sergeant was out traveling all night and is now passed out drunk in a bunk instead of claiming the table for himself. Because of this, we were able to get more sleep than normal and so are able to stay up longer during the day and write letters. You have probably noticed that my letters have become shorter and are more rare. A couple of days ago I sent you a package. I also sent one around 10 December. I packed them rather quickly and so there is no letter in them. In the first are two photos of me taken by a member of the *Propagandakompanie* when a nurse[45] from the NSV visited our position and distributed *Liebesgaben*.[46] One photo is for you and one for Heidi. The other things are for whoever needs them. They're just some small things mostly of no great use, things we get at the commissary, but the sooner I send them off the less I have to carry around.

I showed Father's Christmas woodcut to the CO and he was so impressed that he took it around so that others could see it. That really pleased me, as it should you also, Father. Recently the CO sent me up a small collection of Hölderlin poems. He had it lying around and didn't know what to do with it. I'm in the position now that I feel I can talk with the other men about how I feel and what touches me. Before, that was impossible without being regarded as somewhat strange. I haven't changed any. War has that effect on people. Suffering brings love; love brings truth, and both bring a certain contentment to people. Whenever we hear Ivan singing folksongs across the way, we wonder how we can be shooting at each other. And always one of our men comes up with the idea to sing out an old Russian folksong to see if Ivan is in the mood for a sing along.

Yesterday I received your letters of 27 December. In one of them were four pictures of Wolfgang for which I thank you, and especially Lütte. Each picture shows his face in a different expression. One in his impressive, laid-back, 'don't give a damn' attitude; one smiling; in another his features are composed, earnest, concentrating on some task; and finally one where having business to attend to, he is showing impatience with the photographer. But in all of them, he is reserved, interested, composed, relaxed, the visible and invisible qualities that gave him so much success in life.

Thanks so much and I send greetings.

Your Reiner

4 January 1945

Dear Parents,

Yesterday Mother's letter with the fifth picture of Wolfgang arrived. Also yesterday, one month after Wolfgang's birthday, which was made gloomy by the still recent news of his death, I was informed I would receive the Iron Cross 1st Class due to recommendations and testimonies concerning the retreat of the 6th *Infanterie* Division. I could report things that could just as easily have put me in front of a military court. I'm sure these things will be just as thoroughly investigated. Hopefully something more will come out of this, perhaps a leave. It is not impossible. Actually I'm a bit reluctant about the EK I [Iron Cross 1st]. From the one comes destruction and ruin, and from the other comes life and reward. Basically, I'll only accept it to avoid the uproar it would cause if I refused it. Has anyone ever gained anything honorably? It should only be awarded to those willing to sacrifice their life, not because they're lucky and others died. But then the awarding of medals could not be exploited; the State would gain nothing. Whether I deserve it or not, I cannot say. Others are even less qualified to judge because they were not there. I ought not to be ashamed to accept something that has some advantages. Even so, it's not right. It all comes down to the question of should one yield to the tangible rewards of the world or to the inner feelings, feelings that reject any decoration as a superfluous recognition of the world of idolatry and hypocrisy. My principle has been to do what you can to gain some position in this world so that you can be independent and go your own way undisturbed. And it pains me to think that out of conceit I would coldly walk away from the worthy tradition of the Iron Cross of 1813, but enough of this endless consideration.

It seems Mother is taking my situation here at the front too much to heart. First, one can get used to almost anything. Then, the fireplace in the bunker has been repaired and no longer smokes, the trenches have been dug deeper, and the whole position has been improved. The enemy snipers don't have any telescopic sights, so the company hasn't had a single casualty. In the shallow bunker, things are going all right. Though he is a veteran, the *Unteroffizier* [Sergeant], with whom I had an earlier collision, and I are getting along fine. I'm insightful enough not to question his calculations, and he is agreeable enough to listen carefully to my suggestions as to how best to use our time and limited space. We all have equal time to sleep now, write, or clean our weapons without being robbed of our freedom by some rigid system. Consequently, we are all in a better mood. Now things are done without anyone feeling that they are being ordered around. We even have a fifth person for sentry duty, so we are looking forward to a 'golden age' as long as no one messes up our system.

With the food, things are so good that we have over a week's supply outside in the cold and eight to ten loaves of bread in reserve. This is all because of all the food we got at Christmas and New Year's.

I send my best, best wishes to you and the aunts from your Reiner.

6 January 1945

Dear Parents,

Yesterday evening I received two packages from you. I approve of the one with the salt, but not the one with the sugar. Dear Mother, if you are going to go to so much trouble and effort, depriving yourselves of things you can hardly spare every time I happen to mention something I might like, then I'll have to stop mentioning anything at all. I am not like the Great Orator who constantly repeats the same thing. But I tell you now, we are fine here. I wish I could prove it to you if you don't believe it. If Father could see all the food and alcohol we have left from our Christmas and New Year's celebrations, he would put on a uniform himself. I feel like you think that I do not love you and that by sending me all these things you will bind me closer to you. If that's true, then you don't know me very well. It pains me to think that you are most unreasonably taking from your meager rations and sending them to your overfed son. If that's true, then I'll have to stop sending home any package stamps. If these are hard words, then take them for what they are: a reaction to something that is not reasonable. Now I've had to use up a letter preaching instead of telling you interesting things. The proof of how we are well off is being sent to you today. It is in the form of a container of cheese. It should last you at least two weeks. I still have six sausages and two tins of fish outside in the cold, and they are waiting for packing and mailing material.

For now, I send my greetings to the aunts, Uncle Fritz and the Breslauers, and especially to you from your Reiner.

7 January 1945

Dear Parents,

The package was forgotten yesterday, so it won't get off until today. In reading over the letter, I saw that it was rather unsympathetic and improper in its tone. If you can overlook the tyrannical tone, so common nowadays, then everything will be okay.

I have another package to send off in the next couple of days. It contains mostly old letters from November and December and from the summer, which didn't reach me during the retreat of the 6th Infantry Division. It occurs to me that in the last letter that Wolfgang received from me I used the 'historical pencil' that Aunt Grete gave me on my last leave. It was the last pencil from her father's supply. I used it to introduce the letter and continued writing with it. I don't think it had any influence on my writing though. However, if I use it up now, it means my children and grandchildren will never be able to write with it. It's like Father always said that every thought or action, no matter how incidental, will have an effect on the future. I should stop using this 10 cm long pencil, but I probably won't. Even so, as I use it I will have to think of what Father said.

I still have to clean the machine gun and go to bed. It's already 12.30 p.m. in the afternoon. At four, we have to get up again.

Warm greetings to you all from your Reiner.

                                                                9 January 1945

Dear Parents,

Yesterday I received three letters from 1 January 1945, and I thank you for them, especially to Lütte for her letter.

I think I might have given you a bit of a shock when I described our situation here. We are doing fine here, and as they say, things always seem worse than they are. As proof, we haven't had a single loss in our company. I am in a fairly decent position and with a squad whose morale is good, far different from the squad I was with at the front from 28 October to 8 December. We have a retired, professional soldier for a squad leader. He is good-natured and comes from Regensburg, therefore, from south Germany, which is the country of my choice. He is familiar with the new church built by Böhm. I'm sympathetic to the fact that he is completely devoted to his wife and writes her long letters every day. When he is with the squad, he keeps his drinking under control. An *Obergefreiter* with whom I often do sentry duty, is a typical Swabian with all the outward faults and internal qualities. One thinks of Michael Kohlhaas,[47] quiet, modest, outwardly taciturn, but solid, simple, diligent, and not to be diverted from his goals or task. He is interested in many things and considers himself a reformer and because of his interest in the modern world, his distant, Black Forest village regards him as a modernist. Of artistic beauty, he has little understanding. He looks at Father's work or Christmas cards and hands them back without comment. But he is a true, strong, rural character, determined, correct in his logic and his well-formed opinions. I have often joined him in philosophizing over the highest things and was pulled into his world. It was interesting to see how he sought deep inside himself to find the words to express his thoughts and feelings. That is how you get to know people in the Army where you seldom have the chance to know anyone. This is how I prefer to use my time to profit from it. We also have in the squad a shrewd, slick, merchant type from Cologne-Mühle.

In addition, there is a young, hopeless, childish, and rather dull fellow from Steinmetz, whom I would like to figure out when I have the opportunity. He comes from either an agricultural or hard-nosed business family in Steinmetz, and he always misbehaves. He feels like everyone is watching him, but if you can draw him out of his shell, he's not so obstinate or uninteresting.

With these comrades, we have built a good group, like the one I recently read about in *Fähnlein der Sieben Aufrechten* [by Gottfried Keller], in which we feel free to discuss things openly, even if we don't agree. We show each other respect and consideration. I am quite content with this group, as I am sure the others are.

Well, I must close now. I hope I can go on leave soon, perhaps around Mother's birthday. Three percent here have been released to go on leave. Then you will see your chubby-cheeked son again.

The weather here is mild and it often thaws during the day. We have no more than 5 cm of snow. We had reckoned on a cold winter, but so far not yet. Consequently, we don't have to freeze on sentry duty. The felt boots and winter clothing help a great deal. I send you my greetings and thank you for all your letters.

From your Reiner

12 January 1945

Dear Parents,

Both yesterday and the day before, I received your 39th and 40th letters, and I thank you for writing me. For the past couple days we have been enjoying a thaw and a mild east wind. Before it had only thawed during the day. The 5 cm of snow we had at Christmas has since disappeared. Consequently, we've had to reverse our winter uniforms so that the white side is on the inside. Due to the thaw, our trenches are starting to fall in. That adds more work. Up until now, we've not had a relentless, hard frost. All in all, it has been a short, mild winter—unless it gets a lot worse later.

Tonight I have table duty[48] all night, so I won't have to pull sentry duty. It's much better that way. One can write letters in peace or even finish reading short novels, which I especially enjoy. Also, I can preserve my precious oil lamp, which we've recently had to fuel with a variety of substances: shoe polish, gun oil, frostbite balm, skin lotion, and cooking oil from the canteen. We've found another fuel to use. It's brake fluid, which because of its color, is called 'Eierlikör' [egg-liqueur]. Such is the life of luxury we live here. At least in the bunker one can extinguish these reeking, smoldering, smoking, stinking, bunker-lamps and stare into the burning fire of a wall oven, deep in thought or perhaps not thinking at all. But one does that often enough on sentry duty. I've not had to use my lamp that often because I still have two and a half of the candles you sent in reserve.

Recently I've been thinking often about a possible, upcoming leave, but it has not come yet. The company commander assures me that when leaves come through, I'll be one of the first. He seems to think highly of me, as do my other superiors and comrades. Perhaps because I often make suggestions for improvements, which are always listened to and often adopted. It would be different if I were still a *Gefreiter* and a KOB and always had to be concerned about the opinions of others, dependent on them, and although it is contrary to nature to be completely independent from others, it doesn't hurt to be assertive and speak up for oneself. Even though we know that in this world one can't be anything, except through others. The civilian world is no better that the military in this respect. Angelus Silesius expressed it once: 'He who is substantial is worthy not only to enter into the better world, but able to apply the correct measures in this world and to understand the natural boundaries.'

Or not?

I'll close this letter for today and with you hope for a reunion soon. But sometimes it's best not to hope too much. I send you warm greetings from your Reiner son, brother, and nephew.

12 January 1945

Dear Heidi,

I haven't written to you in a long time even though one package after another arrived from you. I've been counting on your understanding and forgiving nature. There are so many things for which I have not yet thanked you. I want to thank you especially for all your thoughtful efforts and deeds. Though we conduct the war here morally, war often makes us indifferent to everyday decencies and kindnesses. And when I eat up the chocolate you received from the aunts, I do it so Ivan won't get it, even though I hate to think that you will have little yourself and deserve it no less than I. And then I think to hell with it, sending it back would just be more trouble than it's worth and storing it up would have no purpose, so it's 'Ok, Uncle Otto, down the hatch,' and it's gone. I know well that you love me, and it would sadden me if you thought you needed to prove it by sending me all these things. It doesn't make sense for you to send me things that you can hardly spare, but I'd be a real idiot to think that everything in the world is logical. Feelings operate on a far different plane than logic. One can express in a simple thank you far more than in a dozen pages of writing.

But enough of this. Let's talk about the weather. The weather is rather un-January-like and it doesn't even freeze at night. The little snow that we had, which didn't even completely cover the ground, has melted. But there is a strong, fast east wind from which we can expect cold weather. They talk again about us getting leave and that I am to get the Iron Cross I. The war goes on and the mood is bad, I mean the war-mood. Things with us though are good and we really can't complain. As far as rations go, I still have this eternal 'rubber sausage' (from its name you can well imagine its contents). It's lying outside and if I don't soon force those calories into my body, the sausage is going to start to stink in this mild weather. But while we're on the subject, have you already received a package from a certain Gdanitz family from the area around Danzig? The head of the house has often received all kinds of tobacco from me and is supposed to send a package of healthy farm produce to my home through Aken central post office. Have you received it and if so, what was it and how much? The boy seems to come from a decent, diligent family, even if he speaks Polish better than German. His sister looks a great deal like Maria Junghans [Heidi's best friend].

And what else is going on with us? Yesterday a member of a patrol was killed, hence my grim humor. I wasn't there on the spot because I am no longer KOB, but I watched from our position how the whole, shitty mess went down, all because Ivan thought we were up to something. He was a good man, and men like that will be missed after the war. We don't really know yet exactly what happened.

Mother sent me a copy of Rudolph's letter, and the parents sent me nine different pictures of Wolfgang. That was very nice.

I am becoming contemplative again. I should close now and crawl into bed. I send you all my greetings, and also to the Elmering family.

From your brother Reiner.

This letter to his sister Heidi was the last *Feldpost* Reiner wrote from the Warka. Sent back with ration carriers and post-marked on 14 January 1945, it must have been mailed just hours before the Russian offensive. However, in the chaos of the last months of the war, the letter did not reach Aken until 3 April 1945.

The Russian Offensive

After three and a half years on the Eastern Front, German Intelligence at division, corps, and Army levels had become quite adept at divining their enemy's intention. The same cannot be said of the Führer's headquarters. Analyzing the information derived from aerial reconnaissance, patrols, Russian prisoners, and from deserters, Army staff determined that the Russian offensive would begin at dawn on 14 January. In this assessment, they were dead right. At noon on 13 January, the two Panzer divisions—the 25th at Bialobrzegi and the 19th near Radom—were directed to begin moving up closer to the front. On the evening of the 13th, the officers and men on the front line were informed that they could expect the Russian attack at dawn the next day, after a one-hour preparatory bombardment. How well Reiner and his comrades slept that night one can only imagine.

At 4 a.m. on 14 January, the Day of Battle, the pre-dawn darkness of the Warka Bridgehead was suddenly illuminated by the German artillery. They opened up the pre-emptive barrage and brought down destruction on the known Russian jump-off positions. Though limited by plan, it must have caused heavy casualties among the Russian assault troops in their densely packed trenches. However, as *Generalmajor* Brücker lamented, it was not enough.

Two and a half hours later, at dawn, the 8,000 guns, mortars, and rocket launchers of the Russians erupted like a volcano and rained down on the German positions. It was far greater than anything the 6th *Infanterie* had experienced in five and a half years of war. Only some of the more senior officers, who as young soldiers had experienced the drumfire of the First World War, had anything with which to compare it.

The Russian barrage directed its main force upon the positions of Reiner's neighbors to the north, the 18th and 37th Regiments, though the 58th was not spared from its fury. The Russian fire was intense and extensive, hitting not only the HKL but covering the entire battle zone all the way back to divisional HQ in Bierwce (approximately 12 km).

The Germans had expected the usual Russian tactics of a one-hour barrage followed by a mass infantry and tank attack, but the Russians changed their tactics in the Warka and opted instead for the callous and unknown tactic of sending their assault companies forward into their own barrage. It was madness with a definite method. The Russian assault troops did not advance suicidally through their own fire, but rather followed carefully laid-out fire-free lanes. They penetrated deep into the battle zone and surprised the German troops still hunkering down in their bunkers, waiting for the fire to lift. This was a good plan in theory, but in reality, massive blast waves and huge chunks of flying metal do not respect lines on a map, and people lose their sense of direction. The Russians suffered horribly from their own fire.

As the day grew lighter, a heavy fog shrouded the entire battle zone, reducing visibility to less than 100 meters. The German decision to reserve the bulk of the limited supply of artillery ammunition for direct observable fire now proved to have been the wrong decision. There would be no possibility of direct fire. Far better to have fired it off on the known jump-off positions. This weather phenomena had been unexpected by the Germans because there had been no change in the climate conditions from the previous day. There had been no fog the day before and there would be no fog the following day, but on that day of battle, the God of War granted the Germans no battle luck.[49]

Not only would there be no direct fire from the artillery, the German commanders were concerned that the dense fog would greatly reduce the effectiveness of the flanking machine guns and their carefully laid-out fields of fire. They feared there would be no 'kill-box', but they needn't have worried. There would indeed be a 'kill-box' that day—a 'kill-box' for all the young men, Russian or German, trapped within.

Russians were already all over the battle zone. German soldiers, still sheltering in their bunkers, were surprised by a kicked-open door, a flash of a grenade, the burst of a sub-machine gun. That was the last thing they knew—then another grenade, just to be certain. The Russians were no less surprised. Ripped by their own artillery and lost in the fog, they fired upon one another or stumbled unexpectedly into German positions. The one with the quickest reflexes, the fastest trigger-finger, was the one who lived—at least for a few moments longer.

Oberleutnant Willi Stoffels, commanding the 2nd *Kompanie* of the 18th Regiment near Helenow, recorded an account of what happened that day within the 'kill-box':

> The frozen ground trembled under the impact of thousands of shells, and our small bunker shook. Within a few seconds, all of our telephone communications were broken and all of our contact with the battalion, the platoons, and the forward observers were cut.
>
> After I recovered from the first shock, my messenger, *Obergefreiter* Feiser, and I tried to leave our bunker to reach the forward trenches, but in the hail of shells and shrapnel, we could only crawl along the bottom of the communication trenches. After several attempts to leave the bunker, we finally succeeded. I had to find out what was going on in the front line ... Feiser and I crawled our way forward along the bottom of the trench. The drumfire lasted over an hour, and with the fog and smoke, one could not see twenty paces, despite the daylight.
>
> Just before we reached the front-line trenches of *Feldwebel* Rasch's platoon on the right flank, he came crawling towards us, dragging along a wounded soldier, and reported that everything was destroyed up front and that Russians had broken into the trenches. As the furious bombardment continued, I would not believe that the Russians were attacking through their own shellfire. But that was soon apparent when I saw figures, bent over, running towards us through the fog and explosions. I called to them and asked where they were going. To my astonishment, I discovered that they weren't our men but Russians who in groups had overrun our trenches and were storming forward through their own artillery fire. Feiser and I opened up with our sub-machine guns, and at first drove them off. But there were too many of them, and we had to withdraw.

There was no less confusion at the divisional command post in Bierwce. Communication was lost with the 37th Regiment by mid-morning. Its commander, *Oberstleutnant* Lutkehaus, had already fallen. By mid-afternoon, contact with the 18th Regiment was likewise broken. Its last message was that the regimental command post was surrounded by Russian infantry and tanks and that its commander, *Oberst* Graf, had been killed while trying to destroy a Russian tank with a panzerfaust. *Generalmajor* Brücker had but one regiment left in the battle zone—the 58th.

To the north and the south, the Russian assault had also made deep penetrations into the battle zones of *Korpsabteilung* E and the 45th *Infanterie* Division. The Warka Front was coming apart, but where were the two Panzer divisions that were to counter-attack and restore the lines? Again, the fog had caused numerous delays and stoppages such that the Panzer divisions were unable to reach the rear areas of the battle zone as they had been instructed. When the 19th Panzer Division finally arrived, *Generalmajor* Brücker pressed for an immediate counter-attack to relieve his hard-pressed units. *Generalleutnant* Källner agreed to attack at 11.30 a.m., but then put it off until 12.30 p.m., then 2 p.m., until finally canceling the attack altogether. No reason was given for the delays and cancellation, but it could well have been that Källner, a veteran commander, could see that there was no battle zone left to restore and no worthwhile purpose in putting his head into the Russian meat grinder. He then moved his division to take up a blocking position between Zawady and Grabowa Las.

Meanwhile, the *Nebelwerfer Regiment* north of Bobrowniki, which had been pounding the Russians since the attack had begun, was being attacked by infantry and tanks. It fired off its last rounds and went down fighting. Likewise, the artillery regiment found itself under attack at close range. They managed to destroy twenty-five tanks, but by evening they were down to just two heavy and one light *Feldhaubitze*.

In the late afternoon, *Generalmajor* Brücker received a desperate message from his last regimental commander, *Oberstleutnant* Müller, reporting that his command post was under attack by infantry and armor and that he was preparing for all-around defense. Having already lost two of his three regiments in the battle zone, *Generalmajor* Brücker decided that something had to be done to save what was left of the 58th. Major Kapp was ordered to take his *Sturmgeschütz* brigade, break through to *Oberstleutnant* Müller's command post, and rescue whatever remained of his regiment. Joined by *Sturmgeschütz Kompanie Eyrich* and 2nd *Schwadron* (Company) of fusiliers, and with echoes of von Bredow and Mars-la-Tour (*Koste es was es wolle*), he smashed through to Müller's headquarters, loaded the survivors of the 58th—a mere 200 men!—on his *Sturmgeschütze* and then powered his way out, destroying or scattering any Russian tanks in his way.

They were then ordered to take up positions to the southwest, near Lukawa, on the right flank of the 19th Panzer Division, and to go over to the defensive. It was a heartbreaking order to follow. The illuminating flares rising in the night sky over the battle zone and the sounds of combat told the surviving soldiers that some of their comrades were still fighting there—comrades they could not rescue, and comrades they would never see again.

The next day, the survivors of Reiner's regiment were joined by the other remnants of the 6th Division—the Fusiliers, the Replacement Battalion, the engineers, and some 300 artillerymen. The German command intended for them to establish a blocking position along the line Jedlinsk-Bialobrzegi. However, threatened by Russian forces advancing from the northeast and from Radom in the southeast, they gave up all hope of defending the Warka. They were ordered to withdraw 150 km west to Shieratz, where perhaps a new front could be established along the Warthe River. The last survivors of the 58th Regiment wearily climbed aboard the tanks and trucks of the 19th Panzer Division, turned their backs on the Warka, and headed toward the hoped-for safety of the west.

Left behind in the shattered bunkers and collapsed trenches of the Warka Bridgehead were 462 of their comrades (70 percent). Of those, ninety were confirmed dead and 372 were missing. However, Reiner was not among them.

It is still unknown how Reiner escaped the hell of the Warka, but he did survive. Once again, his soldier luck had proven true, and he had cheated death one more time.

Towards the Bitter End: The Final Battles of the 6th *Rheinisch-Westfälischen Infanterie* Division

Hitler's Chief of Staff, Heinz Guderian, had been entirely correct in his assessment of the Eastern Front; when it was attacked, it collapsed like a house of cards. Five Soviet fronts with 250 divisions and 4 million men had broken out of the Vistula bridgeheads, shattered the German Front, and raced across Poland. Warsaw and Radom were taken on 17 January, and Krakow and Lodz were taken on the 19th. The Warthe River was reached and crossed by the 23rd, and at the end of the month the Soviet forces had reached the Oder River. They were now only 60 km from Berlin. The advance had been spectacular. In some twenty days, the Soviet armies had advanced 350 km from the Vistula to the Oder, smashed two German Army Groups, and removed hundreds of thousands of German soldiers from the Wehrmacht's Order of Battle—killed, wounded, missing, or trapped in pockets now far behind Russian lines.

In the west, the German Ardennes and *Nordwind* offensives had burned themselves out. Though they had inflicted heavy casualties on the Allies, they had achieved little more than to delay the Anglo-American assault on Germany by just a few weeks. The Germans had also suffered heavy casualties that could no longer be replaced. In February, the Anglo-American forces began their drive to clear out the German Rhineland and set the stage for the final offensive in the west—the crossing of the Rhine.

Meanwhile, in Silesia, Alfons bid a final farewell to his two sisters in Bad Flinsberg. He and his wife, Lotte, began their journey to the family base in Aken; thanks only to a detour borne of pure chance, they avoided the total destruction of Dresden by Allied bombers on 13–14 February. On the 15th, utterly exhausted, they reached Aken, where they were reunited with their two daughters. Here, they would wait for the war to end and their remaining son to return. They had not heard from Reiner since 12 January.

Withdrawn from the Warka and directed to Schieratz on the Warthe, the 6th Infantry Division found that when they arrived, Soviet forces had already crossed the river at Warthe, 20 km to the north. There was no possibility of establishing a new defensive line there, so they were ordered to continue their retreat another 170 km to the west, to reach the safety of the Oder at Glogów. Perhaps here, along the Oder, the Germans could establish a new line to halt the Soviet advance.

The 6th *Infanterie* reached Glogów on 22 January and were immediately charged with organizing the city's forward defenses on the east bank of the river. Having completed this task, they were finally taken out of the line and sent to Sagan, some 50 km to the rear, where, for the first time since the disaster in the Warka, they could set about organizing their own shattered ranks. The 200 survivors of the 58th Regiment became simply the 1st Battalion and remained under the command of *Oberstleutnant* Müller. The Field Replacement Battalion became *Bataillon Erpenbach,* named after its commander. The remnants of the artillery regiment—320 men without any artillery—were organized as an infantry battalion under Major Brunk. Another battalion of infantry was formed from the communication and supply troops—in all, perhaps some 1,500–2,000 men. Unfortunately, the *Füsilier Bataillon* and the *Sturmgeschütz Kompanie* had been incorporated into other divisions. There would be no reunion.

With their reorganization complete, they were officially (and briefly) classified as the 6th *Volksgrenadier* Division and sent back to the front once more. There, they prepared themselves to fight the last battles of the Reich—and they would fight with whatever men and equipment they could find—local *Volkssturm* battalions made up of older men armed with Italian rifles, Hitler Youth units (enthusiastic but untrained), platoons armed with panzerfausts mounted on bicycles, errant police battalions, ground crews from Luftwaffe airfields, and with abandoned and captured equipment. They would fight to the end of the war; they would fight to the bitter end.

Why would they do this? It was certainly not for 'Final Victory'; that illusion had been shattered long ago. The war, which had progressively revealed ever greater horrors throughout, was now revealing yet another one—the wholesale rape and murder of German civilians by the Russian Army. While in the Warka, the men of the 6th Infantry Division had certainly heard stories of such barbarities when the Russians first entered East Prussia back in September. They could see it with their own eyes in Silesia. They were no longer fighting for the Führer, honor, or even the Fatherland. Now, they were fighting and dying simply to allow the German civilian population a chance to escape the hands of the Russian Army. Such would be the next mission of the 6th *Infanterie* Division.

The Russians had reached the Oder River at the beginning of February. The German command expected that they would soon continue their drive and seek to push powerful armored units deep into Silesia. On 5 February, having had little time to recuperate from their arduous ordeals, the 6th *Infanterie* Division was tasked with establishing a 'Tank Barrier' some 30 km behind the Oder Front using the local Silesian *Volkssturm* battalions and backing them up with the regular units of the 6th *Infanterie* and any other forces that could be found in the area. They did not have much time.

Three days later, on 8 February, the Russians stormed across the Oder at Steinau, broke the German Front, and drove hard to the west and southwest. They turned aside a German counter-attack, encircled the German garrison in Glogów, took Luban, and pressed on. On 9 February, strong armored and motorized units reached the 'tank barrier' that General Brücker had established between Kotzenau and Liegnitz and pressed their attack towards Bunzlau.

Could old men and panzerfausts stop the Russian advance? In a word, no—but they might be able to slow them down and provide the regular German Army units an opportunity to deliver sharp counter-attacks that would cause them to halt for a bit, at least long enough to evacuate the civilian population of Bunzlau. This is exactly what the 6th Infantry Division, now officially renamed *Panzertod* (tank death), did on the night of 10 February. During the afternoon, a strong motorized column of Russian infantry and tanks had emerged from the Lichtenwald and pressed south to the town of Thomaswaldau, 7 km from Bunzlau, where they paused. Now was the time for the Germans to attack. It was decided that Battalion Erpenbach would be entrusted with the assault.

Then, from out of nowhere, arrived a German tank destroyer company outfitted with the ever-effective hetzers (armored tank destroyers). It was *Jagdpanzer Abteilung* 1183, fresh from their training grounds in Bohemia. The 6th Infantry's symbol was quickly painted on their hulls (a white shield with diagonal red lines) and sent to join *Hauptmann* Erpenbach's attack.

Shortly after nightfall, the attack went in. The Russians were taken completely by surprise. The village was in flames, and in the bitter house-to-house fighting, the Russian infantry suffered heavy casualties and a loss of six tanks and numerous other vehicles. Judging themselves not strong enough to hold the village, Battalion Erpenbach and their newly acquired brothers-in-arms withdrew to their jumping-off positions along the heights west of Thomaswaldau. Nevertheless, they had achieved their mission, as evidenced by the fact that the Russians made no attempt to continue their advance on Bunzlau later that night nor in the morning of the next day.

At 5 a.m. on that day (11 February), the last refugee train departed Bunzlau. Having done their duty, the 6th *Infanterie* vacated Bunzlau, crossed over the Bober (destroying the bridges behind them), and withdrew another 10 km to the river Queis, where they rested and waited for their next mission.

However, there would be little rest for them from now until the end of the war. There would always be another city, another town, and another village to defend. Raumberg, Siegersdorf, Hennersdorf, Lauban—only the names would change. For the men of the 6th *Infanterie*, it would always be the same: defend if you can, withdraw if you must, and attack at the slightest opportunity with whatever resources that might be at hand.

At Siegersdorf, a dozen fourteen-year-old youths from a local *Landwehr* (militia) unit asked to join the 6th *Infanterie*. They were given uniforms of a sort and panzerfausts and because of their familiarity with the local area, they were assigned to the division's reconnaissance unit. In the ensuing battle, they rendered the division valuable service and even destroyed several of the new heavy Soviet 'Josef Stalin' tanks as well as some T-34s with their panzerfausts. General Brücker then thanked the boys for their services, gave them Iron Crosses, and sent them home.

For the next two months, the division would fight in the battles that swirled around Lauban. Attack, counter-attack, and attack again. Its scattered units rushed from one crisis point to another to restore the line. General Brücker would be promoted to *Generalleutnant* and receive the Knight's Cross. The division would get its old name back. They would end the war the way they began it: The 6th *Rheinisch-Westfälische Infanterie* Division.

Meanwhile, the war would run its final course. In March, Anglo-American armies crossed the Rhine, encircled the industrial Ruhr region, and trapped the 300,000 German soldiers there defending the vital war industries. On 16 April, the Russians launched their final drive on Berlin. By the 25th, they had surrounded the city, cutting it off from the rest of the Reich. Deep within his Berlin bunker, the Führer continued to issue orders to his armies—armies that no longer existed, or, if they did, were no longer listening. During this last week of April, eastward-advancing American units met up with the westward-advancing Russian forces at Torgau on the Elbe. Very little of the 'Thousand-Year Reich' remained in German hands. On 30 April, Hitler put a pistol to his head and pulled the trigger. Two days later, the last German defenders of Berlin surrendered to the Russians.

The Führer was dead; Germany was overrun. There was nothing left for which to fight. There was no country left to defend, and there was no reason left to allow the dying to continue for even one more day. In the early hours of 7 May, at the supreme Allied headquarters in Reims, France, *Generaloberst* Alfred Jodl, representing the German High Command, agreed to the total capitulation of Germany. The second great European War had finally come to an end.

However, far away to the southeast, in Silesia, the men of the 6th *Infanterie* Division were holding a defensive line just north of Neustadt,[1] a mere 12 km from Reiner's aunts' home in Bad Flinsberg. They were still fighting. In the early afternoon of 8 May, Russian tanks and infantry broke into their positions at several points. It took until evening to throw the enemy back and restore the line.

Generalleutnant Brücker then received a radio order that hostilities were to cease at midnight and that his men were to lay down their arms. Cease hostilities and lay down their arms, perhaps, but surrender to the Russians was not an option. *Generalleutnant* Brücker would not deliver his soldiers to such a questionable fate. He informed the men that any who wished to do so were free to attempt to escape to the west and surrender to the Americans.

How many of the 6th *Infanterie* managed to do so is unknown. As for *Generalleutnant* Brücker, he resigned his command of the division and awaited his fate alone in his headquarters in Neustadt.

However, at midnight, when all hostilities had been scheduled to cease, a group of his staff, with a column of men from the 6th *Infanterie*, arrived at his headquarters to retrieve him. He protested that at his age, he would only be an encumbrance to them. They would not leave him. Finally persuaded, the General resumed his command, led his men to Pisek in southern Bohemia, and surrendered to the Americans, who assured them that they now were prisoners of the United States Army.

When they awoke the next day, the Americans were gone, the Russians had arrived, and there were no options left. *Generalleutnant* Brücker led the men of the 6th *Rheinisch-Westfälischen Infanterie* Division into Russian captivity—a brutal captivity that would last for ten years.

Reiner was not among them. He had been a soldier for three and a half years, sent to the front four times, and wounded twice. He had survived the destruction of his division at Babruysk, and even the massive Soviet onslaught of 14 January 1945. However, somewhere along the line of retreat out of the Warka, in the bleak winter landscape of Poland, Friedrich Reiner Niemann's luck finally ran out.

Epilogue

What happened to Reiner? His fate remained a mystery for over half a century. He was never listed as killed, wounded, or even missing. His military record had only the cryptic bureaucratic statement: 'Reiner Niemann: Disappeared Jan. '45 Radom, Poland'. That, and nothing more.

When the European war ended in May 1945 and Reiner did not return home, the Niemanns still held out hope that one day they would see their son again. His mother, Lotte, wrote in a letter to her cousin Hänse: 'We can only hope that Reiner is alive and that our thoughts and prayers can reach him in Russian captivity.' At Christmas 1946, Alfons inscribed one of his traditional Christmas woodcuts to *dem lieben Reiner*. But where would he send it? To a Siberian gulag? To a nameless grave somewhere in the east?

The family made countless inquiries to the authorities, but in the post-war chaos of defeated Germany, they searched in vain. The deteriorating east-west relations after the war only complicated the efforts of German families to find their missing sons. Still the Niemanns clung to their hopes, but in 1955, when the last German soldiers were released from Russian captivity and Reiner was not among them, Alfons and Lotte were forced to accept the reality that Reiner was never coming home. For the remainder of their lives, they sought to find out what happened to their son. Lotte Niemann died in 1962, Alfons died in 1968, and their daughter Heidi died in 1983. They never learned Reiner's fate.

The task of 'finding' Reiner then fell to the last of the Niemann children—Reiner's eldest sister, Lütte. She and her husband, Knud, had moved to the United States in the early 1950s and settled in New Orleans. There, Knud became the music director and resident conductor of the New Orleans Opera, and Lütte became the music librarian at Tulane University. They established a new life in a new world and raised three children. Still, Lütte was often pulled back into her past. Time and again, she wrote letters to the German government, seeking any information about her brother. However, Cold War politics and Germany's complicated relationships with its eastern neighbors still hindered the search for the missing German soldiers. Her letters always received the same reply: '*Verschwunden*'. Disappeared.

Lütte wrote her last letter of inquiry in January 1991, and the reply she received four months later was no different than the ones before it. However, this time she was assured: '... should we receive information concerning your brother's fate, you will be informed'. She never heard from them again.

Now, there was nothing more she could do but wait. She hoped that the end of the Cold War and the reunification of Germany would facilitate the search for Reiner, but nothing came of it. A decade passed, and still nothing. With age weighing upon her (she was fast approaching the ninth decade of her life) and with the disruptions of Hurricane Katrina, which devastated New Orleans and flooded her house in 2005, Lütte could do no more to find her younger brother.

Fate, however, intervened. Through a curious series of events, Lütte's American daughter-in-law, author Whitney Stewart, took on the challenge of finding Reiner. Hers was not an easy task—an American woman trying to find her husband's uncle, who had disappeared over half a century before. There were false starts, false leads, disappointments, and dead ends. However, armed with determination and Reiner's *Feldpost*, Whitney continued the journey to its end. In January 2013, in a patch of woodland in the bleak winter landscape of Poland, Friedrich Reiner Niemann was finally found.

Afterword

In each of us is the other preserved.

Reiner Niemann

Central Poland: 20 January 2013

Trudging along the edge of the forest, Paweł and I scanned the ground for signs of disturbed land. My hand-drawn map indicated where to search, but it was not to scale and we couldn't judge distances.

'Let's start at the far end,' I said.

Ankle-deep snow slowed our progress, but I was determined to keep going. I had come too far to turn back now. We hiked further away from the warm car until we found an opening where we could slip through the trees. The stillness unsettled me.

'If you trespass like this in the United States,' I told Paweł, trying to sound lighthearted, 'someone might come after you with a shotgun.'

'In Poland, they'd use an ax,' he joked.

That didn't calm my fear about intruding on someone's land. I don't speak a word of Polish and couldn't explain myself if I had to. Paweł and I walked in different directions, but I didn't stray far. He was my Polish interpreter and only friend in this rural region, and I was uneasy.

Without warning, the rumble of an engine echoed through the trees. A black SUV sped across the frozen field and jerked to a halt at the forest line.

'Are they coming for us?' I asked Paweł. He didn't respond.

Holding my breath, I listened hard for sounds. A branch snapped behind me, and I turned around. A man with a rifle slung over his shoulder was taking measured strides in my direction. He said something in a gruff voice, and I tensed.

'Paweł!' I called.

Paweł turned around and moved toward us, talking softly to the stranger. I didn't understand what they were saying, but I watched their body language. The man with the gun wasn't smiling, and for an instant, I wondered what I was doing in Poland and why I had put us in danger.

My journey had started a year earlier, when, on 9 January 2012, I was putting away a Christmas-tree stand in our back shed in New Orleans. In the dark, I stumbled upon a box of moldy documents that had survived Hurricane Katrina in my mother-in-law, Lütte's, attic. I opened the box and discovered a bundle labeled in German, Reiner's '*Kriegsbriefe*'—Reiner's 'war letters'.

I had long been curious about Reiner Niemann—we even named our son after him—but I had seen only one photograph of him. I first heard about Reiner when I read Lütte's unpublished memoir in 1986. Her descriptions of the war years and of losing both brothers stirred my empathy for her loss.

I sometimes questioned my compassion, though, when I considered the horror of the Third Reich and the fact that my two American uncles and my husband's uncles had been enemies in the war. Never did that fact seem more apparent—and strange—than at our wedding, when my uncle Scotty, a former Air Force pilot who had been shot down over Yugoslavia in 1944 and survived, chatted with my tall and distinguished German father-in-law, Knud. They stood there, two elderly men with canes and no hint of animosity. Had they met in 1944, they might have been ordered to kill each other, but one generation later, they could laugh together.

I had wanted to search for Reiner when my family and I lived in Göttingen, Germany, in the early 1990s, but I had no birth or military records to use, and my German was rudimentary. Also, at that time, Germany was still slow to account for its war dead and missing in eastern Europe, so I did nothing.

However, by 2012 the world had changed. The internet had been invented, and my German had improved somewhat. I spread Reiner's moldy documents on my office floor, found his birth and Iron Cross certificates, and searched German records online. Within an hour, I called my husband, Hans, to tell him that his missing uncle was buried in a German military cemetery in Pulawy, Poland—and that we'd have to go there.

I tried to read Reiner's letters on my own, but that proved challenging. I could not decipher his *Sütterlin* script, and his sophisticated and philosophical writing was beyond my comprehension level in German. I could grasp sections, but I wanted to understand every word so that I could follow his trail. I needed a translator for the hundreds of letters.

Denis Havel was the perfect collaborator. He could translate Reiner's text and explain the military situations Reiner faced. Even more extraordinarily, Denis was willing to rush to translate Reiner's last letters first, so that I could take them with me to Poland in July 2012.

That first research trip allowed my family and me to see where Reiner's remains were buried in Poland. It also gave us the chance to meet Lütte's wonderful cousin, Isa Brahe, and her ever-generous husband, Peter, whom I discovered (again by accident) on the internet. They gave me bundles of family letters and documents that were crucial to the Reiner research.

However, the trip also left me with new questions. Where had Reiner been entrenched from August 1944 to January 1945, where had he gathered fresh fruit and vegetables and found drinking water, and, most importantly, what happened to him after he wrote his last two letters home on 12 January 1945?

Back home again, I realized I had misunderstood one crucial point in the German government letters about Reiner. These stated that he had been *reburied* in the German military cemetery in Pulawy; he had originally been buried somewhere else. When was he disinterred? I urged the German War Graves Commission to send me details of Reiner's original gravesite, and they finally emailed me a hand-drawn map of a forest in Grabowa, a tiny village near Potworow. I arranged a second trip to Poland, in January 2013, to find that grave and to experience the same winter cold Reiner had felt sixty-eight years earlier.

'Come on,' Paweł called.

I followed the men, but I was still wary. 'Where are we going?'

Paweł nodded his head to put me at ease. 'These guys helped dig up the bodies. They'll show us where.'

'How was that possible?' I asked myself.

I was amazed at my good luck—that I'd discovered Reiner's letters, met the perfect German translator, Denis, and an energetic Polish photographer, Paweł Wyszomirski, to help me, and that I had found a cousin with more family papers. If that wasn't enough, I bumped into the very men who disinterred Reiner's bones sixteen years earlier.

Had Reiner been leading me the entire way? I looked to the sky, because that's where we think spirits live, and smiled.

'Okay Reiner, I'm here. Now what?'

The men pointed to a small clearing in the trees. 'In there,' they told us, but all I saw were snow-covered branches low to the ground. I walked to the open area anyway and stood where, in 1997, Reiner's body had been found among the remains of 157 German soldiers. Only thirty-seven of them had worn ID tags; Reiner was one of them. The German War Graves Commission reburied their remains 90 km away, but they never contacted Reiner's sister, Lütte, despite their promises to do so in 1991.

In a moment of silence, I tried to feel something of the Reiner I had come to know from his letters. Did he feel fear before his death, or was he calm in the belief that he'd meet Wolfgang in the afterworld, that 'one bright star in the distant southwest'? Paweł took photographs, and we left the forest. However, we came back later, in the dark, so that I could conduct a private ceremony for Reiner. I also gathered dirt and twigs from under the snow. I needed something to carry home.

We later interviewed villagers from the area in their homes and offices. One man told us a story about Russian soldiers who, in January 1945, ordered German prisoners to remove their uniform coats, identifying papers, and ID tags and run away across the Grabowa fields. When the Germans took off, the Russians shot them in the back. A female Russian commander then took up her pistol, shot the Germans again as they lay on the ground, and commanded Polish villagers to bury the enemy.

Perhaps that is how Reiner died. Perhaps not. I have not been able to corroborate the story. But one point is sure—Reiner kept his ID tag on and ended up in a rural forest grave far from home. I'd like to believe he defied his enemy's last command so that someone could identify his body for his family. Reiner, the ever-devoted son and brother.

In 2014, I returned to Poland with Paweł Wyszomirski to work with a metal-detector specialist from Glowaczow, Łukasz Gudkiewicz. We spent days under the harsh sun, digging in Reiner's former battlefields and searching for the pond and village well where he bathed and collected water. We located both water sources, and there we interviewed an elderly Polish man who'd lived in Lezenice when the Germans invaded. He took us to a German bunker where Reiner just might have slept. We also dug up German ammunition, weapons, and equipment, the sort that Reiner once used—German food tins, wine bottles, and tooth-powder containers, and even unexploded bombs. We even found skeletons of German soldiers that await reburial in the Pulawy cemetery.

Denis and I may never know how Reiner survived the Russian offensive at Glowaczow-Lezenice on 14 January 1945, or how he traveled 60 km southeast to Grabowa. Had he run alone across fields and through forests, as he once did at Babruysk in 1944? Had he met up with a German tank and ridden it out of the chaos? Reiner had trusted his luck so many times on the Eastern Front. Did he believe he would escape death yet again? I wish I knew the answers to these and other questions. I wish I could interview Reiner himself.

I ordered a headstone for Reiner that marks the date of his death as January 1945, and it now lies flat over his grave at Pulawy. That stone, however, does not bring closure to a life that still feels so vibrant and indomitable in his letters. I often reread Reiner's words for the wisdom they contain. So many of his passages resonate with me, and especially this one:

War is the father of all things and the root of all evil.

Reiner's letters and short life are a testament to that.

Whitney Stewart

Endnotes

Chapter 1

1. Liselotte Andersson (Lütte), unpublished memoir, Andersson Archives.
2. Alfons' experiences in the trenches of the Western Front would later give him a special appreciation and apprehensions as he read Reiner's *Feldpost*.
3. Liselotte Andersson, unpublished memoir, Andersson Archives.
4. Lotte's maternal great-grandparents, Michael Berendt and Hanna Friedländer, were Jewish. After the death of her husband, Hanna converted to Christianity and raised her children as Lutheran. That would have made little difference to the Nazis; they were only interested in blood and race. Other members of the Elmering family faced difficulties because of the Nuremberg race laws.
5. But not entirely. During the war, the local Nazi *Gauleiter* came across a work of Alfons' and denounced it as 'Bolshevik Art', ordering the search of the Niemann apartment. Nothing incriminating was found.
6. Ages 10–14.
7. In charge of 10–15 boys.
8. Ages 14–18.
9. A *Gauleiter* is a regional Nazi leader. The *Gauleiter* system was used by the Nazis to compete with and later replace the existing local leaders—mayors, councilmen, etc.
10. At this time, 'approved' art tended towards the sentimental and nostalgic (when not 'heroic') and featured the common man—the farmer, the worker, and the townspeople in their everyday lives.
11. Crete fell in May 1941. The Germans invaded Russia on 22 June 1941.

Chapter 2

1. March training only stood second to weapons and tactics in the training of recruits. German soldiers were hardened to routinely endure 50-km marches, hence the continued issuance of the iconic 'Jackboot' and the peculiar gait of marching columns.
2. The 6th *Rheinisch-Westfällische Infanterie* Division was headquartered in Bielefeld. The 58th Regiment was variously based in Minden, Bückeburg, and Osnabrück.
3. Reiner's play on the word '*Kindergarten*'.
4. Reiner will first receive non-commissioned officer training before his officer courses begin. Even so, his rank remained that of *Schütze* (Private).
5. Dr Richard Baum was a Niemann family friend and musicologist.
6. Female division of the RAD (Labor Service).

Chapter 3

1. On 27 August, one month into the summer battle of Rzhev, *Oberstleutnant* Hollinde was severely wounded. He died the next day.
2. *Oberleutnant* (1st Lieutenant) Edgar Leder soon took over command of another company. His replacement was *Leutnant* (2nd Lieutenant) Voss, who took Reiner into his first battle. Leder was killed in action a year later, on 14 August 1943. *Oberst* (Colonel) Furbach was awarded the Knight's Cross for his actions during the summer battle of Rzhev.
3. Slow-flying, obsolete Russian bombers, so-named for the particular sound of their engines.
4. Commander of *Heeresgruppe Mitte*. He had replaced *Generalfeldmarschall* von Bock the previous winter.
5. German soldier slang for Russians.
6. The T-34 was a medium tank of 28 tons, armed with a 76-mm gun. The KV-1 was a heavy tank of 52 tons, armed with a 76-mm gun.
7. Polunino.
8. Either the Russian KV-1 or KV-2 tank. Both are over 50 tons.
9. KVF: *Kriegsverwendungsfähig Feld*. Fit for active duty at the front.
10. By 22 August, the 6th Infantry Division had lost a total of 2,502 men—565 killed, 1,745 wounded, and 192 missing.
11. Knud Andersson, Lütte's husband and Reiner's brother-in-law.
12. Alfons' sisters, Grete and Ella Niemann, in Bad Flinsberg, Silesia.
13. Company owned by the architect Gustav Wolf.
14. Convalescent Replacement Battalion, Regiment 58.

Chapter 4

1. Zum Nussbaum was bombed-out later in the war, but it still operates today in a different location.
2. Rzhev sector.
3. Part of his officer candidate course. He will have to demonstrate his ability to lead a squad.
4. This raid took place on 30 January in the sector of the 37th Regiment, 6th Infantry Division. See Grossmann, *H. General der Infanterie, Die Geschichte der Rheinisch–Westfälischen 6. Infanterie Division.*
5. While in the field, Reiner and his brother, Wolfgang, often employed a family-devised code whereby they could convey restricted information. Alfons would add the decoded message to the bottom of the letters.
6. The German disaster at Stalingrad.
7. Reiner's company commander.
8. Russian civilians often worked in German military hospitals.
9. Leather-bound booklet containing a soldier's ID papers and personal information.
10. Bad Schlema in Erzgebirgkreis.
11. Now a part of Schneeberg, Saxony.
12. Brigitte Pflug, Wolfgang Niemann's girlfriend and a family friend.
13. A colleague of Alfons Niemann.

Chapter 5

1. *General der Flieger* Adolf Galland *Die Ersten und die Letzten.*
2. KV, *Kriegsverwendungsfähig*—fit for active duty.
3. *Wehrbezirkskommando*—recruiting sub-district office.
4. Lt Voss was wounded two days before Reiner was wounded during the summer battle of Rzhev.
5. The regulation manner of wearing the Iron Cross 2nd Class. Only the black and white ribbon was worn in the second buttonhole, not the medal itself.
6. Pentecost 1943 was on 13 June. British 'Mosquito' bombers attacked Cologne on 13 and 14 June.
7. The night of 11 June was a heavy air raid on Düsseldorf.
8. Leo Schlageter actively resisted the French occupation of the Ruhr in 1923. He was executed by a French military commission and became a German national hero.
9. Fritz Niemann or '*Onkel Fietsche*', Alfons' brother, who was an architect in Breslau.

10. Leave granted to military personnel to attend to bomb damage at home.
11. He is referring to bombing raids, of which there were many on Cologne throughout the summer of 1943. The city was bombed in over 250 air raids during the war. The 29 June 1943 raid was the so-called 'Peter and Paul Attack'. It left 4,400 people dead.
12. Unauthorized leave.
13. Western allies invaded Sicily on 10 July 1943, causing Hitler to call off the Kursk offensive in the east in order to reinforce the west. The Russians immediately counter-attacked around Orel and Belgorod.
14. Limited field duty.
15. Base Replacement Company.
16. In both world wars, German troops serving in the east often suffered from a strange illness that resulted in joint pain and inflammation of the heart lining.
17. Reiner's number differs from modern, online sources.
18. Group that clears rubble after bomb damage.
19. The British.
20. The internet offers plenty of information on the bombings in Münster on this day, 5 November 1943. The specific target here was the railroad junction that supplied traffic and war materiel through the Ruhr Valley, both by rail and canal.
21. Unfit for active duty.
22. Fit for active duty.
23. Fit for Home Garrison Duty.
24. Hitler's rise to power on 30 January 1933.

Chapter 6

1. *General der Flieger* Adolf Galland: *Die Ersten und die Letzten.*
2. Considering that German regiments at this time rarely had a troop strength of more than 1,000 men, with such losses as these, it is little wonder that after a year of being classified KVH and sitting around the barracks with little to do, Reiner was pronounced healed (miraculously) and classified KVF.
3. Haas went missing in action in June 1944, Babruysk.
4. Ohms was killed in action on 4 July 1944, Babruysk.
5. 3D terrain map.
6. *Oberst* Wodtke, commander of the 58th Regiment from April–20 June 1944. His replacement was Major Stampe, from the 37th regiment.
7. Also called *Nähmaschine* (sewing machines) by German troops.
8. A stronghold or fortress company—armed, equipped, and designed for a defensive role.
9. 11th *Kompanie* III Battalion.
10. The commander of the 11th *Kompanie* was *Leutnant* Wilhelm Voss. Reiner's

previous commander, Otto Voss, now commanded the 3rd *Kompanie, I* Battalion. Both Vosses were listed as missing in action in June 1944.

11. Reiner is now in the 10th *Kompanie*, commanded by *Oberleutnant* Kurt Haas, who was also listed as missing in action June 1944.

12. For reasons of language, culture, and religion, German regiments and divisions had always recruited on a regional basis. The diverse nature of Reiner's squad is reflective of the great strain on the Wehrmacht's manpower situation at this stage of the war. At that point, whoever was available was sent wherever they were needed.

13. They may have remained where they were and turned in a bogus report of the patrol. This is common with all soldiers in all armies at all times.

14. A wound bad enough to send the soldier home.

15. Soldier slang for the deadly *Nebelwerfer*, or mobile, multiple rocket launcher.

16. British bombing.

17. Allied invasion of Normandy on 6 June 1944.

18. Reiner must be speaking from rumor here. There is no record of an *Oberst* Behrendt ever commanding the 58th Regiment, nor does any 'Behrendt' ever appear on the Officer List of the 6th Infantry Division. However, since numerous command changes were taking place during this period, it is possible that an outside officer from Corps or Army staff was temporarily charged with administering the 58th Regiment.

19. Rolf Hinze: *Der Zusammenbruch der Heeresgruppe Mitte.*

20. Named for the famous general of the Imperial Russian Army during the Napoleonic wars, General Pyotr Ivanovich Bagration, 1765–1812.

21. *Sturmgeschütze* (assault gun) is a Mark III tank chassis with a sloped, armored mantlet instead of a turret, originally armed with a short-barreled 75-mm gun. Later it was up-gunned to a high-velocity 75-mm anti-tank gun, which was successfully employed for both infantry support and tank destruction.

22. Compare Reiner's account to that of the retreat of the 58th Regiment during Operation Bagration.

23. 10 km south of Zlobin.

24. Along the Dobriza River.

25. Along the Dobyssna River.

26. The Ola or its tributary stream at Leitischi.

27. Near Chimy.

28. The breakout route to the northwest.

29. The Mogilew-Babruysk highway near Welitschi.

30. 2 km southwest of Ssergejewitschi.

31. 12th Panzer Division.

32. Sswisslotsch River, Minsk-Babruysk highway.

33. Commander of the 6th Infantry Division, *Generalleutnant* Heyne, was taken prisoner on 29 June.

34. Of these 1,100 men, only 600 of them actually survived the hell of Babruysk. The others had already been in Germany on leave, detailed for special duties, or recovering from wounds.
35. Brücker, '*Generalleutnant*', in Grossman, H., *General der Infanterie, Die Geschichte der Rheinisch-Westfälischen 6. Infanterie Division*, p. 222.
36. Heinrich Himmler, head of the SS, Gestapo, SD, and German Police. The Reserve Army consisted of men called up, trained, and waiting to be sent to the front as needed. In July 1944, the Reserve Army was under the command of General Fromm. The conspirators of the 20 July assassination attempt on Hitler planned to use the Reserve Army to seize and maintain control of Germany. General Fromm was aware of it and was willing to go along with it, but only if Claus von Stauffenberg was successful in killing Hitler. After 20 July, Hitler no longer trusted the Army and put the Reserve Army under Himmler's command to prevent another coup.

Chapter 7

1. Salisbury, H. E., *Die Ostfront: Der Unvergessene Krieg*, (Verlag Fritz Molden, 1978)
2. Technically, Finland had not been an ally of Germany. The Finns maintained that they were fighting a separate war with the Soviet Union.
3. I.R.—Infantry Regiment. A.R.—Artillery Regiment.
4. Brücker, '*Generalleutnant*', in Grossman, H., *General der Infanterie, Die Geschichte der Rheinisch-Westfälischen 6. Infanterie Division*, p. 232.
5. Divisional size *Kampfgruppe* made up of the remnants of the 251st Infantry Division and other units.
6. *Machinengewehrschütze* II. The man responsible for carrying the ammunition and extra barrels and feeding the ammunition belt into the weapon; hardly an efficient use for someone of Reiner's experience.
7. *Zugmelder*. A platoon messenger, one of the more dangerous positions.
8. Reiner's brother-in-law, Knud Andersson, had been seriously wounded in Russia in 1941. Since then, he had been attached to the staff of the II *Panzergruppe* in Yugoslavia. As the Russians had shifted their offensive to the Balkans, the Germans were hastily evacuating their forces there to avoid being cut off.
9. Reiner is referring to the Russian 76-mm anti-tank gun often used in an anti-personnel role.
10. Lütte is working at the Central Library in Trier.
11. Lezenice, Poland.
12. *Nationalsozialistische Volkswohlfahrt* [National Socialist People's Welfare].
13. Age Group refers to the conscription class.

14. Sarcastic reference to the German wonder weapons V-1, V-2, etc.
15. Alfons is now digging entrenchments near Rurich, a town about 10 km north of Jülich on the Rur river.
16. Large numbers of volunteers from the various non-Russian ethnic groups of the Soviet Union joined the ROA (*Ruskaja Oswoboditelnaja Armija*, or Russian Army of Liberation) and fought on the side of Germany. They were deployed on both fronts.
17. French-speaking Belgians who first fought as a Belgian unit within the German Army. Later, they became the 28th *Waffen* SS *Panzergrenadier* Division, or '*Wallonje*', led by the Rexist leader Leon Degrelle.
18. Flak.
19. i.e. Reiner.
20. The Warsaw Uprising began on 1 August 1944. It was not until 2 October 1944 that the Germans were able to crush the last pockets of the Polish resistance. Soviet forces made no effort to aid the Poles.
21. When it was destroyed at Babruysk on 30 June 1944.
22. MG-42, light machine gun; MP-43, the first assault rifle ever issued by an Army; Panzerfaust, one-shot, disposable anti-tank weapon. As it was recently issued, Reiner would not have been familiar with it.
23. He wrote during those five days, but he did not mail off the letters.
24. Reiner has not heard from the family for a while. It seemed as if the front was still in Russia, where the mail took longer to reach him. Actually, Alfons fell ill, was released from digging trenches, and went with Lotte to his sisters in Bad Flinsberg to regain his health—hence the break in letters.
25. Official postcard, with which one could inform relatives of one's status and address.
26. 'Off into the wild blue!'
27. *Kraft durch Freude*—The Strength Through Joy movement of the Nazis' sponsored vacations for the lower and middle classes.
28. Armistice Day 1918.
29. As part of their 'Iron Rations', German troops were issued 3 oz. of schnapps daily; it had to be drunk up to prevent troops from storing it up for a good bash. The Army wanted the men 'feeling good', not falling-down drunk.
30. Gottfried Keller, whose character *Frau* Regula Amrein epitomizes motherhood.
31. The *Volkssturm* was a German national militia during the last months of the Second World War. It was set up not by the traditional German Army, but by the Nazi party on the orders of Adolf Hitler on 18 October 1944. It conscripted males between the ages of sixteen and sixty who were not already serving in some military unit as part of a German Home Guard.
32. Understandably, Alfons wanted nothing to do with the local Nazi party office in Cologne.

33. Concerning his escape from Babruysk.
34. Walter Flex was a popular German soldier-poet in the First World War. He fell in the Baltic Campaign of 1917.
35. Notice of Wolfgang's death on 10 October 1944 near Bologna, Italy.
36. Steal the light from the mouth of the serpent.
37. Reiner's aunt and family in Breslau.
38. *Generaloberst* Heinz Guderian: Panzer Leader.
39. Common German abbreviation of *Sturmgeschütz*.
40. That is 1.30–1.50 meters of earth on top.
41. Alfons' sisters Grete and Ella maintained a successful candy store in Bad Flinsberg.
42. *Oberstleutnant* Müller.
43. German slang for the Russian 76-mm anti-tank gun.
44. Beginning after Christmas, the 18th Regiment (Reiner's neighbor to the left) was the target of several Russian assault parties seeking to probe the German defenses. *Leutnant* Willi Stoffel's account is found in Ernst Rhein's *Das Infanterie/Grenadier Regiment* 18.
45. Sister Leni Magris.
46. Small packages of condiments for the soldiers.
47. A character in Kleist's novel who symbolizes one who struggles against injustice.
48. It seems the schedule that Reiner and his comrades worked out allowed one man to be free of sentry duty each night. The limited bedding was reserved for those who eventually had to go out into the cold.
49. After the war, this led to discussions among the German survivors as to whether the Russians had artificially created the fog.

Chapter 8

1. Nové Město pod Smrkem in the Czech Republic.

Bibliography

German-Language Sources

Andersson, L., *Erinnerungen*, Andersson Archives (Unpublished)

Brücker, 'Generalleutnant, *Die Division ab Juli 1944 bis Kriegsende* in Grossmann, H., *General der Infanterie, Die Geschichte der Rheinisch-Westfälischen 6. Infanterie Division*, (Podzun Verlag, Bad Nauheim, 1958)

Carell, P., *Unternehmen Barbarossa*, (Verlag Ullstein GmbH. Frankfurt am Main, Berlin, 1963); *Der Russlandkrieg*, (Verlag Ullstein GmbH. Frankfurt am Main, Berlin, 1966); *Sie Kommen!* (Verlag Gerhard Stalling. Oldenburg, 1960); *Die Wüstenfüchse*, (Verlag Nannen GmbH. Hamburg, 1958)

Flex, W., *Vom Grossen Abendmahl*, (C. H. Beck'sche Verlagbuchhandlung, München, 1918); *Für Dich Mein Vaterland*. (C. H. Beck'sche Verlagbuchhandlung, München, 1919); *Der Wanderer zwischen beiden Welten. Ein Kriegserlebnis*. (Verlag Beck. München, 1918)

Grossmann, H., *General der Infanterie, Die Geschichte der Rheinisch-Westfälischen 6. Infanterie Division*, (Podzun Verlag, Bad Nauheim, 1958); *Rschew, Eckpfeiler der Ostfront*, (Podzun Verlag, Bad Nauheim, 1962); *General der Infanterie/Dieckert, K. Major der Reserve, Der Kampf um Ostpreussen*, (Gräfe und Unzer Verlag. München, 1960)

Hinze, R., *Der Zusammenbruch der Heeresgruppe Mitte im Osten*, (Motorbuch Verlag, Stuttgart, 1980); *Ost-Front 1944*, (Motorbuch Verlag, Stuttgart, 2004); *Die 19. Panzer Division 1939–1945*, (Döfler im Nebel Verlag GmbH. Eggolsheim, 2003); *Letztes Aufgebot zur Verteidigung des Reichsgebietes. Kämpfe der Heeresgruppe Nordukraine A/Mitte*, (Verlag Dr Rolf Hinze, 1995)

Löhdorf, H., *Infanterie Regiment 58*, (Privately published, 1976)

Rhein, E., *Das Infanterie/Grenadier Regiment 18*, (Eigenverlag Ernst-Martin Rhein. Bergisch-Gladbach, 1993)

Salisbury, H., *Die Ostfront, Der Unvergessene Krieg, 1941 bis 1945*, (Verlag Fritz Moden. Wien-München-Zurich-New York, 1981, translated from the English by Johannes Eidlitz)

Stoffels, W., '*Endkampf im Waka-Brückenkopf*' in Rhein, E., *Das Infanterie/Grenadier Regiment 18*, (Eigenverlag Ernst-Martin Rhein. Bergisch-Gladbach, 1993)

English-Language Sources

Davies, W. J. K., *German Army Handbook, 1939–1945*. (Arco Publishing Company Inc., London, 1973)

Eisenhower, D. D., *Crusade in Europe*. (Doubleday & Co., Garden City, NY, 1949)

Glantz, D. *et al.*, *Slaughterhouse: The Encyclopedia of the Eastern Front*, (The Military Book Club, Garden City, NY, 2002)